D1243695

FROM HISTORY TO SOCIOLOGY

THE TRANSITION IN GERMAN HISTORICAL THINKING

by

Carlo Antoni

With a Foreword

by Benedetto Croce

Translated from the Italian
Dallo storicismo alla sociologia

by Hayden V. White
Department of History
The University of Rochester

GREENWOOD PRESS, PUBLISHERS
WESTPORT, CONNECTICUT

Library of Congress Cataloging in Publication Data

Antoni, Carlo.
    From history to sociology : Dallo storicismo
alla sociologia.

    Reprint of the ed. published by Wayne State
University Press, Detroit.
    Includes bibliographical references and index.
    1. Sociology--History--Germany. 2. Sociology
--Methodology. 3. History--Philosophy. 4. His-
torians--Germany. I. Title.
[HM22.G2A6613 1976]   301'.0943   76-40127
ISBN 0-8371-9282-X

Dallo Storicismo alla Sociologia
was originally published by G. C. Sansoni, Florence, Italy, 1940

Originally published in 1959 by Wayne State University Press, Detroit

Reprinted with the permission of Wayne State University Press

Reprinted in 1976 by Greenwood Press, Inc.

Library of Congress Catalog Card Number 76-40127

ISBN 0-8371-9282-X

Printed in the United States of America

Foreword

An Evaluation of *Dallo storicismo alla sociologia* *
by Benedetto Croce

I limit myself to recommending this exceedingly enlightening book by Antoni only to those who are seriously interested in the problems of philosophy, particularly to those who are interested in the problem of historical methodology. Antoni does not present us with one of those traditional accounts which consist of extracts and compendia more or less ably constructed but examines and exposes the work and thought of six social theorists—Dilthey, Troeltsch, Meinecke, Max Weber, Huizinga and Wölfflin. He masters their thought, exposes their errors and judiciously assigns to its proper place whatever is most valuable in them. The essays are linked together by the theme implied in the title: the decline of the historical concept—the transition from history to sociology—from philosophy to empirical science. It is well worth meditating upon the fact that such a decline could occur in a country with a cultural tradition such as that of Germany, which in modern times has carried the study of philosophical logic to a rather high point and which has given evidence of a profound speculative talent. Antoni shows how these theorists formulated dualisms, insoluble and unsolved paradoxes, how they cling to these paradoxes as " compromises " and multiply entities (*entia*) endlessly. They seem to forget or to totally ignore what is universal and individual: category, ethos, aesthesis, logos, etc. They conclude with spasmodic and sterile attempts to explain causally and psychologically acts of the spirit which are essentially free, original and creative.

For example, Dilthey avails himself of the concept of the

* A review published in *La Critica*, XXXVIII (1940) , 302-303.

Erlebnis, "the elementary reality, the basis of poetry and all other forms of the spirit." It never occurred to him that his *Erlebnis* might be merely the product of a hasty analysis of the spiritual process itself, which, always specified in some definite form, ever has before it all the other forms that, in that act, have become its matter (*materia*) and which has no other reality outside this relationship. The poet thinks and wills in so far as he is a man, and this drama is his *Erlebnis,* a feeling which does not already exist in and of itself but only in so far as it is transformed into poetry. Beyond this it is only postulated abstractly.

Weber did extensive work on the "economic ethic," but he did not begin by inquiring whether or not it were more dangerous to add an adjectival (and hence a modifying) determination which would tend to convert ethics into economics, or if it were possible to distinguish as many moral spheres as there were material existents (*materie*), all empirically distinct, which the morale twists and molds to its own ends. For if one conceives of ethics in this narrow sense, as everything for which man has appetite or which is useful and pleasurable, it is evident that ethics will always be nothing but economics or that it can have for its object nothing but economics. Thus, the adjective is meaningless, suggesting if anything an equivocation on Weber's part.

Meinecke assigns to the state a "double essence" and "makes of power its most indispensable and important but not its only one," as though concepts could be recipients of anything differing from themselves.

Wölfflin sought to construct a history of art. Instead, he presented only the hundredth variation on the dichotomy of classic-romantic, harmonic-techtonic, Latin-Germanic. Since, in his terms, there must be two kinds of art, his dichotomy exists only in his own imagination. He never really asked how there could be two kinds of art, how the true artist could judge, not with the unique criterion intrinsic to him, namely, artistic beauty, but with one which is at one time classic, harmonic, limited and Latin and at another time is romantic, titanic, unlimited, and Germanic, so that one could say: it is ugly, but it is romantic, titanic, etc. This (as Hegel would have said) is conceptual barbarism.

All problems are seemingly resolved or seem capable of being resolved by the laborious construction of types or classes of facts (and this is precisely the method of sociology) —abstractions, which are certainly not the end of thought, since thought dissolves them when confronted by them, in order to penetrate to concrete, universal-individual reality.

Antoni's study is also important in that the authors with whom he deals are all learned, serious, meticulous, genuine searchers after truth—in sum, personally worthy of the highest esteem. In their work one often finds fruitful observations and individual historical interpretations of great merit. Even in that other sterile and tortuous endeavor to which I have already referred there is much that may be considered conceptually useful to the scholar as a stimulus. But this in no way mitigates the fact that the mode of philosophizing which characterizes these thinkers must be adjudged far inferior to that which is currently practiced by the best Italian thinkers. At one point Antoni speaks of a definition " which would have horrified a scholastic." Actually this typological and classificatory method lacks any genuine feeling—let us not say for the great speculative and dialectical logic—even for the more elementary type of logic which was taught by scholasticism.

It is to be hoped that Antoni's book will serve in some way to modify a common tendency to speak of " the provinciality of Italian philosophy." For many, the paragon of civic and worldly good taste would seem to be found only in works written in German or other foreign languages. Such people perpetuate an attitude prevalent at the time when the universities of the New Italy were founded, an attitude which at that time had its good reasons. That one should search out and read foreign works is laudable, but it is also necessary to acquire the capacity to understand, judge and assign them to their proper place in order to extract from them what is genuinely useful—as Antoni has done.

Author's Preface

Here I present in revised and recombined form ten of my essays which appeared earlier in the review, *Studi Germanici*. These examined the transition or decline of German thought from historicism to typological sociologism. I have retained the original, monographic character of the essays because the transitional process itself has neither unity nor continuity; it is instead a tendency which happened to be common to a group of thinkers of the most diverse interests and origins—so much so that for many the title of the collection may seem inappropriate. My work is not a survey of the entire process, since that would have involved a wider examination of the spiritual currents of Wilhelmine Germany. I hope, however, that these essays will serve as a preliminary to such an examination. To the original essays I have added essays on Wölfflin, a Swiss, and Huizinga, the Dutch historian, because both seemed to me to belong, even if only marginally, to the same movement.

I dedicate these essays to Giusseppe Gabetti, who encouraged me to pursue these studies, and to the *Istituto Italiano di Studi Germanici*, which provided me with the opportunity to complete this work.

C. A.

Rome, April 1939

Translator's Preface

I encountered Professor Antoni's work while passing two years in Italy as the recipient of a Fullbright grant. One of the purposes of these grants is to promote international exchange and understanding in the arts and sciences. In presenting the present translation to the English reading public I hope to give voice in some measure to my gratitude to the American Commission for Cultural Exchange with Italy, which made possible my acquaintance with the work of Professor Antoni and other Italian scholars like him.

Carlo Antoni was born in Trieste in 1896, participated in World War I as a volunteer, was wounded and decorated. He was graduated in philosophy from the University of Florence, taught in the *Licei*, was a fellow of the *Instituto Italiano di Studi Germanici* and private docent in philosophy and professor of German literature at the University of Padua. As Croce's colleague, he participated in the formation of the Liberal Party following World War II and was a member of the central committee of that party, a member of the National Council, and governmental commissioner for cultural exchange with foreign countries. In 1946 he was appointed to a chair especially created for him in the philosophy of history at the University of Rome. Currently he is professor of the history of modern philosophy and director of the *Instituto di Filosofia* at that university. He is also a member of the Higher Council of Public Instruction and of many academic and national societies in Italy. In 1952 he received the "Premio Einaudi" and in 1955 the "Premio del Mezzogiorno," testimonies to the high esteem with which he is regarded in Italian intellectual circles.

The work here presented deals with the decline of historicism and its transformation into sociology in the thought of six major European historians and social theorists of the nineteenth and twentieth centuries. It presents sympathetically and completely, yet concisely, an account of a European intellectual tradition which deserves wider hearing in this country for what is living and valid in it. It submits that tradition to criticism in Crocean terms, terms not always familiar to American readers who, if we may judge from the available comment on Croce in this country, have not fully understood the basis and nature of that Italian philosopher's contribution to historical thought.

The general thesis of the book, that the transition from historicism to sociology represents a decline in historical thought, demonstrates that while there are undoubtedly many benefits to be derived from the application of sociological techniques to the solution of historical problems, this application involves serious epistemological, methodological and even moral considerations. Perhaps, as a result of the appearance of this book in English translation, some of the difficulties will be elucidated and can thus be dealt with more intelligently. Perhaps it will serve to help resolve that pointless, because misconceived, conflict between "objective" history and "relativistic" history which breaks out ever so often in the American historical and philosophical journals and which had its origins in this country in a misreading of Croce's early works. In any event, perhaps this book will arouse a renewed interest in Croce's thought in general and in Professor Antoni's cogent application of its precepts in his other works on German historical thought.

The term "historicism" is used in Croce's work in a sense quite different from that employed by Karl Popper and students in America. A recent article in the *American Historical Review* (Vol. LIX, April, 1954, pp. 568-77) lists no less than five different, and often opposed, uses of the term. We thought it wise, therefore, to eliminate the word from the title of the English edition.

The translator from the German is always troubled by the difficulty of rendering seemingly obscure metaphysical and poetical expressions into English. Professor Antoni, as is the custom with European writers, did not translate many of the German terms of prime importance in his exposition of the thought of Dilthey, Weber, and the others. I have translated all of them except those which can be said to be on their way to becoming English, that is, those which appear in *Webster's New International Dictionary*, second edition (1934, imprint of 1957). There is, however, one exception to this rule: the term *Erlebnis*. This term is not precisely translatable because it is used in a special sense by Dilthey to denote a level of being beneath or beyond any conceived by any other thinker. Whether the term is justified or not ultimately hinges upon whether his discovery is accepted as a reality or is rejected as a confusion. The closest I can come to the term in English is "unmediated experience." W. D. Hodges roughly translates it as "lived experience" and uses it to indicate "inner states, processes, and activities in so far as we consciously have them, or 'live through' (*erleben*) or 'are aware of' (*innewerden*) them, or 'enjoy' them in [Samuel] Alexander's phrase, but do not make them objects to ourselves by introspection. This is the normal condition of the mental attitudes, when attention is concentrated on the objective content to which we take the attitude and not on the attitude itself. When attention is turned inwards, lived experience is objectified and becomes *inner preception*." *

I am indebted to la signora Elena Cravera Croce for permission to include the review by her late father, Benedetto Croce, as a foreword; to Professor Antoni, for his kindness in allowing me to undertake this translation and for the stimulation derived from our conversations in Rome regarding it; to Professor William J. Bossenbrook, who encouraged me in the endeavour and who read parts of the manuscript; to the editors of Wayne State University Press, Professors Harold A. Basilius

* *Wilhelm Dilthey—An Introduction* (New York: Oxford University Press, 1944), p. 158.

Contents

On History and Historicisms

The intellectual history of nineteenth century Germany, if indeed not all of Europe, may be conceived as centering about the problem of defining the relation between the human sciences (*Geisteswissenschaften*) and the natural sciences (*Naturwissenschaften*). In no field of knowledge was the problem more acute than in history. Standing as it did halfway between the humanities and the newly rising social sciences, history was neither fish nor fowl, and its practitioners tended to oscillate between the conviction that history was an art, an aspect of *belles lettres*, and the conviction that it was an empirical or possibly even a positivistic science.

A solution to the problem of history's place in the spectrum of scholarly disciplines was demanded by the sudden pre-eminence foisted upon it by philosophers and theologians who thought they had found in historical thought a key to past, present and even future events, the ground upon which nature and man might be unified in a single frame. Historians, yielding to the all too human impulse to accept praise whether deserved or not, did not discourage the popular view, although one wing of historians did assert vehemently that history had no answers: it merely told how things really happened. But even in this empirical school of historiography a difficulty lay in the word "really," for it implied that history contained some means of distinguishing between a true vision of reality and a purely imaginary one. At the same time it was evident to all serious and honest historians that history itself operated without a well defined idea of its proper competence. Thus, the methodological crisis in historical thought was set under way, and a search began for that magic touchstone which, in solving the problem of what history was and how it should be studied, would also resolve the problem underlying the distinction between the human sciences and the natural sciences.

One of the reasons for the central position given historical thought during this period was the high esteem which it enjoyed among the romantics. Unlike the thinkers of the Enlightenment, who viewed the past as an inferior stage in the development of reason and thus intrinsically inferior to the present (and the future), the romantics eulogized the irrational and thus rediscovered historical periods held in disdain by the rationalists for their irrationality. As over against the *philosophes*, the romantics tended to view the past as intrinsically good, for it presented examples of humanity freed from those fetters which were placed on the human spirit by an abstract, mechanical *raison*.

Another reason for history's rising stock in the nineteenth century was the place given it in philosophy by post-Kantian idealism. Here history was conceived as the point of union between the idea and its empirical reality. For Hegel and those who followed him, history was " the development of spirit in time, as nature was the development of idea in space." [1] As Cassirer rightly points out, " We may describe the fundamental tendency in Hegel's thought by saying that he spoke of religion in terms of history and of history in terms of religion." [2] Whatever the negative results of this attitude, it did have the merit of evoking interest in everything historical and inspired in his followers, who were basically opposed to the excesses of romantic irrationalism, the same sort of reverence for the historical existent, whether it appeared at first sight to be rational or irrational. Thus, Hegel destroyed the onesided vision of Enlightenment historical thought, but he did it at the price of an historical vision as radical in its way as that which he opposed.

A third reason for history's pre-eminence in the *Weltanschauung* of the nineteenth century was the appearance in 1859 of Darwin's *Origin of Species*. The popularization of the theory of evolution seemingly demonstrated that the distinction between a growing, living historical reality and a static, mechanical natural reality—a fundamental presupposition of eighteenth century thought, incorporated into the Hegelian world view—was misconceived. Nature itself, or at least a significant portion of it, was shown also to have a history, and this discovery seemed to justify the belief that historical thought held the key to the formation of a total view of reality, both natural and historical. On the other hand, it could be argued with equal cogency that while nature and history now seemed to be parts of the same reality, it was not history but natural science which had discovered this fact. Thus, it could be held that not historical thought but positive science held the key to universal understanding and that history must therefore yield its honored place to science, which would now proceed to the task of analyzing man with the same thoroughness that had yielded a true understanding of nature.

Whatever form the individual appreciation of Darwin's ideas took, the concurrence of an historical attitude in romanticism, post-Kantian idealism and Darwinism resulted in historicism, *the tendency to interpret the whole of reality, including what up to the romantic period had been conceived as absolute and unchanging human values, in historical, that is to say relative, terms.*[3] The emphasis centered upon the idea of change itself, and everything, including ethics and religion, was subjected to an analysis on the basis of a logic not of being but of becoming. This led to the crisis in Western thought which has since been identified as the "crisis of historicism" and to that anarchy of values to which Kierkegaard and Nietzsche reacted so violently. Man was cast out upon a sea of flux, at the mercy of a mythological conception called time, reduced to the status of servant to values which were shown to be mere ideologies.

Thus, even though historicism was, in a sense, born of romanticism, it was re-enforced and justified by findings in the natural sciences as well. It was this second factor in its composition which allowed it to outlast romanticism, which was merely a phase in European intellectual history, and which made the effects of historicism much more dangerous.

The historicist attitude had its precursors in the English pre-romantics, in Rousseau and in German pietism, but it found its first formal statement in Herder's *A Philosophy of History for the Education of Humanity (Auch eine Philosophie der Geschichte zur Bildung der Menschheit)*, published in 1774. Here Herder attacked the eighteenth century view that the history of humanity was a fundamental unity. He held that the determining fact of history was the special peculiarities not of man in general but of this or that kind of man. These special peculiarities Herder considered to be essentially ethnic in character, that is, he conceived them as inherited psychological characteristics, the products of interaction between the human spirit and the soil from which the different races sprang.[4] And not only was man infinitely varied; so too was nature. Both were to be studied not by the abstract *raison* employed by the *philosophes*, a *raison* which blurred the distinctions between the various races in the interest of a fictitious homogeneous humanity, but by *Einfühlung*, a sympathetic communion with the folk soul. Thus man was still for Herder as for the *philosophes* a part of nature, but of a special kind of nature, one which was infinitely creative and variegated, not uniform and regular.

Seen from the standpoint of his own time, Herder's ideas had a salutary effect, for they successfully opposed a vicious tendency in the thought of the Enlightenment to conceive man and nature as machines and to view individual manifestations of human creativity as mere instances of the abstract laws which govern machines. Ultimately, of course, his views developed into a narrow racialism and resulted in that glorification of both nationalism and irrationalism which led to the destruction of natural law and eighteenth century humanitarian cosmopolitanism. But his view of both nature and irrationalism were seemingly given empirical proof in the dark forces unleashed by the French

Revolution and the romantic national revivals which followed it. Since France represented *raison*, cosmopolitanism and civilization, the rejection of France in Germany resulted in an idealization of opposed ideas. The result was both a rejection of a natural law which alone could justify belief in a united humanity and *raison*, which alone could justify a united, peculiarly human, world view. The immediate effect of Herder's thought was to set Europe the task of thinking out the problem posed by his destruction of a distinction between man and nature, on the one hand, and his erection of a distinction between man and man, on the other. This problem was discussed on the ground of the relation between man and nature, and the tendency was to dissolve everything, man, nature, values, in a common crucible, history. Three views, suggested by the three ideas indicated above as contributing to the historicist attitude, were set forth as answers to the problem. These three answers in their extreme or radical forms led to three different types of historicism.

If one assumed that the similarities between nature and history were more significant than the differences, it was possible to resolve one into the other. In this case it was necessary either to see history as one stage of the total natural development or nature as one stage of the total historical development. Depending upon which monistic view was chosen, the result would be either *naturalistic* historicism or *metaphysical* historicism. The first tendency gave birth to an attempt to apply the categories of positive science to historical phenomena and always tended to resolve history into sociology. This transition as it developed in Germany in the late nineteenth and twentieth centuries is the subject of this book.

The second tendency led to a quest for the metaphysical principle which unified the two stages of reality, nature and history, and to the attempt to demonstrate the articulation of that principle throughout the whole of historical time. Metaphysical history found its criterion of discrimination outside of time, either in pure thought (concepts) or in belief (religious faith). This strain of the historicist movement was expounded by post-Kantian idealism as represented by Schiller, Schelling and Fichte, and it culminated in Hegel. It was characterized wherever it appeared by a desire to transcend time in order to find one ideal principle which governed the historical process; it then stated that this process not only governed history but, in a special sense, *was* history. It is a *Weltanschauung* which, according to Professor Popper, holds that "'history itself' or 'the history of mankind' determines, by its inherent laws, ourselves, our problems, our future, and even our point of view ...," but unlike naturalistic historicism, metaphysical historicism discovers not a process but a plan.

Whereas naturalistic historicism sees man as the tool of hypostatized physiochemical process, metaphysical historicism sees man as the tool of an abstract idea governed, in Hegel's term, by the "cunning of reason." As an attitude, metaphysical historicism is dominated by a desire to know the whole of reality, to discover the *Weltplan*, and thus it is an implicit denial of history itself, for it sees change not as the essence of life but as its accident.[5] It is vicious insofar as it invariably leads to the conviction that man must subordinate his freedom to the service of the principle enunciated by thought, thus denying the valid demands of man's physical being, just as naturalistic historicism demands that man ignore his human responsibility and his peculiarly human traits by erasing the distinction between reason and will. In metaphysical historicism action is subordinated to thought; in naturalistic historicism thought is subordinated to action. Both deny that both thought and action are integral parts of human reality and forget that the tendency to resolve one in the other must always result in the formulation of myth, whether that myth be the state, a class, a dialectic or positive science.

Opposed to both naturalistic and metaphysical historicism was another form which grew out of the necessity of asserting man's freedom and individual creativity. This attitude may be termed *aesthetic* historicism. This conception of the nature of historical thought took not historical reality but the historian himself as the center of its attention. It assumed that the point of departure for the construction of a true vision of history must begin not with the object, the past, but with the subject, the historian living in the present. Insofar as it attacked the other forms of historicism and centered its attention upon the creative act of the historian himself, this movement was justified. But it went too far and ended by asserting that the traditional objects of historical reflection, past human thought and action, were less important than the original, imaginative creation of the individual historian. Fact must give way to the creative imagination which confronted it, and in opposing it, it found itself limited and imprisoned. The *effect* of the narrative was considered more important than its truth or falsity.

Such a view, of course, led to a radical relativism, a nihilism, which held that since history was unknowable by any canons of scientific, religious or philosophical knowledge, its proper mode of investigation must lie in art. But art made no distinction between the imaginary world, the world created in the artist's mind, and reality; it did not seek truth, only beauty.

With the triumph of this view, history was released from any obligation to truth in any form in order to become the servant of the beautiful. This attitude of mind was still historicist in that it wished to interpret reality in historical terms, but it represented that anarchy of values which characterized late nineteenth century thought since here historical knowledge was freed from any sort of obligation to find the kind of truth which alone could promote mutual understanding and cooperation between men. The representatives of this view were Michelet, Burckhardt, Carlyle; and its high priest was Nietzsche, whose thought was a revolt against history itself. With the destruction of the quest for any criterion of establishing historical truth in a concept of history as art, it was inevitable that history become subordinated to utilitarian ends, that is, that it be used to serve any cause which at any given moment seemed justified by an irrational will.

This aesthetic historicism, born of a healthy opposition to the monism of both metaphysical and naturalistic historicism, had the effect of pointing up the necessity of an historical view that would give individual human creativity (the demands of the will) and universal human responsibility (the demands of the reason) their proper place in a unified and total vision of reality. But it cut at only one part of the problem, for it erred by abandoning reason completely and centering all power in the irrational will of the Dionysian ego. In so doing it really joined naturalism in its denial of peculiarly human traits. It differed from it only insofar as it stressed the *absolute* freedom of the will (for example, in the superman), whereas naturalism assumed the will's identification with a regularized physiochemical process common to both man and animal. And while one stressed freedom and the other determinism, they both amounted to the same thing insofar as they both denied that reason is anything but the tool of an animal will, having no regulative function whatsoever. Both views were equally destructive of a balanced view of humanity which does justice to its creative and regulative elements at one and the same time.

Nietzsche was right in castigating the " eunuchs " in the harem of history, those empirical historians who merely told what happened and who refused to judge the facts discovered empirically, for he thus revealed that these historians, in hiding behind the cloak of objectivity and refusing to judge the facts, were as guilty of subverting human values as the historicists. At least the historicist was not afraid to view the whole of life and submit it to a judgment by some standard common to all men; he merely erred in mistaking one part of reality for the whole. The objective historians, whose methods were the social equivalent of those of impressionist artists, merely " entertained " the data and consciously tried to avoid interpreting it. Their kind of history was as limited as impressionist art, and in any sane society it would have passed just as quickly as impressionist art. But objective history, like impressionist art, was a bourgeois phenomenon, the history of the middle class; and in refusing to judge the past, the objective historian begged, like Burke, to escape a judgment of himself.

These three types of historicism, along with their polar opposite, the objective history of the bourgeois period, formed the historiographical corpus of nineteenth century thought. It is obvious that they have certain characteristics in common. First, they all share the assumption that all reality must be viewed historically. However, they all deny that there is any such thing as historical thought *per se* and attempt to resolve history into some other form of thought. In the case of metaphysical historicism, that form of thought is philosophy; in aesthetic historicism, it is art; in naturalistic historicism, it is positive science (sociology) ; and in empirical or objective history, it is empirical science. Again, they are all posited on some metaphysical conception (and this includes objective history) concerning the nature of the relation between humanity and physical nature. They all result in a view of history which gives important insight into historical reality, and this truth, which they partially reveal, sustains them in the minds of their adherents. For example, Hegel excelled in his analysis of the history of thought because he assumed that thought was the determinative factor in all of history, but he has little to say concerning economic reality, and when his system attempts to account for the truth discovered by physical science, his work is reduced to downright nonsense. Burckhardt excelled in his analysis of art, but when examining the state in his *Civilization of the Renaissance*, he was led to consider it, not as a manifestation of *kratos*, an eternal moment of human history, but as "a work of art." [6] Marx's analysis of modern society, in which the economic moment predominates in the determination of social development, is brilliant, but when he deals with art, religion and philosophy, his work is patently silly. And Ranke, poor soul, spent a lifetime in his study and ruined his sight attempting to "tell how it really happened," but on those occasions when he issued forth from that study he invariably put his talents at the service of narrow provincial interest and showed his religious and political views to be of the narrowest and most prejudiced sort. Nor have a hundred years of applying his method resulted in any sort of universal agreement on the great problems of history.

The objective gathering of facts, it will be pleaded, has not been completed. Nor shall it ever be completed. It will take to eternity and thus justify waiting an eternity to judge them. But historical time does not know this: if man refuses to judge the facts, they will be judged for him. It is important that he judge them rationally, on the basis of a well thought out and total vision of the world about him which is history. All of the historicisms outlined above gave a partial view of that reality; each raised the curtain on history for a brief glance, and enough truth was glimpsed to make the system constructed on the basis of it resound with its echo. But they were all partial views and thus unhealthy views, and this unhealthiness was manifested in the violence and anarchy that they spawned or justified.

The man whose mission it was to synthesize all of these forms of historicism, to sort out what was living and what was dead in them and to transform the living truth contained in them into a new, autonomous and self-justifying form of thought was Benedetto Croce. Croce's task was to free historical thought from its subservience to other forms of thought, not by denying that these forms of thought had their own function in contributing to the construction of a total vision of reality, but by rigidly defining the competence of each and showing that none had a right to usurp the place of historical thought itself. According to him, the function of history is to reveal to man the story of the creative spirit's eternal quest (and eternal failure) to achieve final form, perfect self-realization, *through* the various forms of thought, art, science, philosophy and history. He did this by "radicalizing historicism," by showing that the historical attitude did not have to justify the object of its knowledge in terms foreign and limiting to it, but that it stood both at the base and at the summit of all genuine truth.

Croce approached his problem with the eye of a practiced historian and with the attitudes and accomplishments of Western humanism built into him by both training and breeding. Particularly, he was sensitive to the demands of art and poetry, and it was natural that he should take up the problem of history conceived as art, where Nietzsche and Burckhardt had left off. In 1893, after a flirtation with Marxism, Croce produced the revolutionary essay which ultimately would lead to the declaration of the independence of history, " History Subsumed Under a General Concept of Art."

For a number of years, Windelband and Rickert had been struggling with the human sciences–natural sciences dichotomy. They had finally concluded that history was one of the human sciences, which dealt with the individual in its uniqueness, while the natural sciences dealt with the general, that is, saw the individual as an instance of a general law.[7]

In his essay, and later in his *Aesthetics* (1901) , Croce asserted that art, not science in any form, dealt with the individual, while science could only be envisaged as the construction of general laws. Since history obviously was knowledge of the individual, history must be an art. But it was also obvious that if history were an art, it must be a special kind of art. Art, Croce held, was pure intuition, and its products were products of the imagination. Its governing principle was not truth but beauty; art did not, after having constructed its vision, go on to determine whether its vision of reality were a true vision or merely an imagined one. Since history purported to give a *true* vision of the individual, and not merely a *beautiful* one, then history must be something quite different. Was it a science after all?[8]

In his next important work, *Logic as the Science of Pure Concept* (1908) , he sought to answer this question. In this work he attacked traditional logic, which assumed that universal judg-

ment and individual judgment were different kinds of judgment. He argued that to "distinguish the individual as a mere
matter of fact, a *vérité de fait*, from *vérités de raison*, implies that
the existence of the individual is irrational," [9] for such a view
results in an arbitrary fissure in reality itself, which is unified.
It assumes that any given individual fact, being distinguished
from universal truth, has no sufficient reason for its existence;
it implies "that the existence of the individual is irrational." [10]
But no individual fact could possibly exist as it does in its
peculiar uniqueness were there not sufficient reason for it. Therefore, to distinguish a universal truth, on the one hand, from an
individual fact, on the other, "implies that universal truths are
not realized in matters of fact." Yet, as Collingwood notes in
his discussion of Croce, "what is a universal truth, unless it is
true universally of the facts to which it applies?" [11]

For Croce, universal truth and individual truth must be inseparable elements in every real cognition: the universal must
be present, incarnate in the individual. Therefore, there must
be only one kind of judgment, judgment which is at once universal (philosophical) and individual (artistic), judgment in
which the individual is intuited and then subjected to thought
under universal concepts. And this judgment, which is at once
universal and individual, is historical judgment. Thus, the relation of history to philosophy is resolved.[12] Philosophy is a
science of pure concepts, not one of which exists in fact but only
in the mind of the philosopher who thinks them and works out
the relations between them. History is cognition of the individual under the terms of the pure concepts, for only when this
universal element is applied, can the world discovered by the
imagination be thought as true or false, beautiful or ugly, useful
or not useful.

And this led Croce to a discussion of science and its relation
to history. Science does not construct pure concepts, but abstractions of individual facts, hence, pseudo-concepts. The world
envisaged by science is a fictional world composed of abstractions

of material reality, abstractions by which the spirit moves in and upon that world. This does not mean that science is unimportant. Without it spirit could not realize itself in time and space, but it is not to be confused with the quest for truth. The only criterion governing the judgment of scientific knowledge is that of utility. One does not ask if scientific knowledge is true or false, beautiful or ugly, but only if it is practical or impractical. Its vision of the world is subject to constant revision on the basis of pragmatic considerations.[13] Thus, Croce accepts the pragmatic view of science and for the first time elevates science to the status of a necessary moment in a world view which is at base idealistic.

Instead of conceiving of one truth which is philosophic or artistic and another opposed to it which is scientific, Croce saw all as necessary forms, albeit partial visions, of truth. He thus conceived the spirit as operating in fourfold complexity: under the categories of the True, the Beautiful, the Good and the Useful. This was really the revolutionary aspect of Croce's mature thought: his attempt to embrace pragmatic science and idealist philosophy in a common, unified system.

He concluded that history is not, as Hegel had supposed, a conflict between opposed realms; reality is not contradictory. It only becomes so when one refuses to accept it in its totality. The only contrasts in history are not those of opposition but those of distinction between the various forms of the spirit as they struggle with each other for a place in man's spirit. It is natural that one or the other moment should dominate in any given individual incarnation, and this imbalance results in historical change, results in that negative moment which demands the passage from one instant to another.

Thus, history is never finished, is never complete, is never over, and at the same time, it is complete in every moment. The task of historical thought is to discover that sufficient reason which brings any given individual into existence and sustains it and that overbalance occasioned by the struggle between the various moments of the spirit in man which results in its passing away. As Professor Antoni wrote of Croce in 1953: " The absolute, that is, the positive, value is put no longer by Croce [as it was for Hegel] towards the end of the chain of contradictions, but is centered in reality, in each historical moment when history assumes form as beauty of thought, as goodness of universal benefit." [14] Indeed, while not rejecting reason, Croce's world-vision is as yea-saying to life as Nietzsche's; as reverent to ideas as Hegel's, while not denying the valid demands of man's physical existence; as scientific as Dewey's, without dissolving spirit into matter. He denies all transcendence and finds the moving force of history there where it is, in the world, without denying the complexity and the burdens of a world in which spirit is made aware of its own creative responsibility to itself.[15]

Thus, Croce, in his most important book, *History as the Story of Liberty*, can conclude that his historicism is humanism raised to a level of philosophical self-consciousness.[16] He does not hypostatize any given moment of the spirit nor deny the existence of any individual manifestation of it but finds each as precious and necessary as the other, here, now and forever, as moments of the one creative spirit which is the world.

vincial clerics; theology now represented merely the bureaucratic side of their ecclesiastical existence. The older, tragic dogmas of original sin, grace, predestination, and justification by faith still survived as tenacious formulas, an integral part of German life, upheld by the church-state organization and perpetuated even more by the amount of hatred, conflict and blood they had once cost. But Dilthey's father, a good friend of his Catholic colleague, refrained from recommending to his son anything more than faith in an omnipotent God, Providence, and the immortality of the soul. All of this was, to be sure, quite far removed from outright unbelief, and it left its mark on Dilthey. In fact, one day Dilthey would insist upon the profoundly religious character of the *Aufklärung*, almost as if thus he might vindicate the essential orthodoxy of his forefathers. In the course of his intellectual development, this aversion to any type of dogmatic formula reappears in his belief in the educative and moral value of religion, based upon his sensitivity to its inner meaning (*Gesinnung*).

Raised in the shade of the old parish house, Dilthey remained the spiritual heir of the pastors, those attentive but discreet observers of the German political scene, the artificers of the German national character and of the *Gemütlichkeit* of German family life of which they were the prime examples. To the lyrical sobriety of this life was added, in Dilthey's case, a musical sensitivity which he inherited from his mother, the daughter of a musician. In his youthful diary are found passages devoted to Mozart, Bach, Handel, Haydn, and Beethoven, acute passages which foreshadow his mature historical abilities: " Our two greatest theologians, Luther and Schleiermacher, realized that music was religion's nearest sister and knew that listening to good music might be an almost religious act." Even in his youth he had dimly sensed what would later appear to him with historical clarity, namely, the pietistic origin of German music, the effusive character of which could be likened, in its consistent evasion of the bonds of dogma, to a form of religious heterodoxy.

Yet it would be misleading to maintain that his intellectual development took its point of departure from theology. He merely represented the general position which his father handed down to him. Even later, at a time of crisis, he did not abandon it. He confessed that he was not a religious person. If one does not choose to penetrate to the deepest strata of Dilthey's personality, where an unresolved conflict between a lyrical, musical temperament and the intellectual discipline of the scholar can be seen, he might even be viewed as a soul almost lacking in emotional warmth. His life was cast in the mold of his forefathers, composed, immune to passions, a little beyond the pale of reality. He did not allow himself to be diverted by politics, although he observed it with acute interest; and he was immune, so it appears, even to love. In this clear intelligence there is not a trace of *Sturm und Drang.* Even at the age of nineteen he undertook to invesigate scientifically the "so-called *Weltschmerz.*" In later years, anxiety over his work, which he realized he would never bring to completion, did indeed disturb his sleep, but the figure of Dilthey as the Faustian professor which Hugo von Hofmannsthal has so pathetically drawn in his famous memorial (*Nachruf*) is hardly more than a stylized distortion.

When he grew older, Dilthey spoke of the "inappreciably good fortune of having lived in the time of Bopp, Trendelenburg, Boeckh, Grimm, Mommsen and especially Ranke." In reality, towards the middle of the century (Dilthey was born in 1833 and began his studies at Berlin in 1853), even the era of the great epigoni had passed. In the letters dating from these years no mention is made of their work, save the philological *quisquiliae* of Boeckh. From Trendelenburg, his most immediate master, Dilthey inherited the idea of the *Weltanschauung* as the metaphysical concept which unifies all knowledge and informs the practical life.[2] He differed from Trendelenburg, however, in his total renunciation of all metaphysics. In this view Dilthey considered himself closer to Kant, now more popular than ever after the breakdown of idealistic metaphysics. And next to Kant stood Herbart. Even though Dilthey later rejected Herbart's psychology because it was based upon an atomistic conception of the world, one cannot account for the influence which the ideal of psychology as a fundamental science exercised over him, unless the great example of Herbart is kept in mind. Moreover, his two friends, Lazarus and Steinthal, the founders of group psychology (*Völkerpsychologie*), were Herbartians.

The dominant theme in Dilthey, the theme which makes him very much the child of his time (the period 1850-70), is realism. He regarded the science invented by his friends as odd, because it did not admit of a collective soul (itself a metaphysical entity), but he agreed with them that the facts of history obeyed laws analogous to those which were observable in nature. In a letter to his brother he explained why theology left him dissatisfied and he affirmed: " Thought is fruitful only when it is based upon the special investigation of some aspect of the real."

This realism was reflected in Dilthey's political attitudes. Like most of his generation, he had nothing but disdain for the declamations of the *Paulskirche*. Even before the rise of Bismarck's star this generation favoured *Realpolitik*, a Prussian solution of force for the German question. Science for Dilthey's generation represented in the intellectual realm what Prussia did in the political. Here was a revolt of sons against fathers: the father, a loyal subject of Nassau; the son, a champion of unity who almost considered Treitschke his master. Although his personal feelings forced him to declare himself in favor of democracy, Dilthey admitted that his intellect " demanded and supported a strong monarchy." For the petty German princes he had little sympathy: " If the interests of the state demand it, they will have to be pensioned off like other minor officials "—only the monarchical ideal was possible in the German state which was " forming itself in war and political affirmation and which had need of a solid, unitary direction."

Nonetheless, even if in 1862, along with his friends of the

liberal right, he deplored the weaknesses of Prussian political policy, even if in 1866 he gave his wholehearted support to Bismarck and the war, even if after that he held that the Prussian state should be maintained with all of its solid monarchical unity—" with both the advantages and disadvantages deriving from such a situation "—around 1870 he was already disposed to indicate to Treitschke the point at which their views diverged. Above all, he wanted historical judgment to remain free of political passions. For him the party struggle was an interplay of forces, each one of which had its *raison d'etre* in a given sphere of needs. Hence, it appeared to him unseemly that an historian should take sides, as Treitschke had done in his essays on Dutch history, with the House of Orange and against the republican forces. If the champions of armed defense were always necessary to counterbalance the apostles of peace, commerce and science, the historian should not ally with the former, because, given the chance, they would reduce all nations to armed camps: " the partisans of the House of Orange could never have created liberal Arminianism, so necessary for the development of science and the freedom of thought and through which Holland became an essential element in the development of European history." Dilthey was himself a liberal Arminian in the Germany of Bismarck and William II, even if his admiration for the Iron Chancellor never diminished.

His aversion to party bias in any form was really an expression of his inherited anti-dogmatism. Through this anti-dogmatism he was led to become the theoretician of *Weltanschauungen.* It was his endeavour, in the era of Zeller and Kuno Fischer, to broaden the base of the history of philosophy by including within it the history of the religious and moral development of mankind. Rejecting the traditional dialectical development of one system out of another, but considering each system the result of needs and states of mind, he restored life to those cold histories of his predecessors. As an interpreter of human activity from a religious and ethical point of view he all but ignored economic and political problems, although he was willing to admit the importance of the social context in the formation of spiritual movements. As an historian of metaphysics who was witnessing the development, or rather the perpetuation, of long genealogies of ideas, he remained aloof from political history almost as if the nature of his profession demanded it of him. The state, the external organization of society, did not, according to him, enter into the play of spiritual powers. On the other hand, he did not envisage an absolute antithesis of spirit and reality. For him the religio-metaphysical spirit was the inner substance of history; to lose sight of this was to divorce oneself from culture, to be deadened to life itself.

It is surprising to note that some have seen in Dilthey an affinity with strains of thought which appear in Nietzsche.[3] Yet none of the intolerance, sarcasm, or revolts of Zarathustra find an echo in this son of Protestant spiritualism, who lived in the universal church of the spirit and who wrote its history. Even in May 1911, on the eve of his death, Dilthey could still write of the *Aufklärung*: " Out of it comes the superiority of the feeling for life of each of us as compared with that of the greatest thinkers, heroes and religious spirits of antiquity. For only now does mankind stand on solid foundations and envision a goal grounded in reality and a clear way to its realization." [4] Indeed, Dilthey's faith in science was never tainted by the slightest doubt.

*   *   *

At the age of twenty-four Dilthey set himself the task of defining the boundaries between the Graeco-Roman world and the Christian theological systems. This, the problem of the origins and structure of the European spirit, was to constitute the fundamental problem of Dilthey the historian. It was at this time that he encountered, almost casually, the great Schleier-macher. Having been asked to collaborate in the editing of the posthumous papers (*Nachlass*) , he soon afterwards assumed complete charge of their publication. Originally he had regarded this task as merely an opportunity to examine at close range a case analogous to those which he had been studying in Philo, Scotus Erigena, and Lanfranc. He had composed an essay, for entrance in a competition on Schleiermacher's hermeneutics, in which he outlined the history of allegorical interpretation from Crates of Mallos to the present. But basically such questions interested him little. Of the entire German idealist movement he was interested only in Kant, the destroyer of metaphysics; in fact, his only wish was that Kant had been more thorough and radical in that destruction. He desired to see the Kantian *a priori* set in motion, so to speak, so that one might describe the process by which human nature, working out of a first dark impulse, arrived at the construction of metaphysical concepts. He envisaged an irrational ground, out of which the "forms" of thought emanated. Psychology and history could be allied in the examination of the geneses of systems coming out of this ground. History would indicate the point at which the dark impulses came to the surface and crystallized, and psychology would be used to analyze and describe the laws which governed the formation of those natural products, those crystallizations which constituted the systems themselves.

Dilthey never came to realize that history and psychology were basically irreconcilable in the same system. It has been said that his real problem was to assist in the fusion of the metaphysical mood of the Romantic period with the realistic empirical currents of his own time.[5] In reality, Dilthey's problem was the problem of his age: to guide a recalcitrant and rebellious historiography into the frame of science, after its autonomy *vis à vis* the natural sciences had been established. With a sort of Calvinistic tenacity Dilthey dedicated his life to that task. In fact, it might well be argued that he dissipated his gifts as an historian by subordinating them to the realization of that goal. The greater part of his activity was incorporated into his *Thoughts Concerning a Descriptive and Analytical Psychology (Ideen über eine beschreibende und zergliedernde Psychologie)* .

In this work he believed himself to be approaching his goal of a union between psychological and historical science, a union which would guarantee to a vague and vacillating historiography the character and dignity of a science.

His so-called " typology " was conceived around 1859. At that time he had already undertaken the task of identifying the basic forms (*Grundformen*) of ancient thought and the impulses which had made of Christianity a new basic form. But he saw these forms as schemata, and he wished to study them naturalistically, in order to derive laws analogous to those which described the formation of crystals. It was at this point in his career that the influence of Helmholtz was manifested. Dilthey considered Helmholtz the "most genial figure" he had ever encountered.[6] He responded to the currents of the time by avidly studying Helmholtz' *Optics* and Fechner's psychophysics. And after becoming a professor at Basle, he plunged into a passionate study of psychology, placing himself in training under a psychologist colleague. The great positivist movement had by this time arrived on German soil.

Dilthey could not resist it and had little reason for doing so. The anti-metaphysical Comte was exactly the figure to capture the sympathies of this avowed enemy of all metaphysics. Positivism satisfied that desire for concreteness which had moved the whole generation.

On the other hand Dilthey could still believe that he was traversing the royal road marked out by Kant. Had not Kant discovered the categories of thought (*Denkformen*), the map of the spirit? And had not Schiller, building upon Kant, derived aesthetic theories from certain universal categories? And had not the Romantics also spoken of style in a similar manner? Dilthey now felt it necessary to generalize the investigation and to explain the genesis of these forms according to psychological laws. In describing the birth of forms and the metaphysical sense, he claimed to have put to profitable use the Fichtean idea of the ego as infinite activity. Nor is he very far removed from

Goethe when he asserts that only he who contemplates all the forms of existence can be considered the whole man. And, finally, in his attempt to correlate all systems of thought, to justify all ideals, is there not a little of the spirit of Ranke?

Sparkling and geometrically formed crystals, musical themes of a grandiose symphony, the basic forms possessed for Dilthey neither any inner logical necessity nor any relation to external reality. But if this is so, the problem arises: How could such a view be saved from skepticism? Solid ground was seemingly offered in psychology, a science of the laws of thought. Law alone guaranteed regularity even in the life of the spirit. Instead of a single, rigid and universal logic, Dilthey sought to establish a classification of forms which did not arbitrarily change or vary but which reflected the structure of the soul (*psiche*).

He did not venture into this endeavour unaccompanied. At the same time Hermann Steinthal was constructing his *Characterization of the Basic Structural Types of Human Speech* (*Charakteristik der Grundtypen des menschlichen Sprachbaus*) and Moritz Lazarus was working on his schematic group psychology. Had Dilthey been less free of scruples, he too might have composed a *Psychologie der Weltanschauungen*. He did not undertake this task because the psychological base upon which his work would have to rest, and which had at first seemed so solid, began to disintegrate before his very eyes. To this detective of metaphysics even associationist psychology seemed a metaphysical construct. The genuine psychological reality which now presented itself to him was the inner life of the individual, the personality in its unity and completeness. This insight had come to him while he was working on the life of Schleiermacher among the posthumous papers.

* * *

In a lecture delivered at Basle in 1867, Dilthey declared that it was the poets who had taught him to understand the world. The systems of Schelling, Hegel and Schleiermacher he held to be nothing but logical expressions of the view of life and the world (*Lebens-und Weltansicht*) revealed by Lessing, Schiller and Herder. The poet is the real creator of a state of mind (*Gemüt*), which lives in a generation and becomes crystallized into a system. Thus, a philosophical system does not stand or fall on formal or logical grounds but in accordance with the rise and fall of the state of mind which has produced it.

The study of Schleiermacher's personality, as it was revealed through his letters, diaries and notes, had taught Dilthey that to understand was above all to re-experience.[7] Schleiermacher himself had made of the *Gemüt* the means by which the soul relates itself to the Absolute, and he had taught that understanding is a gradual re-experiencing (*sich hineinleben*). Those impulses which are presupposed in every metaphysics are therefore the movements of the affective and emotional life. Such impulses seemed to Dilthey to have been present in Schleiermacher's life, in Schleiermacher as the creative source of the last great reform of Protestantism.

Dilthey was not and did not become a follower of Schleiermacher, but his background and his musical temperament gave him a certain affinity with the reformer and allowed him to penetrate into the world which Schleiermacher had himself lived. The pages in which Dilthey describes the community of the Herrnhuter, the correspondence between the young Schleiermacher and his sister, the house of their pastor uncle, the society of old Berlin, and Schleiermacher's relations with his Romantic friends and ladies, make of his biography an unsurpassed example of the sort of thing to which the modern biographical novel aspires but seldom achieves.

With a delicate tread, almost as though he were afraid of breaking the spell, Dilthey entered into that inner realm in which the life of the soul presents itself without veils. Before his vision the usually opaque and complex play of sentiment and emotion becomes marvelously clear and apparent. And here he discovered that before the creative literary act (*Dichtung*), before the expression of word and concept, there is a spiritual act, the *Erlebnis*,* an elementary and immediate reality, the ground of poetry, but also of all other forms of the spirit.

It has been argued that Dilthey was never really clear in his own mind whether the *Erlebnis* was to be regarded as an immediate psychological disposition in the sense which psychology gives it.[8] To be sure, it is an ambiguous concept, perforce, one might say, since it is on this idea that he attempts to draw together historical analysis and psychological description. Yet, if we are to understand him correctly, it must be remembered that he rejected associationist psychology precisely in the name of the *Erlebnis*. He held that associationist psychology erred in taking into account only representations, the cognitive aspect of the spirit as distinguished from other aspects, whereas the *Erlebnis*, residing further down, is an attitude prior to every distinction, the common source (*Urquell*) of all successive activities or impulses. The *Erlebnis* cannot be equated with intuition, for intuition is already knowledge, or with sentiment, for this is one of the forms of the pysche. Nor can it be conceived as pure subjective possibility, as mere virtuality or potential energy of the psyche, for it is already a datum, a vigorous and powerful reality. On the other hand, it is not undefined, pure being, prior to every determination, because Dilthey already disposes here the seeds of distinction, already postulates in its structure the roots of those attitudes which will later manifest themselves as cognition, feeling and will. If a simile were in order here, I should be inclined to liken the *Erlebnis* to the undisclosed bud which is already possessed of all the constituent parts of the flower.[9]

* * *

The *Life of Schleiermacher* remained a torso, but a magnificent one. In the preface to the second edition Dilthey himself indicated how much the biography had revealed that was new

---

* On the meaning of this term, see the translator's Preface.

and unexpected. The Schleiermacher known to Dilthey's time was the man of the later years. Only Schleiermacher's enemies had dared point out the traces of Spinoza in the *Talks about Religion* (*Reden über die Religion*), and Schleiermacher's relations with the Romantics had been generally regarded merely as a period of transition. Dilthey centered his attention precisely upon this period and discovered that the community of life and thought which Schleiermacher had shared with the Romantics had been decisive for him. Even more radical was his view of Schleiermacher's Spinozism. For Dilthey, Schleiermacher's significance as a religious reformer "consisted in his having introduced a kind of pantheistic mysticism into the life of the church and having made that mysticism respectable." Thus, the veiled accusations of Schleiermacher's enemies were collected and transformed into an open title of glory.

Dilthey had rediscovered in the figure of Schleiermacher the great historical problem which had fascinated him from the beginning: the problem of the passage from classical monism to Christian spiritualism. He was convinced that here he was dealing not so much with two historical periods as with two basic forms which were to be found throughout the whole of the historical development. Christianity is theistic, conceiving a personal relation between God and the free human personality, whereas the *Weltanschauung* which marked Schleiermacher in his Romantic period was permeated with a sort of monistic pantheism, into which he had been led by Shaftesbury's influence even before he had become acquainted with Spinoza and Bruno.

As a result of these conclusions, Dilthey was able to conceive the history of the human spirit in new terms. The Renaissance was no longer to be considered as merely a period which had been dialectically superseded by the Reformation, not even in Germany, because it had perpetuated itself throughout the seventeenth and eighteenth centuries, breaking through and flowering once more in the pantheistic motifs of Romanticism itself. Protestantism, with its dogmas of the fall, grace and salvation, was to be viewed as a resurgence of Christian spirituality, while the principal feature of that modern religious spirit was to be looked for in that pantheism which, having already reappeared in the sects, triumphed with Schleiermacher.

It was Dilthey's merit to have led the problem of Lutheranism back inside the boundaries of a definite historical period. Since he recognized that the decadence of Lutheranism was a result of the humiliating subservience of the national churches (*Landeskirchen*), he saw such heterodox thinkers as Spener, Arnold, Franke, and Zinzendorf in a new light: " as men who had exerted an exceedingly beneficial influence on the spirit and culture of the German people." This tradition of religious heterodoxy had culminated in Schleiermacher, the student of the Herrnhuter, who precipitated the struggle for the autonomy and the unity of the churches.

With his description of Schleiermacher's youth spent among the Brethren (*Brudergemeinde*), Dilthey inaugurated the systematic study of the German sects. He was the first to perceive the link between Protestantism and the spirit of economic enterprise, thus anticipating the celebrated thesis of Max Weber and Ernst Troeltsch. But he was less interested in this aspect of his study than in using biography as a prime example of the formation of a new system, a new *Weltanschauung*, on the basis of a new and powerful *Erlebnis*.

The primitive *Erlebnis* of Schleiermacher was a characteristic product of heterodoxy. Born into an environment in which religious discussion, the problem of consciousness, the constant awareness of the movements of the heart and the longing (*Sehnsucht*) for grace permeated the life of family and community (his family belonged to the sect known as the *Ellerianer*, an eighteenth-century group which hoped to construct the heavenly Jerusalem on earth), Schleiermacher had found certitude among the Brethren who preached the mystical and sentimental enjoyment of grace. The original Lutheran concept of certainty, an inner process which offered the guarantee of salvation, was here transformed into a dulcet spiritual mood, a *Gemüt*. Jesus was entertained as an ever-present reality, as the bridegroom of the tranquil soul. A cult took form which was quite foreign to the spirit of Protestantism, a cult of the earthly anticipation of celestial beatitude, an anticipation to be enjoyed among liturgical chants, the splendour of candles, longings of the heart, and tears of compassion. Dilthey observed the similarities between this almost feminine religiosity and the Catholic mysticism of love and was the first to draw scholarly attention to that mentality which has since come to be known as the Baroque.

In his later writings, when he spoke of the *Erlebnis*, he had in mind above all the poetic experience of Goethe. Now, as he contemplates Schleiermacher's career, the *Erlebnis* is identified with a sweet, soft *Gemüt*, the irrational ground of poetry, music, religion and philosophy. Dilthey took this *Gemüt* and, insofar as he was able, purged it of any trace of conventicle and theological polemic, rendered it universally human and proclaimed it the presupposition of all biographical, critical and historical interpretation.

If for Dilthey the irrational individual life could be relived only through documents (through some kind of inner communion similar to that inner revelation with which the mystic comes to understand the Bible), at the same time he held that historical research, true and proper, also had to investigate at least one other problem, that is, the formation of the system. In the case of Schleiermacher, the formation of the new *Weltanschauung* was the result of the confluence of four strands of thought: the *Aufklärung*, Kant, Spinoza and Romanticism.

The peaceful coexistence and intermixture of mysticism, pantheism, and the ideas of the *Aufklärung* were made possible by the character of the last named. Dilthey reinterpreted the nature of the *Aufklärung* by distinguishing it sharply from the Anglo-French Enlightenment and placing it in the main stream of Protestant religiosity. Whereas the Enlightenment was empiricist and utilitarian and broke every bond existing between the world of God and that of man, the *Aufklärung*, though it abandoned the old dogmas, still exalted the beneficent order of the universe, the progressive education of the human race, and the moral perfection of the individual. Thus it conserved and purified the Christian view of the relation between God and man. Few men have sensed the Christian character of the modern world as did Dilthey, and few have proclaimed, as he did, as the heirs of that religiosity precisely those whom orthodoxy long considered its most dangerous enemies.

In an essay on Lessing, obviously a by-product of the *Life of Schleiermacher*, Dilthey described the new *Erlebnis* of which Lessing was the perfect expression. It consisted of the consciousness which the society of the time had of participating in the construction of a free humanity, one which transcended all ethnic and religious differentations and which led to the attainment of a better future, a more serene faith in and a greater enjoyment of life. The Lutheran anxiety, born of the oppressive sense of the Fall, had vanished. The new science had restored to man a confidence in his own powers: " Out of this *Weltansicht* of liberation were born Schiller's *Don Carlos*, the Kantian philosophy of religion, Herder's idea of humanity, and the Ninth Symphony. Lessing stands revealed as the immortal herald of the modern German spirit."

In the *Life of Schleiermacher* there are a number of monographs on the Romantics. Together with the contemporary essays on Hölderlin and Novalis, republished in *Experience and Creative Literary Art (Das Erlebnis und die Dichtung)*, they represent a fundamental re-evaluation of the first generation of Romanticism. Compared to the famous work of Haym, Dilthey's originality lay in the freshness and good sense manifested in his evaluation of the writers of the period—a freshness and good sense born of affection. He does not write of a school but of a " generation," of a group as varied as a generation can be but one linked together by a common climate of ideas and by a community of problems and attitudes. In the Romantics he perceived the advance guard of a revolt in moral concepts and judgments, the subverters of moral dogma in the name of a freer and more realistic moral outlook.

With these essays Dilthey created a history of literature based on the idea of the *Weltanschauung*. The poet is seen as the creator of a vision of life which is the expression of the general feeling of the age.

Did the Romantics represent only an episode in Dilthey's scholarly activity? Did Schleiermacher himself represent only a typical case? One is tempted to answer affirmatively when one reflects that the first volume of the *Life* was completed only with the greatest difficulty (because the author had become interested in the psychophysics of Comte and Mill) and that the second volume was never published. On further consideration, however, it becomes obvious that only through his contact with the poet-philosophers of the Romantic era was the conviction born in Dilthey that poets were the real moral legislators of an age, the creators of new insights into life. From this conviction derived consequences of the highest importance for his historiography.

He rejected Hegel's concept of dialectical development, but he never abandoned his belief in the unitary development of European civilization. But what is it that is formed in a civilization? What constitutes the novelty and originality of an epoch? Development does not occur in any logical way, because the *Weltanschauungen* and the metaphysical systems are already crystals, schematic and static entities, which always remain the same in their type. However, if there is no real development in metaphysics (and therefore no possibility of writing its history), there is still the revelation of the poet, the prophet and creator of the new *Erlebnis*. Since reality is infinitely varied, while the types of *Weltanschauungen* are necessarily limited in number, progress towards a greater awareness of the various aspects of reality, towards a broader vision of life, towards, in sum, a more human humanity, is possible only in the sphere of the *Erlebnisse*, of which the poets are the interpreters. For Dilthey, the

One should not exaggerate, as is sometimes currently done, the importance of his revolt against Comte and Mill. At about the same time in Germany there appeared numerous legal, political, philological and historical encyclopedias, all attempts at synthesis and systematization.[10] From the time of the appearance of Lotze's *Mikrokosmos* a reaction against the excesses of naturalism had been underway. Du Bois-Reymond, in an essay on the limits of naturalistic knowledge, had protested against attempts to describe the life of the spirit under the aspect of a purely mechanical order of nature. Dilthey's originality lay in the fact that he turned the criteria of the positivists against themselves and thus undermined their intrusion into the historical sciences. More positivistic than the positivists, he refused to subordinate empirical facts to laws and methods not growing out of the facts themselves. Like another disciple of the positivists, Bergson, he appealed to the "immediate data of consciousness." Once the particular nature of these data had been ascertained, however, he did not really stray very far from positivistic ideals. In fact, he set himself the task of discovering the "laws" of the spirit which would guarantee to the human sciences—a term borrowed from Mill—a positive character.

It has been asserted that Dilthey's aim was to construct for history a science similar to that which Kant had constructed for the mathematical and physical sciences. The title which he hoped to give to his work "Critique of Historical Reason" ("*Kritik der historischen Vernunft*"), has contributed to the perpetuation of the misconception. In reality Dilthey was quite far removed from Kantian idealism. He was in complete accord with the opinion of his own time concerning the objectivity of the sciences, for the most part agreeing with Helmholtz, whom he cited approvingly: "Science, faithful to its laws, has proven itself richer and more worthy of emulation than all of the efforts of mythical fancy and metaphysical speculation."[11] And the science which he hoped to construct was a descriptive psychology which, on the basis of empirical factual data alone, might rise to the creation of laws of the "psychic structure." If he is to be likened to anyone, he must be seen not as the Kant but as the Bacon of the human sciences. For he sought to give them a method which, if differing from that of the natural sciences insofar as it excluded the idea of a rigid causal connection, remained nonetheless inductive and classificatory.

The premise of any human science is psychology. It must determine the uniform general properties of the individual personality while remaining itself within the orbit of pure description and avoiding any hypothesis. Hitherto such an undertaking had been hindered by the existence of such nebulous and abstract entities as art, science, the state, society, religion, the nation, the national soul, and the national spirit. However, now it could be asserted that the only reality was individuals and their relations.

Therefore, it was necessary to create a new psychology. Dilthey rejected associationist psychology because it perceived in the life of the soul only the play of representations. He considered a representation as an event already penetrated and integrated with feeling and interests.[12] The stimuli of the external world provoke representations, feeling intervenes, colors and evaluates them, and activates the impulses of the will. This division of psychic phenomena into three categories, the cognitive, the affective, and the volitional—a division borrowed from Kant—was for Dilthey a fact given by inner experience. He always felt that it was so apparent and self-evident that he never critically examined or attempted to justify it. It was possible, he admitted, that in their inner workings, one of the classes might be derived from the others, but he held that the psychologist ought not formulate hypotheses on such a matter or seek to penetrate behind the scenes of the psychical experience *per se*.

At first he was convinced that he would be able to pass from such assumptions directly to the formulation of one of the human sciences, that is, aesthetics. Since it was feeling which gave the tone to poetry, one had only to proceed to the analysis of emotions (*sentimenti*) in order to derive aesthetic laws. Fechner had derived them from the effects produced by the work of art on the spectator. Dilthey sought to derive the same " supreme principles " from the simple description and classification of emotions. But it became immediately apparent that art was not only an emotion or a feeling but also a seeing (*vedere*), and that it was impossible to describe its secrets in a series of rules: " The genius appears and forces others to see with his eyes; he thus creates a school, a style, an epoch." [13]

What the artist gives to us is liberation and enlightenment insofar as he makes us participants in a new life-experience. This immediate and concrete feeling for life, a vibration of the individual soul in the world, Dilthey perceived at first only at the roots of art, but he ended by seeing it as the unique positive reality. Thus the belief in the reality of the external world was nothing but an experience of the will feeling itself opposed and limited, a central experience in which the antithesis of knowledge and action is dissolved. Thus, he is driven to affirm: " If from this life we derive a few abstract concepts, we can hope for nothing more or better." [14]

But Dilthey could not or would not allow himself to be lost and flounder in this irrational flux. In such a tranquil spirit the Nietzschean Dionysiac joy of life could not break loose. Yet once the conceptual shells had been broken, he had found himself confronted by pure life-experience, just as another radical empiricist, Ernst Mach, had found himself confronted by pure sensation. But if Nietzsche and Mach had found that they could no longer believe in scientific truth, Dilthey could not abandon the hope of discovering in descriptive and analytical psychology his long desired foundation, a kind of Cartesian *cogito* upon which the scientific edifice might be raised. Nor could he lose himself in a capricious and subjective psychology. If he did, then all the human sciences, composed of psychological concepts and operating with the categories of feeling, will and fantasy, would crumble.[15]

There was yet another reason why a science of psychology was indispensable to Dilthy. Before his eyes the spectre of historicism had already appeared. At one time he could even write: "The knowledge of an age is always transitory and subjective, the expression of a spiritual state. Metaphysical systems, as well as religious and ethical ideals, vary with the age and are historically conditioned constructs." [16] Like Troeltsch, however, he could not abandon himself to relativism completely. An objective reality, raised above the vicissitudes of states of mind, was necessary for life and action. But since it was no longer possible to project an immobile system out of the historical experience, it was necessary to seek salvation in the historical consciousness itself. Amid the infinite number of life and world conceptions, it was necessary to find the universal structure and its uniform articulations through a comparative method. It would then appear that the "forms" constituted nothing but the givens of life with regard to the world. It would then be necessary to relate the "symbols" to the life of the ego from which they emanate, to the psychological structure, and to their corresponding functions. Thus, history is transformed into psychology, and if the result of this transformation is the establishment of the principle of the transitiveness, relativity and subjectivity of all philosophical systems, at least historicism will have been avoided. However, before seeking the uniform structures in the various systems, Dilthey attempted to directly observe the living consciousness in order to examine it as it existed before thought had added anything to it.[17]

Was it possible for the intellect to directly encounter this immediate life-reality? Bergson, as is well known, denied it. Dilthey, in his turn, admitted that what we experience within ourselves could never become clear to the intellect, that, moreover, the vital processes, when brought before the tribunal of the intellect, reveal themselves to be full of contradictions. However, he refused to abandon himself to mystical intuition and submerge himself in the flux. If he had to choose between the immediacy of the *Erlebnis* and science, he would choose the latter. He refused to see the *Erlebnis* as an immediate and undetermined event, as pure inner vibration, in order to fill it with the seeds of the intellect. At a critical moment he abandoned his radical nominalism in order to embrace a kind of conceptualism. If, he argued, in the rapid flow of the inner processes, we isolate *one* of them and observe it, we will find there some constant connections and functions. These are, so to speak, the veins of the psyche which are clarified in logical operations. The intellect is born of the *Erlebnis*: the abstract is already living and present in the concrete. When thought distinguishes and analyzes, it is only discerning a reality which is already a structure, a life which is already a complex of functions. Psychological abstraction has a sure guide in this inner order which spontaneously offers itself, and if it arrives at some hypotheses, these hypotheses will have the *Erlebnis* itself as their point of departure.[18]

*   *   *

In 1894 W. Windelband pointed out the error in which Dilthey was floundering. In a lecture on the relation of history to the natural sciences, Windelband observed that psychology was naturalistic to the core, because it aimed at the construction of general laws, while historical analysis was concerned with the particular alone and its description. Dilthey's response to Windelband was extremely weak.[19] The characteristic of the natural sciences, Dilthey argued, is not the search for laws but for causality. If all of those sciences which seek to formulate laws were naturalistic, then not only historiography but also political science, linguistics, aesthetics, and in general all of the human sciences would have to be considered natural sciences. On the contrary, he asserted, the peculiarity of these sciences consists precisely in their search for the link between the particular and the general as expressed in law.

Thus, the problem of the knowledge of the individual case was presented to Dilthey: How was it possible to know the individual scientifically? In his youth Dilthey had been interested in hermeneutics. Now he saw in this "science of understanding" an unexpected aid in his attempt to construct the human sciences. Every historico-philological discipline was based on the assumption that understanding leads to objectivity. It was thus necessary to determine the rules of such a process in order to guarantee accuracy of interpretation.[20]

To return to hermeneutics meant, for Dilthey, to enter once more into the romantic atmosphere of Schleiermacher's world. Actually, for Dilthey, to understand was above all, as Schleiermacher had taught, to transfer oneself into another spiritual life (sichhineinsetzen), an act which leads then to an imitating (Nachbilden) or a reliving (Nacherleben). And since the experience which is relived is irrational, there is in understanding a fundamental and unavoidable irrationality.

Can one limit oneself to this simple reliving? The human sciences, Dilthey answers, do not offer us only a copy of a given reality; they reconstruct by means of abstract conceptual relations.[21] Thus, he enters once more upon the path on which he had set out so often and which had always led to a blind alley. Because in order to legitimize understanding he was forced once more to postulate a theory of the psychic structure. He had forgotten that hermeneutics had been presented to him as a problem of the understanding of the individual. So once more he was forced to attempt to discover regular and uniform relations in the psychical life, and thus even hermeneutics led him back to descriptive psychology.

Only near the end of his life did Dilthey seem to broaden his horizons. He no longer spoke of functions, relations, structures, but of categories. And he finds in the process of understanding above all the presence of the category of signification (Bedeutung), a category, however, he hastened to add, which inheres in life itself and renders it intelligible by giving order and form to it.[22] It is not, therefore, a Kantian category, a characteristic of the understanding spirit, but still an objective relation of the psychic structure, even if less restricted than the former structural relation.

The development of the category of signification has been hailed by some as a great innovation, as if it were only now that Dilthey had become aware of the fact that in order to construct history, it is not enough to relive it. Actually, as we have seen, the problem of deriving the forms of conceptual knowledge had bothered him from the beginning. The only new element was the exclusive interest in the problem of historical knowledge. But even now, as he is preparing to investigate the process of the construction of the historical world, he is only renewing the old attempt to found the human sciences, to establish the objective value of their operations.[23]

His method is still that of descriptive and analytical psychology: to understand is to rediscover, and thus his categories have to correspond to the life which becomes understood; that is, they have to be traced back into the individual *Erlebnis* and then extended to all individuals, thus acquiring the dignity of a category of the spiritual world.[24]

Later, Dilthey discovered the category of time, which is immediately apprehended in the *Erlebnis*: the relations of simultaneity, succession, duration, change, all are immanent in life itself. From these are drawn those abstract concepts which Kant posited at the base of his doctrine of the ideality of time.[25]

However, immediately afterwards, Dilthey declared that the flow of time is incapable of being comprehended or grasped. If, with a special effort, we should attempt to live in the flow of life itself, we should be dashed against the law by which every observed instant is already an instant fixed by attention and is therefore a remembered instant.

But how do we apprehend real time, duration, if we do not live it, if we live only the single state of mind, the eternal present of the *Erlebnis*? Dilthey attempted to resolve the difficulty with an expedient which reminds one of Condillac's statue: if we live only the present, he argues, we find in it nonetheless some memories, towards which we are passive, and some images of the future, towards which we are free and active. However, he did not ask himself how the distinction between the two types of images occurs. If anything, he explains how the idea of time arises, but that is all. The problem of how real time might be apprehended directly is left unresolved. Duration flows below the *Erlebnis*, in the inscrutable essence of life itself.

To the categories of time and signification Dilthey also added those of end and value. However, he did not stop there. Intrepidly he continued to expand his list, on the basis of empirical observation, to be sure, but without any really precise criterion of selection. In one of his fragments there is the following list: the whole and the parts, coherence, structure, individuality, force, essence, development, creation, configuration. . . . Thus, tired but undefeated, the old philosopher continued to seek the key to the science of history in psychology to the very end. But the analysis of psychical data had yielded him—over and above the traditional Kantian tripartite division—only a few vague and vacillating concepts.

III

In 1889, in an essay entitled "Concerning the Significance of Archives for the Study of Philosophy," Dilthey posed the problem of the relation of the history of civilization to the history of philosophy. Philosophic systems, he maintained, represent the civilization of a people and of an age insofar as they raise life to intellectual self-consciousness and then influence the conduct of individuals and society. The history of philosophy determines the various phases of the spiritual life and permits the ordering of the products of literature, theology, and science into a hierarchy of historical importance.

Thus envisaged, it would seem that Dilthey had assigned a

central historical function to thought. Actually, he did nothing of the sort. What determines the movement of thought? Not internal contradiction, not an immanent principle, but the successive modifications of the sense of life (*Lebensgefühl*). For every modification or change in this feeling there is a corresponding revolution in the systems. From it the philosopher, like the artist and the religious reformer, derives his *raison d'etre*. Philosophy is therefore merely a symbolic projection of a state of mind; it has no life of its own.

In this dualism of sense of life and metaphysics there is something of Schopenauer's dualism. There is lacking in it, however, any feeling of pessimism. Quite the contrary. Dilthey looked upon this dualistic view as a liberation, and not merely as a personal liberation but as the progressive liberation of mankind —or at least of European civilization. The first volume of his *Introduction* contained an historical section in which the growth and decline of metaphysics was described. Before he proceeded, however, to the foundation of a truly modern, scientific philosophy, that is, one which lacked any superstructure, he hoped to demonstrate that the entire development of modern thought was leading to a science of man reduced to pure analysis and psychological description. The second volume of his *Introduction* was to have dealt with the discovery of the individual in the Renaissance and Reformation and then the formulation of the natural systems of the human sciences in the seventeenth century.[26] The practical result of this plan was only a few preparatory essays.[27]

For Dilthey, the Renaissance is the grandiose dissolution of medieval metaphysics as a result of the affirmation of a new sense of life. Feudalism and the church decline and the bourgeoisie and the national states emerge. All Europe is transformed into a huge work camp in which industry and commerce are stimulated by new inventions and discoveries. The whole is a violent explosion of new forces expressed in grandiose personalities, a great literature eulogizing the dignity of man, flaming temperaments and violent passions. Dilthey's view of the Renaissance was truly Shakespearean. He did not treat of a single type, of Burckhardt's "man of the Renaissance," but of a miraculous breakthrough, a kaleidoscope of the most diverse personalities, figures and types. Here one sees the decomposition of the social stylization which characterized the medieval hierarchy.

That hidden residue of Protestant animosity towards the Renaissance which can be discerned even in Burckhardt has completely disappeared in Dilthey, for whom the hedonism of that age was secondary in importance to the vigorous affirmation of the autonomy of man. For Dilthey, the most important development of the Renaissance was the discovery of a realistic psychology, reflected in the secularization of medieval moralistic literature which Petrarch initiated (Dilthey ignores Boccaccio) and which culminated in Machiavelli and Montaigne. Only after the Renaissance had liberated the human sciences from dogma had it been possible for the seventeenth century to arrive at a notion of the domination of man over nature and the concept of a natural system of law, politics, morality and theology.

What part had the Reformation played in this progressive liberation of the spirit? Dilthey's judgment is divided. He was inclined to see Luther, above all, as a violent throwback to medieval dogmatism, a disturbing interruption. On the other hand, he was disposed to recognize one merit in the reformer. He saw in Luther the discovery of a new type of certainty, a certainty which ultimately led to the mystical emancipation of the inner religious experience.

Dilthey's originality, compared with the Protestant historiography of his own time, consisted in his having realized that it was little short of ridiculous to speak of a return to primitive Christianity: the differences between the Reformation and primitive Christianity were total.[28] The central idea of Paul's faith, the eschatological expectancy of the imminent Kingdom of God, was lacking in the reformers. They were intractable in their opposition to the Anabaptists, the one group whose members ardently believed in the Second Coming. In the historiography on the Reformation, therefore, Dilthey represents the surmounting of every confessional or polemical viewpoint. He held that it was not only impossible to understand Protestantism without understanding the preceding Catholicism and its positive contributions, but that "it was a definite damage to Protestantism, for it severed it from the whole of the great Christian religious development." In particular, Dilthey clearly observed, before both Weber and Troeltsch, how Protestantism, far from destroying the old Catholic ascetic ideal, had redefined and transformed it, giving it a new vigour and amplitude. If, therefore, one wishes to speak of a return, one can only point to the revival of the older rabbinical concepts of law, sacrifice and expiation, and above all to the medieval sense of man's complete inability to achieve salvation by himself—a feeling which the German populace of that time, caught between the violence of their customary life and ecclesiastical discipline, were well able to appreciate.

Therefore, it is understandable how Dilthey might hail the progressive victory of humanistic rationalism over Lutheranism and Calvinism as the formulation of the sixteenth-century doctrine of the "natural light" which vindicated moral autonomy even over against the decrees of God. For Dilthey, the new, modern faith was neither Protestant nor Catholic, but the universal theism of the humanists, the serene and tolerant *philosophia Christi* of Erasmus. From the *De libero arbitrio* by way of Coornhert, the Socinians and Arminians, it was developed up through the Deists. However, it also had a certain influence during the Reformation itself in the thought of Zwingli and Melancthon, and it was joined with German mysticism in the work of Sebastian Franck. The identification of the *lumen naturale* with the "Christ invisible within us" was to be the point of departure for German thought up through Kant and Schleiermacher.

It would seem that as a result of the work of the Renaissance, metaphysics had been destroyed forever. But at precisely this point the contradiction which inheres in Dilthey's historical thought manifests itself once more. While studying the youth of Schleiermacher, Dilthey had discovered a pantheistic thread passing through the metaphysical systems of Bruno and Spinoza, Shaftesbury and Hemsterhuys, to Herder, Goethe and the Romantics. Thus all the foundation work which realistic psychology had been engaged in since the Renaissance seemed to be merely a Sisyphean effort. Progress had been more apparent than real, because if medieval metaphysics had fallen away, other metaphysical systems, equally abstract, had been formed to take its place. The humanistic feeling for life which had seemed, at first, so disastrous to the existence of medieval metaphysics, had not destroyed it but only effected a redisposition of three motifs which had been united into a single harmony in the Middle Ages. The religious motif, i. e., the sense of the relation between the individual soul and the living God, had passed into the Reformation. The logico-mathematical motif, i. e., the Hellenic conception of the cosmos, had survived in Grotius, Descartes, and Spinoza. And the Roman motif, i. e., the assertion of the conquering and ordering will, had been conserved in the thought of Machiavelli.

Dilthey was therefore forced to admit that not one step had been gained. There had only been a grandiose re-amalgamation, a new systematization. There had been no liberation from metaphysics; only a liberation of the metaphysical motifs from the cord which had bound them together during the Middle Ages. The modern spirit was as much a slave as the medieval spirit. That liberating, analytical spirit which Dilthey had hailed in Machiavelli was even linked to a metaphysical motif. In like manner, he found a metaphysical motif in that Roman Stoicism which permeated the political psychology of Hobbes, Spinoza, and Shaftesbury,[29] in Descartes, Melancthon, Coornhert, More, Bodin, and Herbert, wherever, in fact, "human reason had arrived at maturity."[30]

Since, then, the age of the systems was anything but ended with the Renaissance and the seventeenth century, and since metaphysics, like a phoenix, had arisen once more out of its own ashes, nothing remained for Dilthey but to take up again his youthful ideas of the schematic forms of thought, the crystallography of metaphysics. Those three motifs of medieval metaphysics would cease to belong to a definite historical period and become elevated to the universal dignity of types or eternal fundamental forms.

*   *   *

The three types are the following: objective idealism, i. e., the aesthetic-contemplative attitude; the idealism of freedom, i. e., the consciousness of responsibility; and naturalistic realism. Dilthey rediscovered them under different names even in the systems of the nineteenth century: in the idealism of Schelling, in the spiritualism of Maine de Biran, and in the positivism of Comte and Spencer.[31]

At this point it would seem that Dilthey had renounced psychological research in order to devote himself completely to history; for he now writes: "We are able to know what the human spirit is only through history; only this historical self-consciousness allows us to formulate a systematic theory of man." But when Dilthey is asked why the types are three and no more, he immediately reveals that his historiography had already assumed a systematic theory of man. The types of philosophic systems had to be three because there were three spiritual moments: naturalism corresponded to the cognitive moment, idealism to the affective, and the idealism of freedom to the volitional. We are still, therefore, in the presence of the Kantian three-fold division, although the primacy of none of the three reasons has been proclaimed. They are all equal in dignity, as are the three types. Each of them is the realization of a sole possibility, the expression of a single aspect of reality. Each is legitimate for itself: they fall into contradiction only when any one of them presumes to account for those aspects of reality which do not properly fall within its own competence. We can comprehend the world under only one category at a time—those of being and cause, value and end—but never the entire system at once.[32]

Why did Dilthey feel that the universe might be comprehended with the aid of the categories? Not only does he not even attempt to demonstrate the relation between the three categories and reality as such, but basically he excludes the possibility of such a relationship, because elsewhere he argues that the universe is infinite in its multiplicity. Nor did he ever clearly confront the problem of the *raison d'etre* of the world view, this burden of which man can never rid himself. Only in an essay published in his extreme old age [33] did he advance a somewhat pragmatic definition of the world view: constituted of a world image (*Weltbild*) which serves to determine the value of life (*Lebenserfahrung*) and therefore to form a practical ideal (*Lebensideal*), it gives order to the immediate experience of life. One can see, however, that even here he tried to maintain the threefold division of cognition, feeling and will.

That which differentiates world views and determines the prevalence from time to time of one type over the others is not the predominance of one of the three moments, but a unilateral accentuation of the subjective life itself, a sort of imbalance in the ground of life. The "aliveness" (*Lebendigkeit*) which exists prior to the *Weltanschauung* is already the assumption of a position *vis à vis* the environment and is determined by the mood (*Stimmung*) of the soul. In the last analysis it is this irrational mood which gives color to life and which projects and consolidates itself into a system.

But then, one can ask, if life already has its direction, if it is already powerful enough to give its tone to the world image, to the valuation of it and to the ideal, what purpose does the order which comes from the *Weltanschauung* serve? It cannot be argued that this is the product of the intellect, because

Dilthey insists on finding it present in all three impulses of the
spiritual life: cognition, feeling and will. Less than ever does
the partial truth of the *Weltanschauung* appear justified: it
should reveal one side of the real, but the nature of the connection between this side and the capricious mood, the subjective
mood which life assumes, remains obscure.

It has been asserted that Dilthey destroyed all faith in the
rationality of the real. In fact, nothing justifies attributing to
him a distinction which, if to anyone, belongs to Nietzsche, with
whom Dilthey had very little in common. It is true that he
declares that the various aspects of the real refuse to be united
within a single frame. In fact, he could even go so far as to
write: "To observe all sides in any one instant is denied
to us. The light of truth is visible only in a refracted ray." But
for him the inconvenience is due to an imperfection in our
eyes, not to reality itself, for he imagined truth to be coherent.
In the universe which is invisible to our mortal sight, all antinomies are resolved.

*   *   *

Dilthey thought that he had found a confirmation of his
theory of types in the history of philosophy, where the types
returned eternally to do battle with one another without any
chance of a definitive resolution of the conflict. This relation
which he posited between theory of the spirit and history be-
speaks an Hegelian influence. But in Dilthey's history of philosophy a concept of becoming is lacking.[34] The types are always
the same. The course of thought is here represented, not by
forces in development, but by three lines which intersect from
time to time and along which individual thinkers are deployed.
But the individual thinkers are deployed, like points on a map,
all on the same plane. Practically, of course, Dilthey admitted
a kind of progress, but it existed for him below the metaphysical
stereotypes, in the feeling for life which always becomes more
rich, intense, and universally human. But this is, after all, only

a postulate, a gratuitous assertion, instead of a demonstration. When he is actually forced to describe a new feeling for life, he has to recur to concepts. Thus, what is offered to us is not the ineffable sense of life but a philosophy, a *Weltanschauung*, the antiquity of which is immediately recognizable. The naturalistic concept of type not only renders historiography schematic, it reduces it to sociology.

The most conspicuous example of Dilthey's sociological or typological historiography is furnished in his essay on the German genius. From his youth on he had rejected the romantic concept of a national spirit as a mere abstraction. In his later years, however, his historical researches were devoted to the description of the formation of the German national genius. In 1900, during the publication of his essay on Leibnitz, Frederick II and the *Aufklärung*, he conceived a plan for a history of the German spirit from Leibnitz to Schleiermacher.[35] Then he perceived that in order to grasp the German essence (*Wesen*) it would be necessary to go back to Luther, thence to medieval poetry, and finally back even to the barbarian traditions themselves.[36]

His conception of the essence of the German spirit was also a result of discoveries which he made in the field of German history. It was he who first pointed out the importance of that seventeenth-century Catholic mysticism which penetrated into Germany with the hymns of Spee and Silesius and there merged with religious pietism. When the hymn lost its creative vitality, the pietistic spirit manifested itself in Klopstock and the music of Bach and Handel. Thus, Dilthey viewed the great German musical tradition as the last creation of Protestant religiosity.[37]

As the heir to this religiosity, the *Aufklärung* had allowed the old dogmas to fall, not in order to destroy religion, but in order to purify the imperishable substance of Christianity. It was the religiosity of the *Aufklärung* which inspired the educational state of Frederick II, and it was " this Christian moral conception within which Stein and the leaders of the wars of liberation had worked and lived, which had, in fact, given the German people the power of resistance." [38]

In Dilthey's view, the historiographical work of the nineteenth century was the continuation of the *Aufklärung*: " In spite of their antipathy to rationalism, Niebuhr, Hegel, Grimm, and Ranke are continuations of the spirit of Semler, Lessing and Spittler." In general, the entire eighteenth century, even today accused of lacking a real historical sense, appeared to Dilthey as the creator of a great historical concept, that of the solidarity of the human race and of its inevitable progress through an essential inner strength: " Only as the result of the historical work of Voltaire, Hume and Gibbon could nineteenth-century historicism have been born." [39]

In sum, the essence of the German spirit was, for Dilthey, represented in the idealism of freedom. Foreshadowed by the individualism of the primitive German tribes, it was being progressively purified throughout the history of German Christianity.

In this sense must Dilthey be understood. As Schleiermacher considered himself a Herrnhuter of a higher order, so Dilthey considered himself a Christian, a participant in a lay religiosity which was purged of the slag of dogma and which had become possible after the work of Kant and Schleiermacher had been completed. Progress for Dilthey was an ever-increasing Christian freedom. Total freedom seemed to him to be possible only after all the dogmas of the churches, all philosophic systems, all artistic images, had been identified as symbols of the deep reality which we directly experience, of that life " in which is woven the consciousness of our higher nature and of our link with the Invisible." Dilthey, like Sebastian Franck, the humanist and mystic, " felt himself above all sectarian loyalties, liberated from those sects among which truth was scattered and dispersed, a member of the invisible community to which Socrates and Seneca had also belonged." The highest goal seemed to him this inner tolerance, this mastery of the spirit over all systems, " a blessing of the supreme freedom and nobility of the soul." The passionate desire of the young Dilthey to free himself from all formulas, found its fulfillment in the contemplation of their history: " The historical consciousness breaks the last chains, the chains which philosophy and natural science could never break. Now man is wholly free."

But was such a total freedom really possible? A *Weltanschauung* appeared both inevitable and indispensable to him in order to give direction to his own life. He therefore advised a restrained trust in one's own *Weltanschauung*, providing that the equal dignity of that of others might be admitted and that one always remained disposed to transfer oneself into the point of view of others. He felt, as had Erasmus and Lessing, that an intransigent commitment to one's own dogma was a prejudice which was completely inconsistent with the many-sided character of life.

He did not, however, ask if it were possible to follow one *Weltanschauung* while recognizing its equivalence with all others. Thus envisaged, it would not be worth the trouble to choose among the three possible types. The situation would be almost tragic were it not for the fact that the irrational mood entered in to make a choice appear both plausible and necessary.

In fact, the last appeal is to this movement of the psyche. But then the possibility of tolerance becomes diminished: for its principle is the same as the universality of reason and even historically is identified with humanistic rationalism. Dilthey's difficulty was this: without assuming a distinctly irrationalist attitude he did not assign a place to thought in his system between the abstract world view and the irrational experience. Therefore, authority ultimately resided in the instinctive mood, which is by its very nature contingent and particularistic. Thus, any sort of Erasmian spirit of compromise is precluded, because even if the mood is more gentle and complaisant than feeling, affection and passion, the mood is at the same time intransigent and blind to the needs of others.

Dilthey had hoped to furnish the philosophical justification of the Historical School. He is therefore considered the theoretician of that moderate spirituality which characterizes the strain of nineteenth-century German historiography based upon the thought of Wilhelm von Humboldt. In fact, he represents the attempt of German historiography during the second half of the nineteenth century to escape from positivism. While his contemporaries believed it possible to attain to objectivity via the document, he sought the criterion of certitude in the spirit. However, when that naïve faith in the fact (*Tatsache*) dimmed and declined, he appeared as the saviour to those who refused to abandon themselves to subjectivism.

But spirituality was only one side of his soul. Beside it existed a respect for positive science and its laws and rationalism. These three elements battled among themselves within his soul and he sought to resolve the conflict at its base, in the undivided nucleus of the *Erlebnis*. But he failed. Since they were truths for him, he decided that they must be partial and contradictory aspects of a higher reality which is hidden from us. Thus, out of his own capacity to overcome the inner turmoil, out of his own weaknesses of thought, and perhaps, out of what were basic character weaknesses, he constructed a theory, the theory of types. Therewith he founded a new enslavement of the spirit which now found itself limited and closed in a shell, but possessed of an incessant and vain yearning for escape.

There survived in his work such a great part of the old, glorious tradition of the *Aufklärung* and Romanticism as to make of it an almost anachronistic affirmation of spiritual values in nineteenth-century Germany. Even if, in his later years, he occupied himself primarily with the German national spirit and, with regard to German education, proclaimed that its methods would not be changed by the introduction of English psychological concepts but only by the national *ethos*,[40] he was still speaking in the spirit of Lessing and Herder. His optimism had something of the eighteenth century in it. He conserved his faith in the *Aufklärung*: if he did not call himself a Christian in the specific sense, he regarded the attempts to reduce Christianity to the status of a mere historical datum with profound contempt.[41] The true aim of his defense of the autonomy of the human sciences was, he declared, to guarantee the independence of the ethico-religious motifs in human experience.[42] And this was also the tacit intent of his doctrine of the *Erlebnis*. Even if he had found enlightenment through the study of poetry, it was the religious experience, the "scintilla" of the mystics, which he always had in mind, so much so that he could write: "The desire to transcend every metaphysics constitutes the heroic and the religious in human nature."[43]

This respect for the feeling of life within us, this sense of the sacred before the human experience and before the history of that experience, gave to his work as critic and historian that power of penetration and sympathy which made him a master. While all about him the philological tradition mired itself down in external detail, he salvaged literary criticism by interpreting poetry as the lyrical expression of a powerful ethical and religious illumination.

However, it is not as the last romantic historian of German literature that his influence was most deeply felt. He is more famous as the interpreter of the history of ideas (*Geistesgeschichte*), the universal history of the spirit, which, more than distinguishing itself from political history, enclosed and subordinated political history to itself. Later thinkers such as Troeltsch, Meinecke, Burdach, Marcks, von Bezold, and Groethuisen advanced on his shoulders. He was likewise followed into his own hopeless enterprises: into hermeneutics, into the doctrine of the understanding, into the attempt to define psychologically the methodology of historical knowledge and to derive from irrational intuition the categories of such knowledge. Spranger, Litt, Freyer, and Gunther are, in this sense, his heirs. Finally, his theory of the types of *Weltanschauungen*, permanent schemes of thought, effected a rupture between thought and life and turned thought into a bond of the spirit. This is the point of departure for that typology (*Typenlehre*) which is to be found everywhere in German intellectual life during the first quarter of the century: in the psychological typology (*Psycho-typik*) of Spranger and Jaspers, in Wölfflin's forms of vision, and in German sociology. In fact, once the real movement and novelty of history were denied, it was inevitable that history be transformed into typology and sociology. The list of his followers should be enough to document the statement that Dilthey, in his uncertainty, oscillation, and desperation, foreshadowed a crisis in the German genius. In the throes of that crisis, the German intellectual world turned to the interpretation of history and life in a skeptical and relativistic mood, and we are met with the so-called " crisis of historicism."

Chapter 2

ERNST TROELTSCH

I

The destiny of Ernst Troeltsch was linked to a typical manifestation of German life in the second half of the nineteenth century: the theology of the Protestant faculties. In the autobiographical sketch which he wrote before his death,[1] he relates that at the time of his youth—in the era of Nordau, Du Bois-Reymond, and Darwinism—theology was the most fascinating and revolutionary of all scholarly disciplines, the only one which still allowed excursions into metaphysics and the great problems of history. In fact, while positivism discouraged and demeaned speculative inquiry into the physiology of the senses and while historiography was being reduced to the reconstruction of the diplomatic-military vicissitudes of the founding of the Reich (*Reichsgründung*) or was being atomized through erudite specialization, the tradition of Hegel and Schleiermacher lived on in the theological schools of Baur and Ritschl. And here also the great philological tradition continued to flourish. The study of primitive Christianity and the church at the moment in which dogma took its place in human history effected a new synthesis of religious and profane history. And, as in the time of Schleiermacher, the polemic against the orthodoxy of the state church was also accompanied by a discussion of the principles of the national political life. While liberalism had been definitely discredited by Bismarck on a strictly political plane, the debate remained open in the sphere of relations between church and state and between the individual and the community. The return to the ecclesiastical ideals of Schleiermacher was also a return to the ideals of Stein, Arndt, and "the patriots of the wars of liberation."

From 1894 to 1915 Troeltsch taught systematic theology at Heidelberg. But even when he went to Berlin to teach philosophy in Schleiermacher's chair, he remained a teacher on the theological faculty, which—unlike the Catholic seminary—found itself in a position analogous to that of the medieval theological schools: it competed with the *magistri artium* and was in constant controversy and compromise with profane science. Modernism, which in Catholicism is only an episode, constituted the essence of this theology. Being directly responsible only to the state in a period in which the state had no particular confessional interests to defend, the faculty was guaranteed freedom of inquiry and protection from the ecclesiastical authorities in the field of dogma itself.[2] Thus was developed the paradoxical situation in which the organ of doctrinal direction of the church was protected by the state from the rigours of orthodoxy. The faculty was the center and motive force of the religious life, limited only by its own sense of responsibility.

This sense of responsibility constitutes the nucleus of Ernst Troeltsch's personality. Insensitive to every worldly allurement, in his writings he detached himself not only from literateurs and dilettantes but also from everything which did not directly relate to the problems of the ethical and religious life. It was said— but it is not wholly correct—that he was insensitive to poetry and music, wit and irony. His prose, while clear and correct, was never brightened by a flash of sprightly humor; he himself is said to have called it "sailor's biscuit." He affirmed a preference for "the hard and cold atmosphere of the stern will to truth." [3] However, that very sense of responsibility prohibited him from becoming a pure scientist. Unsympathetic to the Rankian and

Burckhardtian contemplative attitude, he wished to be, if not a reformer, at least one of the workmen in the construction of a modern, up-to-date Christianity. From the beginning his problem was that of the possibilities of existence of the Protestant church in the modern world. His first scholarly work was an investigation of the medieval character of the thought of the reformers.[4] After this, an endless series of articles, essays and conferences was dedicated to the " religious situation " and to its relations and conflicts with culture, society, science and modern politics.[5] He had few illusions: he knew that " the new church, of which we have such need, cannot be created by theology and science." [6]

Little by little, for Troeltsch—a distant disciple of Melancthon —the problem of Protestantism's fate was widened to embrace the problem of the destiny of Western civilization. In him Christian and humanistic Europe posed the question of its own essence and drew up an inventory of its own values. Like the heir of a great family who examines his own title of nobility, examines charts and portraits of his ancestors in order to account for the depths of his own character and in order to derive from the fortunes of the family an index to his own mission and a guarantee of his own success, he hoped to derive from his analyses a clarification of the energies which had contributed to the rise of the West. He thought, moreover, that it was a duty and a vital necessity to proceed in the direction indicated by history.

It is perhaps too much to juxtapose him to Nietzsche. Yet if one were forced to choose a man in the Germany of the last half of the century who represented in their most worthy form those values against which Nietzsche inveighed, that man would be Ernst Troeltsch. The juxtaposition does not exclude a near relationship.[7]

Troeltsch was the last of the German intellectuals to remain faithful to the old gods, to the Christian order of life, to culture, to liberal progress, to history, to civilization. He was the last to believe in them, in the theological faculties of the Protestant church itself: in 1918, the year of catastrophe, Karl Barth issued his "Commentary on the Epistle to the Romans," which demanded a violent return to apocalyptic pessimism and constituted a bitter rejection of that liberal Protestantism which Schleiermacher had inaugurated and of which Troeltsch represented the concluding phase.

*   *   *

More properly, Troeltsch represents the epilogue to that "theology of compromise" which had begun with the "second reformer," Schleiermacher. The theologians of the *Aufklärung*, Semler, Ernesti, and Michaelis, had had no need of a mediation between faith and science. For them there was no disparity between the Gospel and natural religion but rather an essential correspondence. Schleiermacher, more of a religious psychologist than a theologian, had disturbed the correspondence with the distinction between rational knowledge and feeling. As a former student of the Herrnhuter, he conceived of faith as the kind of baroque religious feeling common among the Brethren, all heat and longing of the heart, and he had affirmed the autonomy of this emotion over against science and ethics, just as his friends of the Romantic school had celebrated the autonomy of art. Thus, religion had been reduced from objective truth to a subjective experience compared with which every formal doctrine was nothing but a symbolic projection, an intellectualistic and practical schema.

Once faith had been concentrated in the psychological event, mediation with science became possible and the widest freedom was conceded to the history of dogma and ecclesiastical institutions, now considered as historically relative, external, and secondary aspects of the religious life.

The theologian was then confronted with the problem of Christianity's claim to a truth superior to that of other religions. A mystic such as Luther would not even have posed the problem: in faith, ignited by the work of the Gospel, he would have found beatifying certainty. But Schleiermacher was not so much a mystic as a theoretician of mysticism. Forced to admit the dignity of all " experiences," he wished to see the primacy of Christianity in the force, purity and nobility of its feeling of love for the Heavenly Father. But it was a questionable solution, because into the criterion of discrimination had entered what were plainly ethical and rational elements. In reality, once faith is reduced to a many-sided immediate experience, the problem of the primacy of one of the historical religions over the others has little meaning.

An attempt to return to an objective authority, to the Gospel, had been made by Albrecht Ritschl.[8] He did not seek to attribute a decisive importance to the present individual experience, but to Christ's experience and to the symbolic expressions adopted by him. Christ himself became a sort of Carlylean hero-prophet. In reality, however, the certainty of Christianity had always been derived from the effect produced by the Gospel, that is, from the miraculous subjective experience worked by Jesus' words, which produced a faith in the will of God, in His love, and in His kingdom.

Meanwhile, the history of the church and of dogma, research in the Old and New Testaments, and the history of the religions of antiquity had removed Christianity from the isolation of its claim to a unique revelation. In his autobiographical sketch Troeltsch records the names of Wellhausen, Kuenen, Reuss, Weiszäcker, Hase, Harnack, Bousset, Wrede, Hackmann, Gunkel and Eichorn.[9] Their work had transformed " historical theology " into a history of Christianity which employed the methods of philological and critical history without reserve. Thus, historical fact on the one hand and the subjective experience on the other produced the concept of the double truth: that which was inner certainty, a subjective experience, when seen from the outside, proves to be a purely human phenomenon, partaking in all of the vicissitudes and developments of history. Thus envisaged, the religion of love which emanated from Palestine was perpetuated through its accommodation to Hellenistic and Roman culture.

The school of Ritschl could still mediate between faith and science, for it could point to the redemptive effect of the historical Christ upon men's hearts as a miracle being constantly repeated. But the situation which offered itself at the beginning of the twentieth century presented Troeltsch with problems of a completely different sort. He wrote: " The situation is serious, serious for Protestantism, which is fighting for the great life which seeps out of its broken and lifeless body, serious also for modern society, which has thoughtlessly broken all contact with the religious forces operating in it." [10]

In a series of lectures delivered at Bonn in 1893 Troeltsch declared that the proofs of the truth of the Gospel were its concordance with the deepest needs of the human heart, its power over the conscience, and the force with which it prostrates and elevates.[11] Beyond this immediate effect, which by itself testified to its own divine origin, he saw no other proof. It was the thesis of his master Ritschl. However, he was not at all satisfied. He asked himself to what extent Christian knowledge could be deduced from this immediate experience and how it could be reconciled to other " facts " which might be presented, by chance, with the same persuasive force.

This crisis of " immediate certainty " is, basically, the crisis of Protestantism itself. The strength of the inner light, the subjective aspect of grace, had allowed Luther to free himself from both authority and tradition. It had allowed Schleiermacher and Ritschl to eliminate from Protestantism whatever vestiges of Catholic dogma still remained in it. But in Troeltsch, faith is no longer strong enough to stand by itself. Ritschl had felt no need for apologiae, only for the exegesis of the Gospel; in Troeltsch, exegesis becomes biblical research (Bibelforschung) and destroys the mysterious effect of the Word. The believer finds himself confronted by a human document. And grace, far from effecting the miracle of inner certainty, is itself reduced

economic interests, between asceticism and the worldly ethic, between history and faith, and between Christianity and the modern world. He made compromise an ideal and maxim of life as well as a theory for the interpretation of history. One might even say that if for Heraclitus and Hegel war was the mother of all things, for Troeltsch this same war was a compromise. He knew that the great creations of history were born and revived only in the flames of general conflagrations, but for him those flames were necessary for the process of fusion.

According to him, state and culture had to pursue their own ends, unhindered by ecclesiastical points of view yet reconcilable with the ideals of religion.[15] For him Christianity was not the unique element of civilization, but one element among many, even if indispensible.[16] He admired the freshness, genuineness, and force of the individual mystical fact, declared himself in favor of a non-dogmatic church, a purely administrative organism,[17] and fought for freedom of conscience, not only within the state but also within the church; but he also recognized that religion always produces a community which lives for itself and requires that its truth be assimilated and perpetuated in some sort of organization. He rejected the hypothesis of Rudolf Sohm,[18] of a " purely religious " primitive church and declared Richard Rothe's dream of a final phase of the religious development, in which the church had become superfluous, unrealizable,[19] because he held that churches were a natural development of the authority of the founder. He assumed the role of champion of a " free " Christianity, but he realized that such a Christianity would, in due time, feel the necessity of an organization and of a common cultus.[20] He rejected Sohm's ideal of a church without ecclesiastical law, because he was convinced that even the juridical organization was necessarily derived from the primitive community; but he rejected the Catholic organization and endeavoured to eliminate from the Protestant churches the last " medieval " Catholic residues. For him the church had ceased to be a " repository of dogma and cultic observances " but was simply the *corpus mysticum Christi*, the community of the spirit, infinitely superior to the individuals who constituted it.[21] As a liberal theologian, he detested the sort of religious individualism which characterized Kierkegaard as anarchical. He envisaged an intellectualized religion (*Bildungsreligion*), but he did not wish to lose contact with the elementary forces of the popular religion (*Volksreligion*). Above all, the church appeared to him to be the most adequate form of religious life as compared with the sectarian and mystical forms of religious experience, because of the moderateness and flexibility which allowed the unification within it of different degrees of religious maturity and the assimilation of the contemporary life which confronted it.[22]

Of course, for Troeltsch the absence of compromise is the cause of conflict and sterility. The dependence of the Lutheran Church upon the state not only brought on that sterility evidenced by the absence of a missionary spirit,[23] it also resulted in a grievous damage to the nation, in as much as it led to the general abandonment of religion by the masses.[24]

It would be inexact to speak of a sympathy for the Catholic church in Troeltsch. Yet he admired it as a "masterpiece of compromise" which had the virtue of providing a matrix for the coexistence of popular religiosity and philosophic dogmatism, absolute authority and revolutionary individualism, asceticism and the modern ethic, and which had, at different times in its history, effected compromises with classical civilization, German feudalism, the culture of the Renaissance, the modern state and even parliamentary democracy.[25] He justified the dogma of papal infallibility by recognizing the necessity of a supreme mediator; but at the same time he justified modernism, because it seemed to him to correspond to the tradition of the church itself; and he saw in Tyrell and Loisy spirits engaged in the same enterprise as himself.

For Troeltsch, the essential compromise and the one to which he dedicated all his energies was that which he wished to effect between Christian theism and historical science. It is an error to think that he ever conceived of himself in a struggle against "historicism" *per se*; he was only engaged in a fight against "unlimited historicism." [26] The discipline of history had forced him to raise the question of the absolute value of Christianity, but it never really shook his theistic dualism. Thus the pathetic figure of Troeltsch struggling to free himself from the mire of history and aspiring to something objective and outside time is only partially correct.

His real adversary was monism, in whatever form it might present itself: mystical, pantheistic, rationalistic, or naturalistic. He purged himself of Schleiermacher's influence because he sensed in his mysticism the "dangerous pantheism of the non-differentiated." Among the pernicious effects of monism, next to utilitarianism, aestheticism, and pessimism, he listed relativism, which was, therefore, for him not a direct consequence of historicism.

According to him, there could be found no serious objection in modern thought to his dualistic faith which separated the world of truth and absolute values from the world of nature and history. The prophetico-Christian idea of a personal God had not been shaken, much less replaced, by other systems of thought.[27]

His was another problem. It was that of the professor of the theological faculty solicitous of the fate of the community and aware of the importance of tradition and communal spirit (*Gemeingeist*): the problem of the relation of the historical individual to the person of Christ, the cultus of which was the only possible bond of a truly Christian community. Here historical criticism had struck at vital roots. At the same time he rejected a view of Christ as the center of the history of all mankind; indeed, he prohibited the tendency to see in him the vertex of a universal revelation, as "liberal theology" tended to do. How was it possible to anchor an eternal truth in an historical personality? In order to answer this question, Troeltsch undertook the construction of a philosophy of religion and history.

*   *   *

Troeltsch's first attempt was to combine the psychology of Dilthey with the science of religion of his other master Paul de Lagarde, the orientalist and Biblical scholar. Dilthey had fashioned the concept of the *Erlebnis*, the life-experience which stands at the roots of poetry, religion, and metaphysics: a concept which, derived from the study of the youthful writings of Schleiermacher, was a translation into modern terms of the idea of mystical intuition. It therefore lent itself to the definition of the primitive religious phenomenon (*Urphänomen*) which Troeltsch sought to isolate from all dogmatic incrustations.[28] Since, however, the "phenomenon" was found in all religions, the problem of the primacy of Christianity and the Christian *Erlebnis* arose once more. Here de Lagarde, with his reduction of theology to a comparative science of religions, could be utilized, because it would be necessary to make a fundamental comparison of the force and depth of the inner life which each of the religions revealed.[29] Here theology threatened to become, for Troeltsch, an historico-psychological science.

He perceived immediately, however, that he was tending towards psychologism, the direct source of relativistic doubt. The *Erlebnis*, a psychological fact, could not in its irrational immediacy offer any guarantee of truth.

Now this was the time in which the new philosophy of value had once more taken up the Kantian method. And Troeltsch turned to Kant's philosophy of religion with the hope of raising himself from the psychical data to the Absolute with its aid.[30] He hoped, as it were, to find within human consciousness a religious *a priori* which stood in an organic relationship to the logical *a priori* and which thus might be inserted into the inner harmony of consciousness with a rational necessity.[31]

Kant, as is known, had founded religion upon morality. The Neo-Kantians—Windelband, Eucken, and Class—had extended the relation to logic and aesthetics, for they saw in religion not a special form of the spirit but only an indication of a transcendent reality to which the consciousness of the norm related itself, a reality inhering in all the forms of the spirit: logic, ethics, and aesthetics. Troeltsch's task can be seen as an attempt to bring Kant and Schleiermacher into agreement. He proposed to vindicate the autonomy of religion by finding a place for "the religious categories" of inspiration and revelation beside the other categories.[32] It was an attempt to broaden the Kantian system in order to leave open a way to the irrational.

On the other hand, in order to be able to demonstrate that this knowledge was not simply a psychological phenomenon, but was a true contact with the transcendental, Troeltsch assigned to religion that central function which Schleiermacher had assigned to feeling: it was conceived as a dark unity of consciousness from which emerged other distinct forms and in which consciousness, by comprehending itself as it were, might become aware of contact with a reality which transcended it. The reality of the contact was verified, according to Troeltsch, by the inner, a priori organization of consciousness which brings about a fundamental confrontation of all values.

It is obvious that such a theory of religion, which in Troeltsch's writing never progressed beyond the outline stage, was only an attempt to correlate varied and contradictory formulae: the mystical experience of divine immanence is here translated into a theistic knowledge of the transcendent, in order to be, ultimately, reduced to the Kantian consciousness of the norm. With this syncretistic theory, Troeltsch proposed to critically sift the various historical religions in order to establish a hierarchy of worth. He realized, however, that in order to isolate them and rank them a preliminary philosophy of history was required.

From the beginning, Troeltsch had aspired to a theology based upon universal history and the history of religions (religions-geschichtliche Theologie).[33] Later he was considered the systemitizer and dogmatist of that group of historians of Christianity

—composed of men such as Wellhausen, Lagarde, Gunkel, Weis-zäker, Wrede, Usener, Holtzmann, and Bousset—who had ceased to regard the truth of the Bible as being revealed in any super-natural manner.[34] Since historical criticism had destroyed the miraculous character of the Bible and the church, he now in-tended to derive from the course of history "the productive element of a necessary truth." Once he had projected the Abso-lute to a place above thought and therefore above history, he believed that he could then rediscover it in history itself.

How could he entertain the hope that historiography might actually accomplish this grandiose task of constructing a hier-archy of values? In the existing historical formations, he argued, we already find some concrete references to the Absolute: it will be enough to impartially compare them; and from that com-parison the standard of measurement will result spontaneously.

Troeltsch, however, was aware that he was moving in a circle; that is, he realized that while he had been attempting to derive a standard of measurement from the hierarchy of historical for-mations, he had already presupposed a unit of measurement by which he was to construct the hierarchy. In order to break out of the circle he had to appeal to an act of will: an individual and irrational act of choice the necessity of which resided only in the certainty of the judicant, forced to judge in that way and in no other. The "faith" of Luther, the "feeling" of Schleier-macher, and the "immediate effect" of Ritschl were thus re-duced to personal choice, the subjectivity of which Troeltsch envisaged to be limited only by the width and depth of knowl-edge of the individual historian. The ultimate and decisive criterion of the hierarchy was not derived from experience but was an individual act of faith which found its own certainty within itself.

This faith was, in Troeltsch's case, the faith which distin-guished and united the Creator and the creature, the person of God and the human personality. This faith allowed one to raise oneself to a sort of unitary vision of the world of history. For the "ethical and religious" man, history could not be a chaos but had to be conceived as an ordered succession in which the life of the human spirit, through all its struggles and errors, had to appear as a progressive development. According to him, history was born of unitary forces and tended towards a unitary goal, and the differences between the great historical blocks or formations were more external and fortuituous than real and essential. They were, more than anything, ramifications and disguises of the great ideas which really operated in the world. He concluded, therefore, that in the apparent anarchy one could discover the "profound divinity" of the human spirit, could discover that faith in God was essentially identical in all its forms, and could find that this faith progressed, i. e., gained in energy and purity, in the degree to which man became disengaged from his original bonds of nature (*Naturgebundenheit*).

In so arguing, however, he did not mean to imply an agreement with the Hegelian concept of becoming. On the contrary, like Ranke, he wished to allow all of the historical formations to retain their individuality and peculiar value: succession ought not "mediate" the individual, nor was it to be considered as a continuous and inevitable growth. Nor did the hierarchy of "formations" coincide completely with mere chronological succession.

But if history had this unitary meaning of emancipation from nature, then for Troeltsch it also had to take on a Christian meaning. In fact, at only one point did the chain appear truly broken: in the religion of the prophets and in the person of Christ the human person had been raised above nature and given eternally transcendent ends. Thus Troeltsch claimed to overcome the opposition between Christian faith and historical science by not lifting Christianity outside the stream of history, by deriving indeed from the whole of history a grandiose testimony of its intrinsic truth, and at the same time not allowing this truth to fall into the status of mere dogmatic formulation, in as much as it did not exclude the possibility of subsequent modifications of the religious forces unleashed by Christianity.

However, the question of the nature of the "historical formations" and in particular of Christianity was still undecided. In a famous book which Troeltsch considered to be "symbolic" of the historical bent of the theology of his time, Harnack had held forth on the "nature" or "essence" of Christianity. The concept of essence, Troeltsch pointed out, under the evident influence of Loisy, was based upon a procedure which was obviously abstract and contained a number of methodological difficulties.[35] This notion of essence, he argued, is a peculiarly historical concept: as Burckhardt had defined the essence of the Renaissance and Ihering that of Roman law, so the history of religion ought to investigate the essence of Hinduism, Buddhism, and Islam. The essence is not the original idea but that which realizes itself throughout the whole historical development by continual conflict with and assimilation of foreign elements, deviations, and enemies. Ranke had spoken of the "ideas" operating in history and had regarded them, not as hypostasized forces, but as forces active in individuals and conditioned by circumstances. Troeltsch preferred to call them the contents of culture. Out of these contents arose the "tendencies" which, although variously oriented, proceeded in a determined manner from their point of origin.

However, according to Troeltsch, "contents" and "tendencies" manifest certain affinities and similarities and are thus susceptible of classification into "types"; around the generalized types the individual phenomena oscillate. Jellinek had distinguished types of political organization, and Max Weber, types of economic organization: Troeltsch proposed to give elasticity and movement to the abstract concept of the essence of religions and then construct a strictly moralistic and anti-historical definition of Christianity with the concept of type. This permitted him to conceive an elastic unity in the history of Christianity and to interpret it as a religious principle which was never complete and finished, a principle conceived as living energy and therefore capable of indefinite development.

* * *

All of the motifs, both metaphysical and methodological, which are contained in Troeltsch's thought are summarized, in what he considered to be a new Christian apologia, in his essay, " The Absoluteness of Christianity and the History of Religion " (*Die Absolutheit des Christentums und die Religionsgeschichte*) .[36]

The title is not wholly correct, for in this work Troeltsch rejects every concept of absolute truth. Earlier he had sought to free himself from the rigid dichotomy of the absolute and the relative, which seemed to him a residue of methodological dogmatism.[37] He preferred the concept of " normative value " to the concept of absolute. He did not attempt to derive this concept by *a priori* arguments, however, because for him even ethics was an historical product. He saw human history as a struggle for the production of norms, as an incessant effusion of tendencies which raised man out of a state of nature and animality. Such creative syntheses remain somehow individual and relative to the historical moment in which they are created. The Absolute remains above, in the inaccessible realm, but history has meaning in as much at it is a presentiment of that realm and an aspiration to it, in as much as it creates normative values which are historically limited forms of the Absolute. All religions point to a normative end, to a transcendental goal which cannot be an illusion, because it is the force which provokes the restlessness and motive power of history itself; in this sense it is a factual datum, not a problem.

The triumph of the purest and deepest religious force is to be awaited. The legalistic religions—Judaism and Islam—impose an *ascesis*; the redemptive religions—Christianity and the Indic religions—seek escape from the natural world. But only Christianity exalts the personality, conceives it as something which is undergoing a process of development through dedication and

action, and which conceives God as a person. In it the great
ideas common to all religions—God, the world, the soul, the
afterlife—have complete autonomy. It is, therefore, the highest
religion which has appeared thus far.

Troeltsch did not exclude the possibility of a later development, but he did regard it as improbable. It was enough for him
to know that he was on the right path to the possession of a
normative truth: to seek an absolute truth in the earthly life
seemed to him the height of folly, a folly which could only lead
to the destruction of faith and the removal of a sense of human
limits.

It is clear that Troeltsch could, from his theistic viewpoint,
argue the superiority of Christianity only because he had reduced
it precisely to a moralistic theism. But the question at once
springs to mind: is this really historical Christianity?

For Troeltsch, Jesus was a person who had enjoyed an incomparable experience of the holy. Redemption was in Jesus'
message, not in His passion and death. The confusion of the
one for the other was, according to Troeltsch, the result of later
apologetics; and the dogma of the Incarnation of the *Logos* was
a compromise between the Christian doctrine of a supernatural
messenger from the Kingdom of God and the classical doctrine
of the divine reason operating in every corpus of wisdom and
philosophy.[38] But is Christianity to be considered as mere faith
in the Message? It might be so considered by a Harnack who
found the essence of Christianity in the Sermon on the Mount,
but not by Troeltsch who refused to separate the egg from the
yolk, condemned the search for an "essence" as a vestige of
eighteenth-century rationalism, and demanded that the entire
Christian historical development be considered as a whole. Yet,
it is patent that at least from the time of St. Paul, Christianity
has taken as its central doctrine the faith in the redemptive
death of Christ.

Thus, Troeltsch found himself trapped between the demands
of his position as a historian (which forced him to consider

Christianity as a historical movement) and the anti-historical spirit of Protestantism. As compared with the Hegelian Bauer and his school, he refused to see history as the development of an idea and Christianity as one phase in that development. This approach, according to Troeltsch, always seemed to redound to the advantage of Catholicism in as much as it was able to boast of its uninterrupted continuity and its effective development of its own dogma and institutions. In Troeltsch's view, Protestantism by its very nature demanded a conception of history as a series of breaks or ruptures. Thus envisaged, Catholicism might be seen as a deviation. Yet, how can a Protestant deny the Pauline faith?

As was his custom, Troeltsch overcame this difficulty with a form of compromise. He conceded that even the Pauline message might be considered a new religious element which operated alongside the Messianic element throughout the Christian historical development. Once started on this path, he ended by also accepting Platonism and Stoicism as elements acquired by Christianity during its historical development which were now inseparable from it. He could not deny that a certain kind of development had taken place. In medieval Catholicism, in the Reformation, and in " Christian humanism " he perceived the development of elements which were already present in the primary phase, which had come forth under new circumstances with their own peculiar accents. These were not therefore developments true and proper, but simple " effects " of the spirit of Christ in different historical circumstances.

He was able to hold that elements as diverse and contradictory as the Catholic idea of the church, Protestant individualism, the Augustinian ideas of sin and grace, and Christian humanism were already contained in the primitive message. In fact, it was precisely in this contradictory plurality of possibilities that the richness of Christianity was to be found. It is a religion of redemption and at the same time a world-accepting religion, and this fundamental dualism is continually transcended in faith and in action and by the simultaneous affirmation of the value of the individual personality and a sense of community. These diverse aspects he saw crystallized into the different Christian formations —into the church, sect and mystical movements—all legitimate, because all, in some way, were directly descended from the Gospel.

Thus Troeltsch was able to boast of not having been halted by the definition of Christianity as the Sermon on the Mount and of having taken into consideration the entire history of Christianity. On the other hand, it is obvious that he made no concession whatever to the principle of development (*svolgimento*). History, for Troeltsch, was only the separation of elements originally united, even if they were not distinct. The so-called "developments" were only aberrations, variations, and violations of the primitive happy compromise.

Far from adhering to historicism, therefore, Troeltsch assumed a negative attitude towards history itself. On the other hand, was not that very theological movement to which he belonged an attempt to reconcile Christian faith with modern science and the modern world? Did not the term "modernity" itself imply a conception of the positive value of history?

Actually, the term "modern" did not mean "superior" for Troeltsch. The "modern world" was only a period objectively different from the other periods, a "type," the beginning of which he placed at the end of the seventeenth century, as Dilthey had done.

Closer analysis revealed to him a disquieting problem. He could easily enough interpret the earlier phases of Western civilization as unfoldings or "effects" of the primitive Christian message; they were all more or less variations on the message, or at least could be so conceived. But the characteristics of the modern world constituted a different problem: besides the discoveries and capitalism, the characteristics were individualism, the sense of immanence, and, above all, the new natural and historical sciences, all free from dogmatic premises. As opposed to medieval ecclesiastical civilization, it had made man the principle of civilization and morality, affirmed the positive worth of the earthly life, and discredited the ideas of original sin and a transcendental existence. Was a compromise with these principles still possible?

Troeltsch neither rejected nor castigated the modern world. He did not delude himself by regarding it as Christian but made of it a " type " in itself, differentiated from the other type which was Christianity. According to him, the modern individualistic, immanentistic and rationalistic world was derived directly from the Renaissance; the Reformation had been nothing but an interruption. Over against this new type only Catholicism had remained faithful to the old, medieval type, projecting itself into the modern world like a monstrous, foreign body.[39]

But in like manner the Protestantism of Luther and Calvin was medieval; it was a transformation but still a continuation of Catholicism. In his *Protestant Christianity and the Church in the Modern Age* (*Protestantisches Christentum und Kirche in der Neuzeit*),[40] Troeltsch continued the analysis begun by Dilthey; here he interpreted the Reformation as a resurgence of medieval thought, which, by destroying the rudiments of a free secular civilization, had forced Europe to live two centuries longer in the medieval world.

Since he was not predisposed to repudiate this " free secular civilization," Troeltsch undertook to separate the medieval from the modern in Luther's thought. Here he distinguished between primitive Protestantism and neo-Protestantism as two sides of the Lutheran Reformation, the one side medieval, the other modern. It was the Reformation, he concluded, which had saved the idea of the church as an objective institution by responding to the Catholic doctrines of predestination, work and penance with the Pauline idea of redemption. To be sure, its concept of grace was Augustinian and medieval, even if for it grace was no longer sacramental *medicina* but *favor*, i. e., revelation of God's love. The reformers' view of justification had remained Catholic and their concept of faith itself was only the apex of a process which stood in the tradition of monasticism, mysticism and nominalism. The condemnation of monasticism as a special class did not mean the exclusion of asceticism, but was, on the contrary, an accentuation of the idea of original sin. Finally, it conserved the principles of conformity of thought and coercion by maintaining the institutions of censorship and even developing its own scholastic philosophy. The essential novelty, according to Troeltsch, resided in the destruction of the concept of the sacrament, in the reduction of faith to grace, i. e., to the miraculous affirmation of God, a purely internal, psychological event, even though it is a predestined gift granted independently of all human action. The emancipation of this idea from medieval incrustations had been effected by the heresies of Protestantism —in the Baptist movement, spiritualism, the *Aufklärung*, and German idealism. It was these " Protestant heresies " which constituted the essence of neo-Protestantism.

It is evident, however, that even Luther's novelty presupposed and implied some medieval ideas: the doctrine of original sin, the concept of grace and redemptive faith, the pessimistic principle of the *servum arbitrium*, the doctrine of supernatural revelation. Troeltsch would eliminate these elements; but, then, what would remain in his Christianity that could be distinguished from the " modern world "? And was not this " last phase of neo-Protestantism," of which he proclaimed himself a herald and champion, really that German idealism which in Hegel was outright monism, immanentism and historicism?

Troeltsch avoided these consequences by conceiving history as a simple juxtaposition of " types " or " civilizational forms." As Dilthey had described the perduration and intermixture of different " types " of *Weltanschauungen*, so Troeltsch was able to conceive history pluralistically as the constant interaction and cooperation of diverse " bodies," " types," and " organisms." Thus, the unitary development of history, any kind of dialectical development of history, is completely eliminated. Ranke's ideal, which prohibited the mediation of epochs and civilizations and their subordination to any unitary plan, was maintained. The individuality of the epoch was safeguarded.

It is obvious, however, how schematic is this division of European history into parallel types. Troeltsch could detach the modern world and make of it a type in itself only by eliminating every religious element, making of it a schema. And here an unconscious influence upon him is manifested: his " modern world " is nothing but Comte's " third stage," the civilization of science and positivistic interests, immune from theological and metaphysical influences. This was a positivistic residue inherited by Troeltsch from Dilthey.

As a Christian, Troeltsch should have rejected this *regnum hominis*. He did not reject it because he admired the " amplitude of its horizons, the efficiency of its technical and political organization, the freedom of the working classes, and scientific progress in general." He preferred a compromise which would reconcile religious truth with scientific truth, and allow the co-existence of the patrimony of Christian ideas with those which were non-Christian.

Like all doctrines of the double truth, his neo-Protestantism was nothing but a symptom of crisis and an age of transition. If one were allowed to employ the jargon of business, it might be said that it was a friendly agreement which concealed an inner deficit and pretended to avoid bankruptcy thereby.

However, liquidation was unavoidable. That modern world which Troeltsch could not bring himself to repudiate pressed in about him. All of a sudden he was snatched away from the atmosphere of the theological faculties and ecclesiastical conferences by what he called " the arrival of the German people at political maturity." And the modern world was revealed to him to be not only historical criticism, scientific progress and aristocratic individualism but an arena of violent social and political struggles in which power and self interest predominated, a cruel and merciless world which rejected completely every type of compromise with the Christian ethic of love.

II

In the course of the nineteenth century the crisis of German Protestantism scarcely penetrated beyond the orbit of the university faculties, the sphere of higher cultural interests, and at most the bourgeois intelligentsia. Generally the masses had not been disturbed by disputes over the origins of Christianity and its dogmas. Here and there among the lower middle classes the writings of Strauss had become known, but the large mass of artisans and peasants reacted to this new "science of the gentleman" with a renewed pietistic fervor manifested in the *Stille im Lande* movement. It was the rapid transformation of patriarchal Germany into a country of steel and coal near the end of the century which really shook the old evangelical church organism to its popular foundations. Bismarck had responded to worker agitation with his anti-socialist laws *(Sozialistengesetz)*, and the church had given its approval, just as it had approved the massacre of rebellious peasants and communistic Anabaptists during the sixteenth century. The old Inner Mission, born of the pietist movement, could only heal a few wounds which existed on the edge of the system. The masses responded by wholesale desertion of the churches. Compared to Catholicism, which could boast of a certain success in the organization of the workers, German Protestantism appeared possessed of a thorough-going sterility, incapable of speaking one new word. The attempt of the court preacher, Stöcker, to found a "Christian-social" worker's party served only to point up the naïveté of Stöcker himself. He had absolutely no support among the workers, and Bismarck, who was completely unsympathetic to the idea of having to deal with a Protestant evangelical democracy similar to that of the hated Catholic center, undermined Stöcker's plans and heaped ridicule upon their formulator.

Naturally the question did not end there. William II, who had not concealed his sympathy for Stöcker and had spoken in favour of the Inner Mission and the " new tasks " confronting the church, allowed it to be rumoured about that an ecclesiastical reform was imminent. The anti-Semitic preachings of Stöcker had found a wide audience among the landed aristocracy, and a movement took shape which had the flavor of an anti-capitalistic *fronde* in that it did not attack race as such but concentrated upon the Jewish " spirit," i. e., capitalism. In Stöcker there still existed the old Prussian " Christian-Germanic " ideals, which stood in violent opposition of " Mammonism," to the perverse " new spirit." But among the liberal clergy and the young pastors of the industrial centers the ideals of social democracy were beginning to find favour. Those theologians who had once concerned themselves solely with the relation between the Christian faith and historical criticism now gave themselves enthusiastically to the analysis of the relation between the " social question " and the Christian ethic. At their head stood the most fertile publicist in the Germany of William II, Friedrich Naumann, who was fighting for a " national social " alliance between Christianity, democracy and the German imperial idea.

The question was taken up by Troeltsch rather late in his career, in the first decade of the twentieth century. In his autobiographical sketch he states that this sudden change of interest was brought about by the cessation of his interest in the philosophy of religion.[41] The way in which the problem presented itself to him was characteristic, through an insignificant book on " the social tasks of the evangelical church " which he was supposed to review. The task revealed to him the complete ignorance which prevailed in German religious thought concerning the problem, and he immediately undertook the task of determining the character of the Christian social ethic of which everyone was speaking. In place of the review was born *The Social Teachings of the Christian Churches and Sects (Die Soziallehren der christlichen Kirchen und Gruppen)* .[42]

*   *   *

In those years Troeltsch entered into the sphere of Max Weber. The extent to which Troeltsch, the mild theologian, was able to maintain his intellectual independence once he had entered into contact with the robust, powerful personality of his friend Weber is difficult to determine. Under the influence of Catholic and Protestant attempts to resolve the social question on the basis of a Christian ethic, Troeltsch gave himself to the study of the social doctrines of the Christian churches, of the Christian sects, and in general the relations between religious life and economic organization. But the stimulus to undertake an assault upon the Marxist theory of the "superstructure" must have come to him from the sociologist and economist Weber. Thus, undoubtedly it was Weber who played the dominant role in the formulation of the famous thesis on the birth of the "capitalist spirit" out of "worldly asceticism" and Calvinist dogmas, even if Troeltsch did speak of the thesis as the fruit of a collaboration between Weber the sociologist and himself the theologian.[43]

Also, the inspiration of his friend is evident in the formulation of the circular scheme by which religious life was to be correlated with the economic life, a scheme which takes on the character of a sociological mechanism.[44] Finally, it is also from Weber that the distinction between the "types" of social organization of the Christian idea, employed by Troeltsch in his *Social Teachings* (*Soziallehren*), is derived. The types of social organization were: the church—an objective institution of grace and salvation which exists independently of the subjective perfection of its members and operates through sacraments and a clergy; the sect—a union of free and elected disciples who ignore the objective value of the sacrament and the special dignity of the sacerdote; and the mystical—an expression of anarchical individualism which admits a community and a collective consciousness only in the most relative sense, as a stimulant to the personal religious life. One may add that this sociological schematism weighed heavily upon Troeltsch's work as historian, for, once obliged to recognize that the three elements had been indistinct in primitive Christianity and that even later they appear in different degree in all religious formations, he thereby raised the question of quantitative proportion, and he was forced to deal with individual religious formations as though he were making a chemical analysis. This gave to his work that character of ordered clarity and detached objectivity which is proper to the naturalistic technique but also lent to it the monotony of a classificatory exposition which lacked any trace of dialectical development. Instead of problems one is presented with different ideologies which follow one upon the other as in a lexicon. There is lacking in this indifferent plurality of doctrines the negative moment, the insufficiency which translates itself into the painful need for and progression towards the new. This absence of drama gives to the work the character of a list of formulae which, while clearly illustrated, pass before the eyes like the images of a magic lantern, totally lacking in weight and substance. It is the tribute paid by Troeltsch to the genius of his friend Weber and the sociological method expounded by him.

Yet this was not the deepest influence of Weber on Troeltsch; there was another which weakened his own vision and interpretation of Christianity. Weber held a Tolstoian idea of Christianity, conceiving it as an otherworldly religion of love and its prime attribute, a radical rejection of all worldly values. Such a view was, virtually, the criticism of a liberal Protestantism determined to reconcile faith and science and of a Christian democracy intent upon finding a " social " ethic in the Gospel. In a profession of faith composed at this time, Troeltsch reaffirmed his belief that Christianity was the most complete breakthrough of the spirit of God into the world, the purest of God's revelations, but he also added that being the most pure, spiritual and universal religion, Christianity was perforce lacking in the means of descending into the realm of social and political reality.[45] The relation which existed between the national religions and the socio-political life here appears severed. A hiatus is opened between spirit and nature.

Troeltsch did not see any paradox or dilemma in this. On the contrary, he felt that Christianity had come to terms with the world that it despised. Nor did he consider such compromise as decadence, corruption or betrayal. On the other hand, since he was averse to every immanentistic interpretation of history, he could not see in this submersion of the religious idea in social and political reality any sort of conquest or progress. He was limited to maintaining that compromise was inevitable, because no matter how intolerant, rebellious and ascetic the spirit might be, it was always obliged to halt itself before the insuperable and uncontrollable forces of human nature.

The immediate effect of the adoption of Weber's view of Christianity was the resuscitation of the old pessimism, the fruit of the Lutheran, Augustinian and Pauline conception of nature as fundamentally evil. For Troeltsch lacked the ancient courage and decision of the mystic. Nature, politics and force were not for him to be either romantically celebrated and consecrated or ascetically condemned. Having discovered a fundamental dichotomy between spirit and nature, he posited the necessity of compromise. The character of the compromise would vary with the times and according to historical circumstance, but this did not imply for him any amelioration of the situation or any alteration to the advantage of the spiritual.

It is obvious that Troeltsch did not think through this problem of the relation of nature to spirit. Instead, he searched for guidance in the history of compromise itself. How had Christianity, although it lacked the proper means, been able to descend into the realm of socio-political reality? Who or what aided it in this difficult transition; who or what was the mediator? This is the theme of the *Social Teachings* and the *Essays in the History of Ideas and the Sociology of Religion (Aufsätze zur Geistesgeschichte und Religionssoziologie)*.[46] In these two works Troeltsch sustains the thesis (which he considered a discovery) that the mediation was accomplished by the doctrine of natural law.

The idea was suggested to him by one of his earlier works in which he had indicated the importance of the Stoic concept of the *lex naturae* in the elaboration of the Christian ethic.

In that earlier essay he had likened the adoption of this principle by Patristic theologians to the adoption of the Logos concept by Christologists. But the historical importance of the Christian natural law tradition had been recognized some years earlier by Gierke in his work on Althusius; [47] and Dilthey, in his essays on " the natural system of the sciences of the spirit in the seventeenth century," had pointed to the transition from the Christian idea of natural law to the profane conception of it as one of the most decisive developments in the formation of the modern spirit.

Seizing upon the idea of natural law as the great link between the Christian ethic and the " world," Troeltsch made of it the nerve of the social doctrines of Christianity and therefore one of the principles of Western civilization. Besides posing the problem of the attitude of Catholicism, Lutheranism, Calvinism and the Protestant sects towards this Roman Stoic idea, he was able to give new insights into the socio-political history of Europe. The question of the relation between religious faith and political ideas had arisen once more in the Germany in the early nineteenth century. It had been centered in the polemic between conservative Catholics and Protestants when Jarcke had attributed the revolutionary ideas of the period to the Lutheran Reformation and Ranke had accused the Jesuits of having been the first to legitimatize resistance to authority. But it was only through the dispassionate investigations of Troeltsch that the relation between the confessions and the socio-political ideologies of the various European nations became clearly defined. More important, Troeltsch demonstrated that those ideas of natural law which the Romantic and historicist publicists attributed to the abstract, modern rationalistic mentality, belonged to a tradition which went back to Cicero and Seneca, St. Ambrose and St. Augustine, even if it was only in the seventeenth century, in the climate of ideas created by the rationalism of the mathematical sciences, that they had been cast loose from their metaphysical and theological moorings. Western democracy was seen to have its roots in the doctrine of absolute natural law as expounded by Calvinism and the sects; Catholicism was shown to be less radical in as much as it admitted a relative natural law; and Lutheranism was shown to be in its social ethic resolutely conservative and authoritarian. To round out the picture, Slavic Christianity, the heir of Byzantium and the Greek Fathers, was characterized by monastic, apolitical and anti-legalistic tendencies, as Weber had argued, precisely because it was lacking the natural law tradition.[48]

Troeltsch's analysis was, as noted above, most dispassionate. He took no position himself, being content to clarify and explain. He described the grandiose history of this idea of natural law without ever raising the question of the nature and value of the idea itself. He did not make himself the champion of an idea which from the time of Althusius and Thomasius had found little favour on German soil; however, he did regard it with a certain benevolence and even with a certain sense of pity, as the mediator of the compromise between the Christian faith and the " world."

Furthermore, he felt that a compromise was demanded between the idea of natural law and the world. Without really taking into account the fact that the idea of natural law is, as much as Christianity, a dualistic doctrine which opposes an ideal of perfection to an imperfect human " nature " and that, therefore, far from mitigating the conflict, it really aggravated it by bringing it down to earth, Troeltsch began by making a distinction between absolute natural law and relative natural law. It was the latter (which is already a compromise) that had effected the compromise between natural law and the world. He felt that the church had been able to overcome its original indifference towards the world and to formulate its own doctrine of state and society, only when it had become able to apply the distinction made by the Roman Stoics between an ideal golden age without struggle and violence, without slavery, property and class differentiation, and later ages of corruption and violence in which the ancient natural freedom and equality had been transformed into the orders of state, law and property. Taken up by the Latin Fathers and fused with the myth of original sin, this doctrine had permitted Western Christendom to justify the existing socio-political order as *poena et remedium peccati*. The acceptance of absolute natural law had been left to monasticism. This accounts for the power and attraction of the monastic ideal and, at the same time, for the vacillations of a Christian thought confronted with the values of a worldly existence.[49]

Now, aside from the question of whether or not it is permissible to attribute a natural law aspect to monastic asceticism, it is far from correct to identify a doctrine which justifies the socio-political realm by considering it a *poena* with a relative natural law theory. The natural law idea was that heritage of the classical world which had, after the disappearance of the *polis*, sought to salvage for the individual a universal dignity as "citizen of the world." Thus, as handed down by the Roman Stoics, it was a positive acceptance of the world, a proclamation of its fundamental rationality (even if ruffled by passion) and an assertion of the possibility of its betterment through positive legislation and the work of the state. Cicero, Seneca and the *jurisconsulti*, inasmuch as they claimed to release law from the arbitrary judgment of the law giver and make it dependent upon a universal, rational norm, must be seen as guardians of the ancient concept of the sanctity of the law, the dignity of the legislator, and the belief that men are capable of reforming their society for the better.

Along this same path, within certain limits, moved Thomistic Catholicism. In the Fathers there are indubitable traces of the natural law ideal, but only in so far as those elements won distinction later in their Thomistic elaboration can one really speak of a relative natural law. Troeltsch's view, consequently, would have value only for Catholicism, in which the unstable compromise, and often an outright conflict, are to be found.

Troeltsch was concerned, however, with separating primitive Christianity from Catholicism, which he considered to be a medieval creation of the Pseudo-Isidorian and Gregorian papacy. In " an extremely important addition " to the *Social Teachings*, the essay on St. Augustine, he sought to correct not only the old opinions of Protestant theologians, who had made St. Augustine their master, but also the modern view, which made of him the father of the medieval world view. He sought to show, that is, that the thought of Augustine had to be interpreted within the framework of the practical problems which confronted him in his own time, the problems of the dying classical world. Similarly, he attempted to show that Augustine's concept of the *Civitas Dei*, of the kingdom of grace, had little in common with the medieval idea of the church, just as his political ideas had little in common with the medieval notion of the *sacrum imperium*.[50]

Since he was utilizing the sociological method and interpreting Catholic social philosophy as a type different and separate from Patristic social thought, he could not clearly appreciate the significance of the Thomistic doctrine of the double order, of the higher *lex Dei et Christi* and the lower *lex naturae*, as an effort to penetrate into and conquer the world, as a denial of mystical renunciation, as a deliberate attempt to institute and maintain a natural moral order through the help of a servile state. In all that, Troeltsch saw only a form of compromise.

Much more original is his analysis of the social doctrines of Protestantism. Here he was aided by a distinction which he had made in *Protestant Christianity and the Church in the Modern Age* between the emotional, internal character of Lutheranism, mystically absorbed in faith, i. e., the light which grace ignites in the hearts of men, and the practical character of Calvinism, which had made of predestination a test of the ability of man to execute the commands of God. Troeltsch held that the two different points of orientation of the central dogmas of the two confessions determined their different attitudes in the social, political and economic realms: Lutheranism was indifferent and Calvinism aggressive. In these conclusions, Troeltsch paralleled the work of Max Weber.

Above all, Troeltsch shows how Luther, after having initially envisaged a reform of Christianity through the spontaneous power of the Spirit and the Word, had been obliged to abandon himself to the force of the state, because the destruction of the hierarchical order of the church had led to anarchy in those areas in which the political authority had not assumed direct control: in the choice of clerics, the definition of doctrine, and the direction of morality, a system which was extended even to the feudal lords who had to exercise the power of ecclesiastical patronage over their own lands. With Weber, he called attention also to the Lutheran notion of calling (*Beruf*) : the idea of a holy vocation and a means of sanctification through which Lutheranism placed its stamp of approval upon an agrario-feudal society, rigidly divided into classes and corporations. It is one of the merits of Troeltsch to have courageously brought to light this conservative-authoritarian character of the Lutheran social idea. However, this character is attributed by Troeltsch essentially to the new " meaning " which Luther gave to the concept of natural law, " inherited " by him from Catholicism. Indifferent and pessimistic towards the world, Luther had transformed the idea of the *lex naturae* by defining the essence of the state as force and power, justifying its function as an institution established by Providence to the ends of discipline, and imposing upon the subjects of the state an attitude of obedient resignation both towards the impious prince and the tyrant. From this precept Troeltsch then deduced the respect of the Lutheran populace for the police and the bureaucracy, the spirit of voluntary subjection, and the sense of official duty.

But it is obvious that Luther did not " inherit," mucn less give a new meaning to, natural law; instead he actually destroyed it.

Since Troeltsch lacked a preliminary definition of what exactly constituted natural law, he was able to ascribe to Luther a natural law theory deprived of the rational and individualistic element. But such a concept of law can hardly be considered adequate. In fact, even if one does find in Luther's writings a few hints of *lex naturae*, his concept is essentially opposed to that of *jus naturale*: he conceives of an historically formed order, of the actual situation, with all of its class differences, functions and powers as consecrated and sealed by Providence. Any criticism, any ascertainment of abuses and institutional irrationalities is excluded *a priori*. And all this is not merely the result of Luther's misreading of the natural law idea, but derives directly from his reaffirmation of the dogma of sin and grace, from his pessimistic attitude towards the world, from his denial of the doctrine of works, and his doctrine of the enslaved will.

Troeltsch clearly demonstrated how Calvinism, as a result of its original dogmatic orientation, had not abandoned the world to itself but had been constrained to Christianize it through a rigid discipline and an aggressiveness intensified by a fanatical certainty among the faithful which made them conscious of being instruments of God's will. What is not clear, however, is the extent to which natural law had served as a mediating factor. Moreover, Troeltsch himself derived the principle of active resistance to authority in case of violations of natural and divine law by the sovereign from premises which are not religious but socio-political, i. e., from the particular situation at Geneva, a merchant republic, and from this beginning he sees arise in France, the Low Countries and Scotland the idea of constitutional control over the sovereign, the right of revolution, and the idea of popular sovereignty. On the other hand, it is to the mystical and fanatical sects that he attributes the revival of natural law, that attempt to institute a free and egalitarian society, from which Locke (after purging it of its dogmatic elements) then derived the doctrinal bases of liberalism and democracy.

The grandiose *Social Teachings* remained without a conclu-

sion. Possibly Troeltsch was content to conclude that the "con-
joining" of the different confessions with the idea of natural
law was at every time different, being determined by the general
spirit of the confessions, and thus could avoid taking sides with
one compromise over against the others. As for the question
which had first inspired him to take up his pen, that of the
Christian social ethic which might serve to resolve or at least to
mitigate modern social conflicts, he refused to commit himself at
all, noting that those social doctrines of Christianity which had
been evolved as a response to past social situations were not
adaptable to the solution of modern problems. Thus envisaged,
the *Social Teachings* is a remakable example of that brand of
history of ideas (*Geistesgeschichte*) which avoids the theoretical
problem in order to linger with consummate finesse and erudi-
tion upon the exposition of past solutions. The result is a list
of opinions which through its very neutrality contributed to
the discrediting of historicism.

Lutheran and liberal, Troeltsch should have been able to
utilize his research abilities to discern how varied and contrasting
were the sentiments which made up his own spirit. He esteemed
a neo-Protestantism purged of Lutheran dogma and tended
towards an Anglo-Saxon type of Christianity; nonetheless, he
remained a Lutheran. With his friend Weber he remained
Lutheran in that sad realization that religion has no real part
to play in the modern world and in his belief that politics, which
is the organization of sheer power, will never be able to function
without its Machiavellian traits.[51] He pretended that he no
longer believed in the doctrine of original sin, but he continued
to hold that human nature could never become subordinated
to spiritual laws. For him nature was basically wicked, had
rendered vain every dream of the theoreticians of natural law,
and had legitimized—with a natural legitimacy—violence, war,
and political force. His friend Meinecke, who was floundering
in the same dualism, would dedicate to him his exposition of

the theory of this nature, his *The Idea of Raison d'État* * (*Die Idee der Staatsraison*) , and would describe, in his *Origins of Historicism* (*Entstehung des Historismus*) , the end of the concept of natural law.

III

Troeltsch was not one of those strong personalities who, fortified within their own systems, advance imperturbably to a preestablished goal. He proceeded cautiously, continually searching for points of orientation, attentive to all voices, and ready to register all vibrations of the atmosphere about him. He conceived of the mission of the scholar as that of living in his own time, thinking with it and suffering with it. But the place assigned to him by Providence was a hapless one: theologian, professor, and patriot, he was destined to witness (and even to aid) the precipitous decline of those faiths and ideas into which he had been born and within which he had grown to maturity. His entire existence was tormented by the realization that something which was a part of his very soul was in peril. The malevolent would call him " the man of crises ": the crisis of Protestantism, the crisis of the middle class, the political crises of his native land, the crisis of liberalism (to which he rather vaguely adhered) , the crises of science, culture, society. Yet, unlike the professional prophets of doom, he did not wish to abandon himself to complete despair. He gained solace from the view that the crisis of the Protestant churches had been a preparation for a Christian renaissance. And he hoped that after the catastrophe of the Hohenzollern empire, there would emerge a new and freer life for his country. In like manner, he saw in the crisis of science

* Published in English under the title of *Machiavellism: The Doctrine of Raison d'État and Its Place in Modern History*, translated from the German by Douglas Scott (London: Routledge & Kegan Paul, 1957) .

and culture the opportunity for a salutary revision of their fundamentals and a guarantee of their vitality. He devoted himself, therefore, to opening the road to the future which he believed he dimly perceived ahead.

In the last years of his life, he devoted himself to the study of Europeanism, to the study of the formation of the spirit of European civilization. He was urged on in this task after World War I by the oppressive sense of *senescens saeculum* which pervaded German society. In his younger days the question of the objective truth of a Christian idea which had been historically born had led him into an examination of the idea of historicism. Now the question was widened. His research in the history of Western Christianity had shown him how far removed it was from Byzantine and Slavic Christianity and how much farther it was removed from Copto-Abyssinian Christianity. The efficacy of the original Christian idea appeared to him to have been diminished or at least narrowly limited in its action by the national and social order. Western Christian civilization, having formed itself on the base of classical culture and among the life conditions of the Romano-Germanic peoples, appeared to him as a unique totality, a peculiar organism. But investigation of those values which had assured to Europe its marvelous destiny once more rendered acute the problem of the relation between absolute value and historical relativity: Europe, having arrived at the apex of its intellectual development, having arrived at the knowledge of the historicity of all ideals, seemed threatened precisely as a consequence of this knowledge, by this " unnerving " relativism, by its inability to believe and act. The problem of the historical relativity of Christian truth was widened to the problem of the relativity of all those values in which Europe had trusted and which had constituted its life norms. Thus Troeltsch posed the problem of historicism. That term, which up to his time had been used only sporadically by economists and theologians in a polemical sense,[52] soon became common usage as

one of those terms which indicated the great currents of thought
and cultural epochs.

However, Troeltsch's own position relative to historicism is
not particularly clear; in fact, one cannot even say with certainty exactly what he meant by the term. He rejected as
absurd and unnatural the ideal of historiography as a pure
science or as disinterested contemplation. He attributed to that
ideal itself the origin of that "evil historicism" which had resulted in mere fatuous play with ideas, in unlimited relativism,
and in a paralysis of will and life. The attempt to justify it with
an appeal to aesthetic taste was completely repugnant to his
moral sense.[53]

On the other hand, historicism was for him "the radical
historicization of our knowledge and thought," that is, the application of the categories of change, contingency, and individuality to the products of our thought: "Here everything is seen as
existing in the river of becoming, as unconfined and continual
individualization, determined by the past and directed towards
an unknown future. State, law, morality, religion, art, are all
dissolved in the stream of history's becoming and are intelligible
to us only as constituent parts of historical developments."[54]
What is not seen is where some brakes or limits might be placed,
as he claimed to be able to do.

That he was not really clear as to the problems implied is
indicated by the similarity which he found between historicism
and naturalism. He declared that "naturalism and historicism
are the two great scientific creations of the modern world" and
that "modern scientific thought is divided between historicism
and naturalism." Having thus conceived naturalism and historicism as analogous and peacefully juxtaposed entities, he could
not see them as contradictory or grasp the nature of historicism
which, as a total order of thought, had completely destroyed or
absorbed naturalism and had replaced the naturalistic logic with
a logic of its own.

This misconception allowed him to undertake the task of

eliminating the onesidedness and danger of "unlimited" historicism, just as he had wished to eliminate the excesses of
naturalism, and could lead him to write: "Unlimited naturalism
leads to a terrible naturalization and devastation of all life; historicism leads to relativistic doubt."

This uncertain posture before the problem—in fact, he speaks
of the "problems of historicism," not of historicism itself as a
problem—results from his fundamental equivocation.

He repudiates every universal norm, every abstract precept.
As an enemy of ecclesiastical dogmas, he was unable to escape
being an enemy of lay dogmas as well. He was violently opposed
to such "empty" concepts as "humanity," "reason," and "progress." With a certain pathos, he asserted that it is necessary that
we free ourselves from all Eleatic and Platonic residues and that
we cease regarding universality and invariability as aspects of the
real. On the other hand, he never abandoned his theistic dualism, an idea which he had possessed from the very beginning and
which he had sustained in the lectures posthumously published
with the rather arbitrary title, *The Conquest of Historicism (Der
Historismus und seine Uberwindung)*. In reality, he had no
need of overcoming historicism, because he had always believed
in an absolute, universal and extra-historical truth which for him
was not only a faith placed on the "margin of science" but
which he also declared to be the presupposition of any historiography. So little was he suffering from the "waves" of historical relativism that he was able to entertain the ambition of
elaborating his faith into a metaphysical system. In his autobiographical sketch, he declared his hope of constructing a metaphysics by following in the direction indicated by Leibnitz, Malebranche and Hegel, and in *The Problems of Historicism (Der
Historismus und seine Probleme)*, in fact, one is presented with
an attempt to systematically amalgamate monadology, the doctrine of the vision of the ideas in God, and the dialectic.

But as he hoped to derive from history itself the proof of the
extra-historical, absolute character of Christianity, so now he pro-

posed to derive from the study of history the antidotes for
unlimited historicism, that is, the proof of the absolute character
of the values of Western civilization in their historical formations. And as at one time he had felt the need of a preliminary
philosophy of religion, so now he felt the need of a logic of
historiography.

*   *   *

As a theologian Troeltsch had believed that only by breaking
up the movement of history into a number of great historical
individualities would he be able to guarantee to Christianity a
" relatively absolute character." He now followed a similar procedure in regard to Western civilization. Nations, states, civilizations and religious communities become, for him, only so many
" individual totalities." These individual totalities, even if composed of innumerable psychical processes, he conceived to be
actually given, real and concrete historical entities. And just
as the various religions had been for him revelations of the
divine spirit in varying degrees, so also here these entities were
animated by revelations or " thoughts " of God.

Ranke had been the first to speak of historical individualities
animated by " tendencies " or " principles " or " ideas " which, in
the last analysis, were " thoughts " of God. Thus, in Troeltsch's
work, in the middle of the question of historicism, the figure
of this nineteenth-century historian reappeared. One day
Troeltsch's friend, Friedrich Meinecke, would conclude his history of the origins of historicism with a eulogy of Ranke as the
historian who had introduced into the vision and interpretation
of history the Goethian and Romantic sentiment of the incomparable value of the individual.

But to envisage a return to Ranke was absurd. Ranke had
lived in what was still the climate of Goethe, Humboldt, and
Boeckh. That very doubt which Troeltsch considered a consequence of the ill-starred contemplative attitude had been, in the
beginning, the Goethian joy of the inexhaustable variety of the

real, the humanistic will to the enrichment of the spirit in Boeckh and Humboldt, Ranke's enthusiasm for understanding and justifying everything, and later, in Burckhardt, the appreciation of the culture of the free personality. Troeltsch himself was too deeply immersed in the life of the community to be able to appreciate the humanistic contemplative ideal, the last of the aristocratic educational ideals. Goethe's personal development pattern (*Bildung*) had become, in the meantime, a scholastic program, and the idea of humanity (*Humanität*) had been relegated to a place in the manuals of literary history. The invective of Treitschke had discredited any attempt at impartiality, and Nietzsche's scorn had rendered ineffectual any effort by the "eunuchs in the harem of history." And had not Troeltsch himself condemned as immoral any attempt at purely disinterested contemplation?

Furthermore, the aesthetic concept of individuality was descended in a direct line (as Meinecke has shown) from a metaphysics which saw in the infinite multiplicity and spontaneity of things the immediate manifestation and creativity of God. It was a line which went back to Shaftesbury, Bruno, to the Neo-Platonism of the Renaissance, to Pseudo-Dionysius, and so forth. There was nothing more alien to Troeltsch, the enemy *par excellence* of any monism. In fact, it is with Troeltsch that the idea of individuality, which had once exercised such a fascination over Ranke and his followers, is rejected. Here is lost that quality of indefiniteness, lightness and elasticity which the idea received at Ranke's able hands. It is no longer something to contemplate with the joy of the artist, for now the individual becomes merely an object.

It was Troeltsch's task to demonstrate the possibility of knowing such objects. Historical knowledge, given that it was derived from knowledge of individual entities, had to be an "intuitive representation." However, since one was dealing with the knowledge of these individualities in their "inner principles" or "ideas," it was impossible to exclude the intervention of something which was not simple, immediate intuition. Ranke had spoken of "presentiment." Forced to specify, Troeltsch finished by calling his totalities "individual concepts," the results of abstraction. That is, the abstraction would encompass the *vinculum substantiale*, the salient traits and characteristics, the symbols, of an immeasurable mass of particulars. What criterion would guide the choice? Reverting for the occasion to the philosophy of value, Troeltsch attributed the choice to our feeling for values which finds in every individual totality the immanent "unity of values." The task of bringing the abstract and the concrete into correspondence was entrusted by Troeltsch to the talent of the historian.

To this same talent Troeltsch entrusted the practical solution of another difficulty which was the direct consequence of the objectification of the "individual totalities": the question of their relation to those other objective individualities which are individual persons.

But the greatest difficulty lay in defining the relation between the totalities themselves. Here Troeltsch had proposed to restore continuity, mobility and fluidity, so that the historian would be able to perceive a general unity of becoming notwithstanding the plurality of historical objects. Yet the movement of which he was a representative, that is, the individualistic historicism of Ranke, had arisen in opposition to such an idea—against the Enlightenment idea of progress on the one hand and against the Hegelian idea of development on the other. In his own mind, as an apologist and historian of Christianity, he belonged to that movement of reaction against the Hegelian dialectic which had triumphed in the Protestant theological schools and in general throughout the whole of Germany in the nineteenth century. Consequently, it was paradoxical that he should recur to such concepts as development, unfolding, and progress. For him, history was but a series of "objects." Therefore, he was forced to adhere to a logic of objects, that is, a logic of being, not of becoming. Thus, it was inevitable that in his thought the "continuity" of becoming should be resolved into the only possible relationship which can exist between objects: the mechanism of action and reaction, or contacts and encounters. Here pluralism is reduced to atomism.

Troeltsch was also forced to deny any development to the individual totalities. As the totality is limited in space, so too is it limited in time. It had a beginning and an end. And here, of course, the inevitable idea of the cycle presented itself. The impression of development, Troeltsch declared, is only an illusion: there is only the cyclical movement of the rise from a primitive stage to the stage of hyperculture (*Ueberkultur*), after which follow inevitably the stages of tiredness, disintegration and ruin.

With an exultant pride, he hailed his "logic" as a "liberation from the naturalistic exigencies of the abstract laws of the natural sciences, from a mere necessity without meaning and purpose, from an atomism which artifically divides and reassembles everything, from an enervating determinism, and from those equations which render everything insignificant." [55] But there is a fundamental confusion here: what greater naturalism, atomism, and determinism can be found than is here contained in this theory of historical individualities conceived as being closed cyclical entities completely lacking in development? In the beginning, he had esteemed a sort of balanced and divided authority between historicism and naturalism. In the end, he reduced historicism to a kind of naturalism. It had already been pointed out how historical "facts" might be likened to physical "facts" and how they might be considered an abstract "nature." [56] To the objective "facts" Troeltsch added objective "totalities," each of which incarnated or incapsulated a "value." He forgot, among other things, what political economy had been teaching for a long while: that in nature, in objective reality, there is no value.

*   *   *

It is difficult to understand why Troeltsch found it necessary to add to his "formal" logic a "material" philosophy of history. His logic had little about it that was formal, postulating as it did the existence of the past as a given reality composed of series of objects and governed by cyclical laws. A second philosophy of history could hardly do more than duplicate the first.

His motive lay in the desire to find a path which would lead from contemplation to action, lead, that is, to the liberation of historicism from the accusation of passivity and inertness. What was the purpose of knowing those individual totalities which, closed in themselves and belonging to the past, had run out their cycles and were dead to us? Humboldt, Ranke, Boeckh and Burckhardt had found a purpose in the joy of pure contemplation. But Troeltsch, as was seen, rejected this form of aestheticism. It only remained for him to discover some vital link between the past and the present, an "intimate and vital" relation which would justify contemplation.

Troeltsch did not wish to confront the problem of the contemporaneity of the past. For him, the past and the present were two separate entities, and to seek to establish the fact that the past might be somehow alive and present seemed to him to lead into metaphysics. He sought, therefore, to reveal the present as a construction in which the single "totalities" of the past constituted the "pieces." The task of determining and describing the pieces which serve to make up our present is assigned by Troeltsch to the philosophy of history.

Thus, the present emerges as a state of consistency (*Bestand*), a composite heritage, which we must receive and clarify to the end of forming the future. In this way, the philosophy of history acquires for Troeltsch a practical importance in as much as it gives foundation, content and direction to the new cultural synthesis (*Kultursynthese*), which will be projected into the future. Thus, Troeltsch could maintain that he had escaped from the bonds of pure contemplation and had "philosophically mastered" historicism.

In his view, historical knowledge could not transcend or go beyond the limits of its own cultural cycle (*Kulturkreis*), which for us is Western civilization. Everything outside the cultural cycle must remain outside it, because we are able to know only one totality by being able to " reexperience " its value and meaning. We can understand, he argues, only that which is contained within us as an essential part of our being, and since the East, for example, does not enter into our composition, we will never be able to understand it.

Furthermore, it is unimportant that we can never understand it, because for Troeltsch only the knowledge of the composition of our own cultural cycle is necessary and desirable. We are faced only with the necessity of attentively studying the civilizational blocks (*Kulturmassive*) which have entered into the construction (*Aufbau*) of our own world. That requires, of course, a delimitation of the blocks, that is, an exact division of historical periods. Troeltsch, as is obvious, is unable to admit the conventional divisions merely on the basis of conventionality alone. On the contrary, he was so anxious to establish their objective existence that for the moment he was forced to admit a progress. The divisions utilized by the medieval theologians, by the humanists, by the *philosophes*, by the Romantics and by the positivists formed, according to him, a " logically progressive series " of ever more penetrating attempts at definition; they were not merely changes in conceptualization. At the vertex of the series he placed his own division into periods, based upon the changes in the socio-economico-juridical life, the only series which offered to him solid and externally recognizable structures.

*   *   *

Troeltsch's use of terms is singular. What he called " the material philosophy of history " is what is traditionally called " the history of Western civilization," while that which is generally called " philosophy of history," that is, the doctrine of civilizational cycles, was, for him, a formal logic. But this is not all that is strange. He enumerates seven civilizational cycles: the Ancient Near East, which finds its unity in Islam, the Egyptian, the Indic, the Chinese, that of pre-Columban Central America, and the Mediterranean-European-American complex. And he did not realize that by assigning to non-European cultures the dignity of civilization cycles which were endowed with peculiar values and meanings, he had overstepped in some way that limit which he had imposed upon himself. He differs from Spengler and Keyserling, who penetrated into similar alien cycles, only in the consciousness of his incompetence, his prudence, or (if one wishes) his modesty.

In reality, Troeltsch's history of Europeanism is only a revision of that chapter in *The Decline of the West* (*Untergang des Abendlandes*) which deals with our own civilization. Naturally, Troeltsch lacks the bold improvisation and pomp of Spengler, but the criteria and the methods are the same. Whereas Spengler saw three cycles in chronological series, Troeltsch saw only one. But this cycle has a special structure. It is a true *monstrum*, with two souls, one classical and one modern, the two being conjoined by the church. His formula is complicated because he did not wish to consider the modern world as a synthesis of the classical and the Christian, but as a world in itself, which runs through the stages of its cycles according to the rule, just as the classical world ran through its stages. But the modern world, even though it is new, is " conditioned and filled " by the ancient world and is composed, therefore, of contradictory substances.

But this idea of a European world closed in itself led Troeltsch to even more strange judgments and artifices. A first difficulty was offered him in the determination of the spatial and temporal limits of the civilization. Hesitating to receive Russia into the European community, he admitted America. The beginning of the modern world he placed " in a general sense " in the fifteenth century, with the inception of the absolute monarchies, and " in a strict sense " in the seventeenth century with the English Revolution, that is, at the time in which these monarchies were beginning to disintegrate.

The content of this world, he argues, is made up of four " blocks " or " fundamental forces." The first, alas, would seem to be of an indubitably oriental origin: the Hebrew prophetic tradition. So in order to exclude from our civilization any oriental influence, he declares with a certain candour that we can ignore everything which comes before the Greeks. But we cannot ignore the Bible. So he then denies the oriental character of that aspect of the Bible which has penetrated into our world. Employing an observation of Keyserling without citing it, he finds that there is an elective affinity between Judaism and the Hellenic *ethos* which permitted the latter to receive Christianity into its own humanistic ethic without the oriental element. Needless to say, such a view is at the very least tenuous. His second block consists of Hellenic civilization. The third is the Hellenistic-Roman monarchy. The fourth is the medieval Occident, informed by the church, Byzantium and the Arabs.

These he posits as the four pillars which support our world. In conclusion he exclaims: " This is the edifice which we have been seeking." And he adds: " Only with this image in mind can we proceed to our present cultural task." And the task? The formation of the new cultural synthesis which he hoped to be able to offer to his confused and disoriented contemporaries.

But it is obvious that he could offer them little. Out of the mass of pages composed by him, pages devoted to the collection of materials for his new cultural synthesis and dealing with such diverse subjects as Einstein's theory of relativity, occultism, Sorel's syndicalism, Wells' universal history, and so on, there emerges only one original idea, and that is a religious one. As he had imposed upon the Christian the necessity of continuing to believe in Christianity because it was the revelation allotted to him by fate, so he imposed upon the European the necessity of remaining loyal to the Western civilizational ideal because this ideal was the manifestation of the Absolute assigned to him by destiny. Here was a far distant echo of the Lutheran ethic of vocation: the European must remain a European because such is his place in the world, because history has made such of him, and because any deviation would be unnatural. But what is the meaning of this Europeanism? Was it not derived from a multitude of forces which were basically contradictory? Was not the history of Europe itself, when compared with the idyl of other continents, a drama? With a certain pedantry not completely lacking in pathos, Troeltsch patiently began to draw up an inventory in order to weld these historical forces into a new synthesis. His death, which halted him at the very beginning of his labours, was perhaps a merciful release.

Chapter 3

FRIEDRICH MEINECKE

I

In the first real proof of his historical talents, a biography of Marshal von Boyen, Friedrich Meinecke expressed his basic position thus: "An historical interpretation which took the national unification of 1870 as its point of reference could assume that everything had transpired exactly as it should have and, by ignoring the clouds gathering on the horizon, could exult in the bright dawn revealed in those events. But it may be permitted a younger generation, groaning under the burden of social problems which seem almost insoluble, to turn with a feeling of nostalgia towards those luminous thoughts of the age of the reforms—an age in which the state and the ideal of humanity were conjoined and every class was offered fully the opportunity to live fully its own life, giving and receiving, learning and teaching. Luminous, eternal thoughts, however much conditioned by the time." [1]

To reinvoke the figure of Boyen, the friend of Stein, Gneisenau, and Humboldt, was to draw attention once more to ideals which the *Realpolitik* of Bismarck had all but erased from the German spirit—ideals more ethical than political. But immediately after the fall of Bismarck, while the empire which he had founded was beginning to reveal its structural debilities, Meinecke's reevocation of those ideals could only be seen as an expression of the doubt which resided in the mind of the young historian. It revealed a belief that perhaps the Bismarckian

solution had not been the best possible one and that perhaps the
renunciation of those old ideals had been a political error which
had cost the nation dearly. It also represented a decided break
with the school of Bismarckian historians who had sanctioned
the formula of the Chancellor, and it marked the beginning of a
critical revision of the period of the establishment of the Reich
(*Reichsgründung*).

Yet the relationship between Meinecke and the great national-
liberal historians of that period was an intimate one. The man
who had suggested the theme of his work and who had opened
the doors of the Prussian military archives to him was Heinrich
von Sybel, with whom Meinecke collaborated on the *Historische
Zeitschrift*, as he later collaborated with Treitschke. As successor
to the posts formerly occupied by Sybel and Treitschke on the
great review, he was their heir and the continuator of their work.
The problem of national unity, a profound and intimate unity,
remained always at the center of his thought. And even when he
broadened his intellectual vision to encompass the problems of
raison d'état and historicism, his interest always remained centered upon his own country's history and its ethico-political
problems; his problem was always the same. In his anguished
questioning, in his speculative torment, the deepest impulses of
the souls of Droysen, Sybel, and Treitschke, those impulses which
they had deliberately (and not without profound effort) re-
pressed in 1856, once more asserted themselves. And both the
limits within which he placed the problems of modern German
history and his virtual critique were borrowed from the tradition
of the national-liberals.

The national-liberals, who at first had waited for " empirical "
Prussia to reveal itself as the " true " Prussia and to fulfill its
" mission," interpreted the reason for the frustration of their
dream—rather superficially—as the defeat of idealism. The result
was a political idea permeated with disillusionment, which
separated the ideal from the real and spirit from power. They
tried to accomodate themselves to the reality of the situation,

because they felt that the national unity was a goal to which every intellectual prejudice had to be subordinated. Nonetheless, a fundamental hostility remained, buried in the formula which envisaged Prussia as a mere military-bureaucratic force, a power state (*Machtstaat*). " Spirit " and " culture " remained to the other side, in their impotent " a-politicality." It was a distinction born of pessimism and the realization that a victory of spiritual ideals without the help of the secular arm, the triumph of an idea without force, was an illusory dream.

Meinecke accepted this dualistic distinction between *ethos* and *kratos*, although it pained him to see them separated. He criticized Bismarck and Roon, masters in the manipulation of the national idea and national conscription for their failure to have attained to that marvelous harmony of political and spiritual convictions which had motivated the men of 1813.[2] He did not castigate Sybel and Treitschke for their adherence to Bismarck's victorious solution, but he did point out that with their conversion something precious had been lost. When Sybel suddenly proclaimed that his earlier opposition to Bismarck and Roon had been wrong, Meinecke observed that Sybel had failed to realize exactly how much of the previous criticism had been justified. In Treitschke he saw and admired the man who loved " with a sacred conviction " the great national state, made up of both spirit and power, respectful of the ethical freedom of its citizens, and resting ultimately upon the citizen's sense of a sacred duty towards it.[3] But by going back to the origins of the nationalist movement, back to a time when the movement was still identified with the cause of freedom, Meinecke was necessarily led back to the heroic age of the wars of liberation, to the age of Stein, Arndt, Scharnhorst and Gneisenau.

Traditionally, the German development during the nineteenth century was described in terms of a symbolic juxtaposition of Weimar to Potsdam, the literary-humanistic tradition of Herder, Goethe and Schiller being opposed to the military tradition of the Great Elector and Frederick II. Meinecke's originality lay in the fact that he was committed to neither of the two poles, but to Königsberg, the homeland of Kant and at the same time the stronghold of the Prussian rebirth after Jena. As a Prussian and a Lutheran, Meinecke found there the genuine Prussian and Lutheran traditions, the synthesis of the two elements, ethical-religious and politico-military. For Stein and the heroes of Leipzig, homeland and humanity, the struggle for national independence and the struggle for a kind of Kantian freedom, were the same thing. Thus, from the very beginnings of his activity as a historian Meinecke was confronted with the question of the relation between morality and *raison d'état*, the question of the juxtaposition of Kant to Machiavelli. But for Meinecke, the student of the Bismarckian historians, the primacy was reserved for *raison d'état*. For him the problem was not, as it had been for Kant and Humboldt, that of guaranteeing the freedom of the individual, but of insuring the strength of the state through the utilization of new and fresh forces which might confront it in the course of its development. He made no concession to any universal law of nature, nor did he see the individual as the end of the state. On the contrary, he believed that the individual would serve the state best whenever appeal was made to his sense of responsibility and his inner discipline. In this subordination of the Kantian ethic to *raison d'état* lies the kernel of Meinecke's liberalism, a liberalism which might be better called historistic nationalism: a nationalism which invokes liberal reforms in relation to the historical situation by requesting a reformation of the state on the broad and solid base of the entire nation.

The life of Boyen was meant to be a description of that happy moment in Prussian history in which the conjunction of the two elements had born its most precious fruit: the rebirth of the state and the liberation of the fatherland. It was meant also to show how the separation of the two elements, the abandonment of the patriots' political policy in 1819, had resulted in the loss of Prussia's tradition of greatness. The aggravation of internal discord, the consolidation of the aristocracy in its privileged position, the radicalism of a bourgeoisie driven to opposition, the revolt of March 1848, and the agrarian crisis of the late nineteenth century, were all, according to Meinecke, the result of that first fatal error. Even more tragic appeared to him the damage done to Prussia's international prestige with the fall of Humboldt and Boyen. Hailed with jubilation in Vienna, their fall signalled the inauguration of a series of humiliations for Prussian foreign policy, culminating in the disgrace of Olmütz in 1850.

But even more important to Meinecke was his desire to demonstrate that the liberalism of the patriots, far from being the importation of a foreign ideology, was in reality the natural development of an indigenous Germanic tradition. If Stein, Scharnhorst, Gneisenau, non-Prussian in their origins, were more devoted to Germany than to Prussia, Boyen, the descendant of an ancient family of Prussian officers, was of an unquestioned loyalty. Meinecke found in him the old, pure religiosity of the Frederickian armies, the religiosity which had been elevated by Kant to moral consciousness. However, not even in the other "liberators" does he find any taint of an abstract doctrinairism of foreign importation, but rather a moral enthusiasm of pure Prussian and German lineage.[4] True Prussianism had its champions in them, not in the *Junker* or in the court party. And the reformers were the real heirs of Frederick II even in the hegemonic political policy in Germany, whereas the conservatives were the enemies of the idea of national unity and remained bound to the world circumscribed by little Prussia.

The fecundity of the union of *ethos* and *kratos* is demonstrated in that part of the biography which at first sight would seem to be the most dry, that is, in the description of the technical reorganization of the army. Here military history is transformed into the history of ethical ideals, for the new firing tactics which replaced the eighteenth-century geometrical line maneuvers are confided to the initiative of the individual soldier, not to any mechanical discipline, and implied thereby a "general spiritual revolution." With Boyen as minister of war, the Kantian principle of moral autonomy was infused into the most minute administrative provisions, into the tactical rules, the army regulations, and the disciplinary code. However, his greatest reforms were those which transformed the mercenary standing army into the national conscript army and the creation of the Landwehr, a reserve militia officered by middle class non-professionals. He concluded that such a reform, indispensable to the safety of the country, signalled the transition from the enlightened despotism of the eighteenth century to the national state, presupposed the liberation of the serfs,[5] and implied the abolition of the highest privilege of the *Junker*—that of defending the fatherland—and thus the disappearance of the *raison d'etre* of their caste.

How did it happen, notwithstanding all this, that the *Junker* not only resisted these incursions upon their privileged position but ultimately triumphed? Meinecke could not accept Treitschke's explanation of the reaction of 1819 as being caused by the Prussian monarchy's need to avoid any rupture with Austria. Given the Austrian situation in Italy and its rivalry with Russia, Meinecke argued, Austria would have had no choice but to show a good face if confronted with a constitutional Prussia. Nor would he admit the thesis that the liberal movement of that time was weak and superficial.

Although he was willing to admit that when compared with the compact feudal aristocracy the middle class still lacked complete self-consciousness and was somewhat immature, he still held that the "impetuous force" of the liberal movement did have some chance of success. When confronted with the triumph of the court party, it only remained for him to speak of a "betrayal by the Philistines."

In an essay, "Vaterländische und religiöse Erhebung am Anfang des XIX Jahrhunderts," [6] the search for the indigenous roots of the German national-liberal idea was pushed even deeper. If the "elementary religious force" of German Protestantism had appeared in Stein, it was in the prophet of the

German national state, in E. M. Arndt, that the same romantic spirit was manifested which had led Schleiermacher to bring a new life to a Protestantism formerly reviled by the *Aufklärung* and which opposed to the state of the Enlightenment the idea of a state born of the land, sprung from the folk as a natural and organic community. And this as early as 1802, so that Meinecke felt able to assert that the new national sentiment had been born prior to the rise of the foreign menace, even if its rapid development was favored by it.

But much more acute was another problem facing the historian and the patriot, the problem of the failure of the marvelous national energy, the fundamental problem of modern German history.

Cosmopolitanism and the National State (Weltbürgertum und Nationalstaat) [7] is the answer to the problem: the idea of national unity had to undergo a long and painful elaboration before it could be translated into a reality. Thus, Meinecke was able to conclude that it was not in the weakness of the men themselves nor in any egotistical resistance to that idea that the reason for its failure is to be found, but in the idea itself, in its immaturity and in its incompleteness. Thus the history of the establishment of the Reich acquired clarity and the character of logical necessity.

*   *   *

With *Cosmopolitanism and the National State* Meinecke transformed political historiography into the history of ideas. The new method was the result of his historiographical experience: in Boyen, Arndt, and Stein he had witnessed the germination of the idea and had traced its practical productive breakthrough. Against the backdrop of the wars of liberation he had perceived the profile of Immanuel Kant, and even further back that of Luther. While working on the *Thoughts and Reflections (Gedanken und Erinnerungen)* of Bismarck,[8] he had admired the way in which the old chancellor had been able, in his narration of the relations with Austria of 1863-64, to show them as a kind of spiritual process which embraced the whole history of the Austro-Prussian dualism. From that time on, his main interest was in pursuing the origins, the oscillations, and the compromises of ethico-political ideas. Not that he enjoyed following their fortunes in and for themselves, as stars spinning in the sky of history, but because in the fortunes of those ideas he hoped to find a clue to the destiny of his country, of Europe, and of the world. That is, he believed it possible to grasp the most vital and concrete forces of history in the study of these apparently abstract principles.

On the other hand, since he was much closer spiritually to Humboldt and Ranke than to Hegel, he imposed no rigid schematic development upon the history of ideas. He felt that as they passed through different environments and situations, the ideas became tinged with foreign colorations. If they developed, they were also deformed, dragging slag along with them and becoming limited psychologically in the various historical personalities who embraced them. Still, there throbs within them a wealth of plastic possibilities.

This agility is granted to Meinecke, however, because of his essential dualism: the idea is not the whole of reality. Beside and beneath it is the social and economic world, the world of passion and power. And it is this world which stamps the idea with its historical determination.

There is not, therefore, a true and proper dialectic in the movement of ideas. Their advance is represented by a process of progressive purification through the elimination of extraneous elements. The task of the historian is to penetrate into this historical process and to reveal the progress of the idea towards purity in its linear development. There is no contradiction within the idea itself which might motivate it. Its movement is due to the disturbing elements and obstacles which have grown up around it and penetrated it from the outside.

Meinecke never fully and systematically elaborated a theory

in which the relation of the ideas to reality was defined. However, it is obvious how he could avoid the danger of reducing the ideas to the status of mere ideologies or instrumentalities and thus escape relativism or pragmatism. For Meinecke, the idea of the national state, the idea of the *raison d'état*, and the historicist idea of individuality and development are for him discoveries of the truths which not only impose themselves upon ethico-political practice, but have also enriched our understanding of life and history. In the preface to *Cosmopolitanism and the National State* he speaks of the opportunity which historiography offers through its contact on the one hand with philosophy and on the other with the problems of political life. He does not, to be sure, arrive at any identification of the two, but he does unite in a single process Fichte, Novalis, Gneisenau, Arndt, Droysen, and Bismarck: philosophers, poets, generals, political agitators, historians and statesmen. And it is Bismarck who appears at the end of the process, not so much as the man who brought to practical realization the ideas of others, but as the man who solved a problem common to them all.

As no other German historian had done, Meinecke pointed out the decisive importance of philosophic thought for political history. He could penetrate with a sure hand to the vital nucleus of any given action, and with the care and patience of a goldsmith, he assigned to each thinker his contribution to the whole of the German historical development. It is only when he sheds the clothes of the historian in order to don those of the philosopher, that is, when interpretative insight must yield to a rigour of argumentation, that the capacity for psychological penetration (*Einfühlung*) becomes a weakness.

This weakness is already revealed in the formulation of the problem which is the motivation behind the work, *Cosmopolitanism and the National State*. In his historical reconstruction, he utilizes a kind of sociology of nations, a classification which divides all national groups into cultural nations (*Kulturnationen*) and political nations (*Staatsnationen*). Thus in place of a description of the slow formation of the German national consciousness, arising out of a linguistic and literary unification and attaining to a political one, we are here presented with the story of the transition from one type of nation to another.

In reality, the supposed transition of the German nation from the cultural to the political type is the process of its formation out of an imperial phase (F. K. Moser, 1765) into that of Bismarck. If elsewhere a nation was that unified community which a monarchy imposed upon ethnical and linguistic, class and religious differences and which became a self-conscious entity during the seventeenth and eighteenth centuries as the subject of law and history, the German nation, which had its first politico-communal experience in the Holy Roman Empire, did not come into existence until the nineteenth century. Meinecke begins with the moment in which, according to him, the cultural nation is already formed, with the year 1790, when " under the powerful influences of the French Revolution, the state and the relations between nation and state now become, even for German thinkers, an object not of active participation but of the most interested reflection."

Humboldt, writing in the last decade of the eighteenth century, still considered most worthy that national character which most nearly approximated the essence of humanity. In such an ideal, argued Meinecke, the concept of nation is still an eighteenth century one. Only when the ideal of humanity had been removed to the supernal spaces and man had learned to regard himself and his nation empirically and realistically, limiting himself to the ascertainment of national differences, did the concept of nation become applicable to the realization of the ends of the state, and above all to the ends of the Prussian power state.

It was necessary that the state be purged of any universal ethic. Meinecke reproved Stein for not having wished to admit that the state was, above all else, pure power; and he reproved Humboldt for not envisaging the state in its crude nature, in its autarchy and autonomy, in the immediate expression of its power instinct (*Machttriebe*), as Ranke and above all Bismarck had been able to do.

It is obvious that once it had been assumed that the true idea of the nation is that of an empirical particularity and that the true idea of the state is that of the power instinct, Bismarck will have to appear not only as the stateman who adapted the idea of the nation to the ends of the Prussian power state, but also as the thinker who freed the idea of the national state from all eighteenth-century ideological fantasies and offered it in its purity to the German people.

At this point it would seem that Meinecke had abandoned his youthful enthusiasm for the " eternal thoughts " of the age of the reforms. He appears to be converted, like his masters Sybel and Treitschke, to the ideals of *Realpolitik* and power egoism (*Machtegoismus*). Yet he discovered in a memorandum written by Humboldt in 1813 the most grandiose political words of that time, because in it " power and spirit, nation and humanity, politics and culture were in ideal balance." The state remained for Humboldt a " natural " reality; not spirit, but drive (*Trieb*), instinct, nature, that which Kant had wished to suppress. Meinecke, on the other hand, recognized it and accepted it as a fatal inevitability. Thus, it is obvious why he was totally unsympathetic to the idea of the ethical state of Hegel; he accepted from him only the denial of an international justice, that is, only as much as agreed with the concept of the state as power instinct.

Yet Meinecke did not wish to deny to the state any ethical justification. He castigated both the cosmopolitans of the *Aufklärung* and the Romantics for having considered that which resided in the " nature " of the state itself as blind desire for domination and for not having taken into account the fact that morality, besides having a universal side also had an " individually determined " side, and that from this side the " apparent immorality of statist egoism could be morally justified."

Thus he found himself confronted by the problem of *raison d'état* as an internal problem of German national history, and he resolved it, then, with a distinction between the two " sides " of morality.[9]

*   *   *

If Meinecke had demonstrated how the German nation had been obliged to sacrifice its universalistic ideals in order to achieve national unity, he was obliged to show also how it had been obliged to renounce the idea of a full and total unity, that is, how the champions of unity from Stein to Treitschke had erred not only on the grounds of contingent opportunity but in their ideas as well. This is the thesis of the second part of *Cosmopolitanism and the National State.*

Up to that time German historians of the establishment of the Reich had examined the various phases of the Austro-Prussian struggle and the final expulsion of Austria. The problem of the relations between Germany and Prussia had remained in the dark: Sybel had not taken them into account and Treitschke had halted his work at the year 1848.[10]

Fichte, Stein, Niebuhr, the patriots of the wars of liberation, and later those of the *Paulskirche* had been for unity and against particularism, even if most of them had seen in Prussia the instrument of the unity. Even in this ideal of unity Meincke detected a survival of the non-political spirit of the eighteenth century. The champions of the united empire, who wanted the Hohenzollern dynasty but not Prussia, had miscalculated. But their gravest error, according to Meinecke, was in believing that the concession of a constitution to Germany would have opened the way to national unification. On the contrary, he argued; had Prussia become a constitutional state, it would have concluded its own development by becoming a Prussian national state and would have been lost to Germany.

To anyone familiar with the " sacrifice " of Piedmonte, the hope of Fichte and Stein appears to be anything but " a-politi-

cal," just as it is difficult to see how a Prussian constitution
would have presented an obstacle to unity: the concession and
maintenance of the *Statuto* were not a menace to Italian unity,
nor did it favour the formation of a Piedmontese nation. The
year 1848 did see a conflict between the National Assembly at
Frankfurt and the Prussian Assembly at Berlin, but this was a
conflict between the liberalism of the upper middle classes and
radicalism, not between two national ideas. The only supporters
of Prussian particularism were the members of the feudal party:
Stahl and Bismarck himself, the heirs of the court party which
in 1819 had defended the interests of little Prussia.

Meinecke's explanation of the hope of the patriots seems too
narrow: he sees it as being born of the fear that the Prussian
Assembly might predominate over the *Reichstag*, because of a
" parliamentarian prejudice which saw constitutionalism and
parliamentarianism as the same thing." In reality, his belief
that the hope for a full national unity after centuries of
separatism was due only to a parliamentarian prejudice is mitigated by the fact that its champions were men like Droysen and
Treitschke.

According to Meinecke, what was needed was an idea which
would reconcile the unity and power of the whole with the
freedom of the parts, that idea which Bismarck had given to
Germany by destroying the parliamentary movement by the
creation of the *Bundesrat*, the repository of the authority of the
Reich, and by opposing the institution of the imperial cabinet
(*Reichsministern*), the apparent oppressor of the freedom of the
individual states.

Meinecke himself explains how the most profound justification
in the mind of Bismarck for the feudal empire was not so much
the feeling of respect for the particularism of the other German
states as his desire to protect the existence of a semi-feudal
Prussia within the new national framework. This did not represent a development of the idea of the national state, a liberation

from the vestiges of the eighteenth century, but was a concession to the spirit and interests of the old Prussia of the *Junker*.

The reason for Meinecke's difficulty thus far is obvious. He rejected the idea of the nation as *volonté générale* as a product of the abstract natural law theory of the eighteenth century. Therefore, he naturally adhered to the Romantic idea of the nation as it had been developed by Herder, Arndt and Grimm. The Romantic conception of the nation was born in opposition to rationalism, was thoroughly sentimental, and was grounded in the tradition of folklore, language, custom, fable, and popular poetry. Such an idea was anti-centralistic and anti-political, born as it was of an opposition to the centralizing tendencies of the eighteenth century. Savigny and his school affirmed the originality and peculiarity of the "national soul," which they juxtaposed to the abstract intellect of the politicians, and fought against the codification of the law. Such a concept, opposed to any sort of nationalistic centralization, penetrated to the lowest strata of the population, and consecrated regional particularities and folk traditions. Even Bismarck, himself a disciple of the Romantics, when he arrived at the end of his career, exhorted the younger generation to maintain that variety in unity which had been realized in the federal empire created by him, to resist the levelling influences of the West. The German nation remained a politically unfinished product conseqently, standing as it did midway between unity and regional particularism. Particularistic federalism, which Meinecke considered a sort of political perfection of the national idea, was in reality the result of a non-political conception of the nation. In fact, since it was originally conceived in opposition to the arbitrary character of enlightened despotism, such an idea was not really related to the national will at all but to the national "nature" which, totally lacking any sort of political will, was conservative, inert, "vegetative," idyllic. It was precisely the idea of the cultural nation. As a non-political ideal it could be used by Bismarck for the realization of the ends of the Prussian state by serving as that "imponderable factor" in the struggle of the Prussian monarchy for hegemony. Spontaneous and irrational, antecedent to the human will, the nation could have no decisive political initiative, no political destiny of its own. So the political initiative would have to come from something external to it, from the Prussian state, the repository of the political moment, of pure *Machtpolitik*.

Meinecke considered this idea of the nation the true one. Moreover, he deprived it (with a certain positivistic dryness) of that Leibnitzian universalism which it had still possessed with Herder and reduced it to an idea of mere empirical particularity. And he considered such a reduction to be an improvement on the idea, as an emancipation from an eighteenth-century cosmopolitanism which he regarded as a-political. In reality, such an idea might serve as the matter for which Bismarck, as minister of a power state, could play the role of *demiurgos*. Never again could it serve as an active principle in the formation of a political nation endowed with a will of its own.

Moreover, Meinecke himself recognized that a unity was lacking in the new German political life and that with a monarchy which was both Prussian and German, which had two souls and two nationalities, any real development was impossible. But he hoped that one day middle-class, industrial Germany would show itself capable of satisfying the demands of *Machtpolitik*, a vital necessity for a great European state; Prussia would then become superfluous, and the German national state would finally be complete.

A proof of the thesis presented in *Cosmopolitanism and the National State* was the great biography of Radowitz, which is also a history of the German revolution of 1848.[11] It was Radowitz who first attempted what Bismarck had succeeded in doing. To expose the reasons for his failure was to test the logical necessity of Bismarck's success, to give it a demonstration *per absurdum*.

To Meinecke, the historian and interpreter of the movements

of Germany's political soul, rich materials were offered by the adventurous life of the former official of the kingdom of Westphalia who became a Prussian general and confidant of Frederick William IV, who launched the idea of the union and who, as minister of foreign affairs in 1850, sought to lead Prussia into war with Austria. Bismarck characterized him as an "able caretaker of the medieval fantasies of Frederick William." Meinecke, however, discerned in him a certain political shrewdness and demonstrated how in effect he had opened the road for Bismarck. To Meinecke, Radowitz represented in the history of the German national idea the intermediary zone between the Romantic age and that of the establishment of the Reich.

Here too the basic theme is the transition from universalistic idealism to political realism. Radowitz's error, according to Meinecke, was in having conceived of a German *Bund* before 1848 which, instead of being a national state, was an ideal entity whose members (including Prussia) would have been obliged to follow a heteronomous policy which was contrary to their political power interests (*Machtinteressen*). The question at hand was not, as Treitschke held, one of "fanciful confusion" but of the expression of a concept of state which was contradictory to the nature of the state itself. However, the course of practical events succeeded little by little in raising the romantic ideological fog: in 1848, at Frankfurt, Radowitz was able to oppose to the national-democratic utopian idea the concept of the modern national state, a concept which did not subsume a universal law of nations in processes of self-determination, but which posited at the very base of national life a vital impulse which affirmed itself in a particular and egoistic way, through struggle, and compelled other nations to resort to the same weapons. Radowitz aroused a "tempestuous storm" in the Prussian Assembly when he declared that Venice should remain under Austrian rule for strategic reasons, that is, for the defense of the southern borders and the way to the Adriatic, an artery of German maritime and commercial existence.

However, Radowitz's weakness was in never having arrived at a conception of secularized politics, in never having liberated himself from the last universalistic bonds. He was too much a product of his own past to be able to deliver the final blow against them. That task was reserved for Bismarck. Radowitz thought too much of Prussia's national mission and too little of its real interests.

What were Prussia's real interests? Meinecke rejected the traditional interpretation of Radowitz's fall and the "disgrace of Olmütz" as being due to Prussian military unpreparedness and Russia's menacing attitude. The Prussian army was in good shape in 1850 and well able to undertake a struggle with Austria. It was numerically and qualitatively superior to the Austrian army, and Russia, if the question of Holstein could have been resolved according to its desires, would not have intervened. And even if Russia had intervened, it would have permitted Prussia to settle the matter before any disastrous blows had been struck and to obtain better conditions than those of Olmütz. For Meinecke, here was another instance of the failure of a national political policy before the cold Prussianism of the reactionaries. As formerly in 1819, the conservative prejudice and the class interests of the Prussian nobility had frustrated the Frederickian instincts of Prussia: Radowitz fell from a blow struck by the court party (*Kamarilla*).

Thus, the contradiction emerges once more. On the one hand, Meinecke hailed the progress towards pure politics, free from all ethical and universalistic considerations, and on the other, he condemned the policy of the reactionaries as a sin which had been translated into political betrayal.

These oscillations between realism and idealism, between Bismarck and Stein, appeared to have come to an end with the advent of World War I.

The great day of German unification seemed finally at hand. In the supplement appended to the third edition of *Cosmopolitanism and the National State*, in 1915, Meinecke declared that at last industrial Germany had shown itself capable of defending the state. For him the war was the consecration of national unity, the realization after nearly a century of struggle of the hopes of the patriots of the wars of liberation. In a lecture delivered near the end of 1915, he praised the achievements of the Landwehr and the Landsturm, creations of Boyen, and he saluted the great secular processes of " militarization, nationalization, and democratization " which alone had permitted the organization of armies composed of millions of combatants.[12]

That cry of exultation was the death sentence of Bismarckian Germany and the Germano-Prussian compromise. Meinecke never dreamed that within a few years that declaration would be transformed into an accusation and that he would be forced to return to his youthful doubts. In November 1918 he accused the Bismarckian concept of the state of being ultimately responsible for the German defeat. Like the Prussia of Jena and Olmütz, it had been unable to adjust to the demands of the modern world and above all to the exigencies of modern war.[13] In December of the same year, he confessed: " We historians played the major role in the canonization of our process of national formation; we never tired of showing how fragile, unfeasible, and utopian had been all previous attempts at solution of the German national problem and of measuring them by Bismarck's work as though it were an infallible unit of measurement." [14]

II

The experience of the lost war revealed a new contradiction in Meinecke's thought. Up to that moment he had conceived the national state as an impulse to the infinite development of power which found its proper limits in the power of others. The contradiction was born out of his attempt to deal with the in-

ternal means to this end, with the internal structure of the power
relation. Now that the *Entente* [Allied Forces] was no longer
confronted by counterforces which might limit its oppression,
Meinecke felt the need of discovering some inner limits to the
expansion of power. However, he guarded himself well against
rejecting all of his past and the tradition from which he had
sprung and against going back to a theory of natural law or to an
ethical ideal of community among nations. He preferred to find
limits in the concept of politics itself, by distinguishing between
a wanton *Machtpolitik* and " true " politics. Furthermore, he
realized that *Machtpolitik* had been the last German sin against
realism, against politics itself. He confessed that he himself had
once thought it necessary to reject the naval agreement offered
by the English in the name of honor and German autonomy:
" We forgot that in questions of power, not sentiment, but only
raw *raison d'état* has to decide issues." [15] And he inveighed
against the annexationist campaign, which rendered impossible a
peace acceptable to both sides, as well as submarine warfare,
which he considered the German " Sicilian expedition." [16]

Thus Meinecke conceived a fundamental fissure between " elementary passions " and " pure *raison d'état* in the deeper sense."
The entrance of the masses into the life of the state, which he at
first regarded with admiration and then enthusiastically hailed
as a completion of the national state, was now suddenly revealed
as the entrance of " elementary passions " into the life of the
state. Precisely at the instant in which he had denounced the
work of Bismarck and invoked a national community of the
people (*Volksgemeinschaft*), a mass state, he recognized that
during the war what had been lacking above all in Germany had
been a Bismarck who would have respected the limits which
" true " politics imposes. The necessity of some higher brake
appeared to Meinecke's thought, and Bismarck was suddenly
revealed in a new light, as the man of wise moderation in victory, the man of prudent balance.

In various essays Meinecke outlined the damages done by the

German government to "political tact," to "true" *raison d'état*, before and during the war.[17] But the problem could not be solved with a series of critiques and retrospective recriminations. That concept of *raison d'état* which Germany had betrayed and for which betrayal it had paid with defeat, appeared to Meinecke full of latent possibilities. In the gust of Wilsonian moralism which now swept the world, a resurrection of the old, almost forgotten *raison d'état* held forth the possibility of solving the problem of the relation between morality and politics which, now detached from a capricious *Machtpolitik*, was foreign neither to the tradition of nineteenth-century German thought nor to the rediscovery of the autonomy of politics.

The Idea of Raison d'État (Die Idee der Staatsraison) is an apologia and an examination of conscience. In it Meinecke writes: "We were castigated for having given ourselves totally to the cult of power and *raison d'état*, and it was therefore assumed that we could be treated not as a defeated people but as criminals." [18] For Meinecke, such accusations were only the mask for the *Machtpolitik* of the enemy. Furthermore, he pointed out that the idea of *raison d'état* was born on Latin soil with Machiavelli and that it had grown to fruition in the France of Richelieu and Louis XIV. On the other hand, he argued, German thinkers had not been disposed to accept it at first. Luther invoked the Christian state, and Kant, Fichte and Stein stood as proof that the autochthonous tradition was anti-Machiavellian. How did it happen, then, that the ideas of Machiavelli had found new life in Germany during the course of the nineteenth century? Meinecke is not above repeating the motif of the directness and sincerity, the love for imprudent truths of the German people who, having only in the nineteenth century opened their eyes to a truth, did not have the hypocrisy to conceal it.

But what is this truth?

The state, Meinecke explains, is grounded in the elemental will to power. This will to power awakened men to the historical life and drove crude despots and ruling castes to found political unities. Beyond this sphere of activity, in another sphere altogether, there are unconditioned values, morality and law.

This dualism of ethics and power is defined in terms of a "double polarity" of the "realm of the spirit" and the "realm of sin." It belongs to the essential nature of *raison d'état* that it must stain both ethics and law with violations. In sum, the state must sin. This is the most terrible and basic fact of world history: that the human community which comprises and informs all others, and should therefore guide them with an essential purity, has no moral nature, is not even able to enjoy a theoretical purity.

Yet Meinecke mitigates his conclusions by holding that power is not "evil in itself," but is indifferent to good and evil alike. The true and inevitable tragedy is that the possessor of power is always tempted to abuse it. And even *raison d'état*, the foundation of political activity which the state must obey if it wishes to live a free and independent existence, is broadened and ennobled in Meinecke's eyes: it is certainly not identified with *Machtpolitik*, but is the bridge between the power instinct and moral responsibility. The state itself does not have as a single root the power instinct, but has a dual character, standing as it does halfway between an elemental nature and the spirit.

The two elements oscillate in such a way that now one prevails and now the other. Is there any sort of development? Is there any progress of the moral element in history? Meinecke answers that state egoism, the instinct of self-preservation and power, is universal and timeless.

On the basis of this summary the criticism of Croce, who finds some confusion in the theory, seems fully justified.[19] On the one hand, it would seem that Meinecke considers power to be rooted in the evil nature of man himself and sees the state as the result of some kind of original sin. On the other, he is able to maintain that power, in itself neither good nor evil, can become evil when the possessor of it abuses it. In fact, Meinecke insists on the "excesses" of *Machtpolitik*. In sum, he recognizes that the state has to sin by its very nature, is unable to enjoy even a theoretical purity; at the same time, he attributes the sin to an "abuse" or "excess" on the part of the possessor of power, that is, to a completely independent and contingent responsibility which does not inhere in the essence of the state itself.

The total result of this oscillation is a dualistic vision of life and the world with the two poles consisting of Kantian spiritualism and naturalistic positivism. Meinecke never ceases proclaiming the unconditional superiority of moral values which are unable to renounce their essence, not even before the state itself. But he is also disposed to accept "all the facts of the natural and dark side of human existence, the causal, mechanical and biological relations which modern positivism rather narrowly but with a certain heuristic fertility emphasizes."

In place of a "happy faith in the identity of spirit and nature," there is in Meinecke a desolate recognition of an incurable, eternal conflict of the two principles. History is in no way seen as a redemption, but as a perpetual mixture of moral life and instinctive violence, a Manichaean struggle. The evil, fraud and violence perpetrated in history remain evil, and no higher synthesis can change its fundamental nature. Nor does the world tend towards perfection. In brief, history is without hope.

Yet from time to time there is a chance for compromise, compromise imposed more by circumstance than by the effective force of *ethos*. In Meinecke's view, the new *raison d'état* will serve as the instrument of this compromise, for "it is able to penetrate into the ethical sphere, even though it does not always do so."

One could argue that this "nature" which Meinecke considers an intrinsic, constituent and essential part of man and of the state belongs also to the human spirit. And since he admits that power in itself is morally indifferent, one might add, also, that he recognizes in this instinctive process the most elementary of

practical forms. Thus envisaged, the state would appear to belong to the sphere of ethical indifference, as a pure practical fact.

But Meinecke would rebel at such a Crocian conclusion. In
fact, he had castigated Treitschke for having regarded the state
as pure power and for having thereby led the Germans astray.
With an observation that would have horrified a Scholastic, he
ascribes to the state a double essence, and he finds, or at least
pretends to find, as an integral part of the state, besides power,
law, morality, and religion. Thus, for him, power becomes the
basic and most indispensable " factor " in the composition of the
state, but not the only one.

It would be too simple to merely smile at the contradictions in
which Meinecke's thought flounders. He would probably maintain that the contradiction in his thought is a reflection of a
fundamental contradiction in human nature itself, a human
nature in which spirit and matter, divine aspiration and daemonic
passion, are strangely interwoven and intermixed. To arbitrarily
heal the fissures in his thought would seem to sanction some
sort of monism of the whole man, to repeat the optimistic error
of Hegel, and even worse, to repeat the dangerous error of
Treitschke, who was not content to recognize the elemental
natural character of power but also sought to give it an ethical
consecration. An error such as this would justify the accusations
of the *Entente* propagandists. The Germans would have committed the sin of optimism by illuminating with an ethical light,
as Treitschke had done, the elemental dynamic of the power
struggle and by believing, as Hegel had done, in the fecundity
of such a struggle: " Up to the eve and during the first days of
World War I, we Germans lived in the reflection of this state
of mind, although dark clouds had already begun to form
over us."

The war, and even more the defeat, destroyed the German
historian's faith in the cunning of Reason and in the positive
character (*positività*) of history. Confronted with the fact of
defeat, the patriot could not find it in himself to admit it as a

had considered the national-liberal ideal of cultivating and difus-
ing power as the greatest title to glory,[21] the admirer of Boyen, of
the general conscription and of the Landwehr, the herald of the
national state who had castigated Burckhardt for having refused
to participate in the struggle for the perfection of the state and
for having defined power as " evil in itself," [22] now realized that
the national state invoked with an unprecedented violence the
daemonic forces, that the general conscription created a new
militarism, and that the democratization of the state meant a
mass nationalism which would be complicated by all of the
popular passions and instincts which it introduced. He did not
go so far as to rehabilitate Metternich, but he did discover that
Bismarck, by fighting as he had done against parliamentarianism,
saved Europe from disaster, had been the last champion of true
raison d'état and the last great moderator of the power instinct.

The disappearance of this wise *raison d'état*, overwhelmed by
popular passions, made him fear for the old Europe and for
Western civilization. He now felt that one of the most pernicious
of all ideas was that which maintained that the " republicaniza-
tion " of states would diminish the possibility of war, an idea to
which Kant had subscribed. And he turned to Burckhardt, for
whom any possibility of security had disappeared after politics
had become linked to the internal agitations of the masses.

Twenty years earlier, while analyzing Burckhardt's *Reflections
on World History* (*Weltgeschichtliche Betrachtungen*) , he had
discovered there, with C. Neumann, echoes of the Enlightenment,
of Rousseau, of Humboldt, of Romanticism, and even some
shades of Haller, the other Swiss patrician-historian. By returning now to the wisdom of Burckhardt, to what degree was he returning nostalgically to the world of eighteenth-century cosmopolitanism and romantic Europeanism? Having perceived the
daemonic character of the forces unleashed in the nineteenth
century, he was forced to go back to the eighteenth century to
find spiritual sustenance in the pages of Goethe. *The Origin of
Historicism* (*Die Entstehung des Historismus*) is a history of

eighteenth-century thought and concludes with an apotheosis of Goethe.

*   *   *

In *Cosmopolitanism and the National State*, Meinecke had accused Humboldt of having remained bound to a belief in the necessity of a supernational community. Meinecke regarded this as a residue of an a-political view, but he did grant him the merit of having made a step forward in as much as he had strongly felt the spontaneity and autonomy of the individual and had been able to appreciate the value of the individuality of nations. This sense of the incomparable individuality of nations seemed to him to have been derived from the secular standpoint from which the Germans had investigated, to its very roots, the essence of the individual. And he had exclaimed: " Individualism, spontaneity, the impulse to self-determination and the infinite expansion of power: thus it is in the state and the nation also! " It was *Sturm und Drang* transferred to the field of international politics. Thus, *Machtpolitik* received an unexpected justification and an ethico-metaphysical legitimation. Similarly, the idea of the national state itself had found an unexpected starting point in the Goethean tradition.[23]

In *The Idea of Raison d'État*, which is dedicated to Troeltsch, this sense of the value of the individual is called " historicism." And the investigation of the idea of historicism is held to be a necessary examination of conscience: " Since with this idea the break with the natural law tradition of the Western world as well as the spiritual isolation of Germany is realized, there is a profound need and obligation to undertake the examination of this historicism."

It is strange that in a work on the dualism between nature and spirit, between good and evil, in which their absoluteness is postulated, there is also an acceptance and defense of a historicism which, while justifying history in a new theodicy, denies radical evil as well as transcendance. Actually Meinecke moves along lines laid down in *Cosmopolitanism and the National State* but in a different direction: instead of following the progressive adaptation of the idea of national individuality to the idea of *Machtpolitik*, he went back to its eighteenth-century origins. In fact, he argues that the major defect in the historicist thought of the nineteenth century was the idealization of a *Machtpolitik* to which a higher morality was attributed. This was Hegel's error, and his influence had been such that in the last analysis the historicism of individuality was separated from that other form of historicism, the Hegelian idea of identity which fused heaven and hell, the real and the ideal, in the dialectic of history.

By rejecting such Hegelian immanentism and by leading historicism back to its origins, Meinecke hoped to free it from relativism and to reaffirm the absolute: " To attain once more to the faith that there exists some absolute is necessary in both a theoretical and practical sense."

Up to that time the question of historicism had been discussed in an aura of conceptual uncertainty and vagueness.[24] Meinecke's *The Origin of Historicism* [25] at least succeeded in giving the term a clear definition. For him historicism is the application of the principles of Leibnitz and Goethe to the historical life in which an object is considered in its individual aspect rather than as an instance of a general law. And even though this ideal had some precursors—especially in the Neo-Platonism of Shaftesbury, Vico and the English Pre-Romantics—Meinecke considers it the second great German cultural contribution since the Reformation. Similarly, he holds it to be the highest stage thus far achieved in the intelligence of things human. The idea that it might lead to relativism and paralysis of creative forces is a consequence of the " concealment and intrusion of foreign elements."

However, the concept of individuality implies that of development. But historicism is a mode of thinking in which the concept of development is different from the idea of progressive perfection found in the *Aufklärung* and from the vulgar idea of progress in as much as it attributes spontaneity, plasticity, and unpredictability to the historical life.

Meinecke had faith in the future of this historicism and in its capacity to heal the wounds produced by the relativization of all values, but he in no way gives a justification of that faith. In returning to the origins of historicism, he was able to call attention to a period in which the individual had not yet come to be considered the opposite of the universal. He could then conclude his work with a consideration of Ranke and his concept of the unity of the Latin and Germanic nations, his Europeanism, and his concept of historical development, which, by admitting not only an unfolding of innate attitudes but also the action of the forces of the time and then by transferring the concept of individuality over into the fields of political history, could imply a universal history. To be sure, the history of the human spirit from Shaftesbury to Goethe is a marvelous story. And, in fact, it could be said that contact with these sublime spirits had transported Meinecke into a benign atmosphere in which the anxiety that vibrated the pages of *The Idea of Raison d'État* had been stilled. The eighteenth century is indeed studied with major interest centered upon that nascent nationalism which anticipates and informs German thought in the nineteenth century. However, in the precursors, there is also to be found the cosmopolitan and idyllic spirit of eighteenth-century Europe. Here historicism exists in a stage of unconscious innocence and the joy of first discovery. It has not yet assumed the role of open subverter of natural law, an idea which "for two thousand years had been the polar star of Western civilization." Here historicism has not yet scratched the faith in the stability of human nature and the universality of reason but is limited to appearing as the integration of knowledge, as a more agile and a tighter mode of interpreting life, art and history. Among the precursors, Shaftesbury, Vico, Herder, Goethe and Ranke, it is permeated with a breath of Neo-Platonic pantheism, with a sense of joy before the reality of infinite forms which, in their divine

essence, become one. This revelation of the variety and multiplicity of the universe cuts at the very foundations of the dry
rationalist system. Yet the new sensitivity to primitive poetry,
the new respect for fantasy and sentiment, imply a finer sense
of conciliation, a more tolerant and human comprehension of a
greater portion of humanity and history. In this pantheism, in
this moral-aesthetic vision of things, humanism may be seen to
enjoy its last and most delicate flowering. Goethe represents
the last instant of a miraculous balance within the idea, a balance
maintained only by a conscious effort.

Inevitably the concept of individuality had to lead to the
anarchical individualism of the nineteenth century, to the dissolution of universal norms and values. Meinecke sees an absolute in the pure moral law. But it is impossible to reconcile the
absoluteness and the universality of law with individuality, a
law in itself. At the very beginning of the movement, Shaftesbury
had denied the reality of evil. Later, Lessing had deduced from
the Leibnitzian monadology the conclusion that the norm of
individual action was obedience to the nature of the individual
entity, to its own law, and he had halted there, thoroughly
frightened by the enormity of his discovery. But Hamann had
already transformed the idea of individuality into the theory of
the genius, the original creator, ignorant and mad, the subverter
of every norm, the rebel archangel. And finally Schlegel had
arrived at liberalism. Thus, already in the eighteenth century,
nature in its particularity had been substituted for the idea of
absolute law. Even if one could admit, with Dilthey, that
Romantic individualism expresses the need for a more intimate
and spontaneous morality, the fact remains that it not only dissolves natural law, as Meinecke holds, but also any universal
ethical norm. The absolute was restored by Kant, but as a move
against nature, against the idea of the empirical particularity of
the individual, for which he substituted the idea of moral personality, which was identified with universal law. According to
Meinecke, the flaw in historicist thought was the idealization of

Machtpolitik, to which it had attributed a higher morality. But is there not a similar flaw to be found in Meinecke also, insofar as he ascribes a higher morality to individuality itself?

Meinecke's discovery of the Neo-Platonic current in the development of historicism is considered by some to be a lasting contribution to the history of ideas.[26] But one might ask whether it is permissible to designate Pre-Romantic individualism with the term "historicism." The real target of individualism was not natural law but French poetry. Seen in terms of its aesthetic theory, it was a eulogization of spontaneity, sincerity, grandiose wildness, and fantasy which were a rebellion against the rules of French Neo-Classicism. To be sure, in its political orientation, on the continent, there was an aversion to French absolutism, to the French *raison d'état*, which was perceived behind that poetry as well as behind the French courtly etiquette. It was a protest against despotism which drove Bodmer, Möser, Hamann, and Herder towards Shakespeare, Milton, Addison, towards the English Pre-Romantic aesthetes, with their cult of Homeric and Biblical poetry. Here was a primary form of liberalism which was opposed to Voltaire, the ideologue of enlightened despotism.

But what does this liberalism have to do with history? It was concerned with the old liberties, with the civic virtues of the past which Bodmer had found in the free Swiss communes of the Middle Ages, Möser in the fabled agrarian communities of Saxony, and Herder in the Hanseatic cities. From that happy state of vigorous and healthy freedom there had been a fall into decadence and corruption. Thus, their nostalgia was something less than a justification of history, and can be seen as a movement which incorporated a social view not radically different from Rousseau's nostalgia for the state of nature. A historicism based upon a justification of history began only with Lessing, who fused the idea of profane history with the idea of Revelation in the concept of the education of the human race. It is this new theory which Kant elaborated in his " Idea of a Universal History from a Cosmopolitan Viewpoint " (*Idee zu einer allgemeinen Geschichte in weltbürgerlicher Absicht*) and which triumphed in the Hegelian dialectic, the ill-famed identification of heaven and hell.

Meinecke thought to mediate the dangers of individualism by refusing to conceive the individual as a monad and by linking its development to the processes of the external world. The resultant relationship is therefore conceived as an intermixture or interweaving, a reciprocal determination of two entities, remains, that is, an extrinsic and, in the last analysis, purely mechanical relationship.[27]

The individual is not considered a moment of the universal or its concrete realization but as a reality in itself which responds to influences of the environment. The accent remains on the individual with all its consequences. The postulate of universality, the need to mitigate individualism, remains a goal to be attained rather than an achievement of Meinecke. The idea of the individual remains much stronger, for the individual is a substance in itself, even though it recognizes its own "plasticity" and the pressures exerted upon it by the universe. Moreover, the individual will try to resist these influences, affirm itself, save itself, will see the universe and its norms as a menace and an oppression, and its own existence as a perpetual rebellion. If the universe is only an entanglement of individualities, these remain the true subjects and arbiters, and all values are reduced to the status of servants to these capricious entities. Thus, all values become relative.

Romantic individualism broke the barrier between nature and the spirit by refusing to grant value only to the rational and universal aspect of man and by attributing genuine value to his particular and irrational aspects, to his sentiments, passions and instincts. Thus, from the era of *Sturm und Drang* up through Nietzsche and Isben, one could celebrate the right of the individual to demean and violate the conventions of society in order to live "according to his own law."

In *The Origin of Historicism*, where hints of external dangers are to be found, there appears not even a suspicion of the errors and dangers which individualism nourishes in its breast. Meinecke does not seem to realize that those "crude, external elements" which appeared only in the nineteenth century, are to be found in a nascent state in the eighteenth-century idea of individuality, and that they were nourished, moreover, in Hamann and Möser by libertinism more than Platonism.

Meinecke reminds one more of Herder than of Goethe and Ranke. His method, which was constantly being refined, is most Herderian in his last work, in as much as he attempts to understand individualities through ideas, to give to the ideas themselves an incomparable coloration as they are passed from hand to hand and are reborn in individual thinkers. The account is monographic in character. But in every case, however powerful and original the individuality is, the threads which link it with the universal are infinite. They are monads with doors and windows open to receive the spiritual history (*Geistesgeschichte*) of the age. A unique flame burns in the single individuality. In the movement of ideas which culminates in the "German movement," Italy participates with Vico, England with Shaftesbury and the Pre-Romantics, and France with Montesquieu. And the Enlightenment itself, the enemy, contributes Voltaire, Hume and Robertson to the movement. The only real adversary remains unmentioned—the doctrine of natural law, here identified with the denial of natural differences and individuality. In this unity and multiplicity, in this *concordia discors*, in this polyphony, there is still a movement, a progressive purgation of the slag of natural law, but it is a movement without a dialectic. Here also Meinecke remains the Herderian. Those who prepare the way for the Hegelian dialectical idea receive little if any comfort: Lessing is remembered almost with ill will and Kant is passed over in silence.

Behind Herder stands Leibnitz. In fact, it is the monadology of Leibnitz, even more than Shaftesbury's Neo-Platonism, which forms the metaphysical base of this historicism. The other de-

fender of historicism, Troeltsch, the friend of Meinecke, also envisaged a return to a Leibnitzian metaphysics. Troeltsch dreamed
of a sort of syncretism of Malebranche's doctrine of the vision of
the ideas in God with the Hegelian dialectic. In Meinecke, however, there is a tendency to incorporate monadology with Neo-
Platonic pantheism in order to posit a pre-established harmony:
monads are seen as basically obscure and ineffable, arising out of
irrational forces, but also as participants in a universal life. One
may doubt, however, if such a hypothesis is acceptable for an
interpretation of history. For even if the monads are capable of
absorbing external movements, they still must be seen as absolute beginnings and must remain dark energies (insofar as they
are ineffable individualities) which become clear only when they
cease to appear in their extemporaneous and punctual " nature "
and enter as instants into the course of history. Only then does
the individual become reconciled with the universal; only then
does reality become one with it. Here, however, the universal
has its limits, that is, finds its negation, in the individual.

Thus historicism, understood as the subversion not only of
mathematical and mechanistic *raison* but also as a denial of faith
in the unity of human nature, arrives at pluralism, the denial of
the universal itself, and therefore at the dissolution of faith in
thought. Meinecke refused to be led to this conclusion by holding fast to the humanism of Goethe, Herder, and Ranke, which
still lived in him.

Chapter 4

MAX WEBER

I

The figure of Max Weber is one of the richest and most complex to emerge from the world of Wilhelmine Germany. In his manly conscience he bore the weight of the contradictions of a society and a culture vainly seeking to reconstitute themselves upon new foundations. It is therefore extremely difficult to define his work. Karl Jaspers, his friend and student, hailed in him "the true philosopher of the time in which he lived," adding, however, that "he did not teach a philosophy, but was a philosophy"—ambiguous words which seem to betray a certain perplexity. In fact, after having presented some examples of Weber's political, scholarly and philosophical thought in the profile dedicated to Weber,[1] Jaspers was constrained to reunite them under the vague term "German character." The full biography which his wife wrote—one of the most impressive tributes of love and devotion ever rendered by a woman to the memory of her husband—describes him as a vigorous old champion (*Recke*) a hero girt for battle but groping in the dark.[2] The nervous stroke which prostrated him at the height of his virility and from which he recovered only with the utmost difficulty appears almost as a symptom of an inner weakness lurking beneath the semblances of imperious vigour.

It is difficult to follow the line of his scientific and scholarly development. After a promising beginning in the history of medieval commercial law,[3] he became interested in the history of Roman agrarian law. Thence he passed to an investigation of the condition of the East German agrarian worker, and finally plunged himself into social polemic. Having recovered from the crisis, he undertook to investigate the problem of the methodology of economic science, but he interrupted these researches in order to study the ethico-religious origins of modern capitalism. He soon abandoned this research in order to begin an examination of the socio-economic premises of the great religions and to immerse himself in the study of Hinduism, Buddhism, Confucianism, and Judaism. Yet he never completed any of these studies, which were meant to serve merely as a point of departure for his general history of Western capitalism. Meanwhile, he had composed a long sociological tractate and found at the same time the energy to undertake a history of Western music in its social aspects. All of this work, fragmentary and unconnected, was buried in journals or left unedited. It would have been lost had his wife not devoted the remainder of her life to its collection and publication.

Not less erratic, apparently, was his political development. The son of a national-liberal deputy, nephew of that Hermann Baumgartner who was the adversary and critic of Treitschke in the name of the ideals of '48, he broke with liberalism and won his political spurs on the reactionary *Kreuzzeitung*, professing himself an economic nationalist. Soon, however, he revolted against the *Junker* and Pangermanism, became a follower of Friedrich Naumann, " the poor people's pastor," and adopted a position similar to that of Socialists of the Chair. He was opposed to the personalistic *politique* of William II, agitated for the introduction of a parliamentary regime and universal suffrage, and was among the founders of the Democratic Party. Yet all his life he remained faithful to the monarchy, and it was he who had written into the Weimar constitution those clauses which granted discretionary powers to the president of the *Reich*. Having embraced the doctrine of politics as pure power, he spoke of German "colonial fragments," spoke in favour of an international power politics (*Weltmachtpolitik*), but opposed the annexationist programs advanced during World War I.

It was his belief that the scholar should not pose as a prophet or master of life. He passionately denounced the use of the professorial chair as a platform for political propaganda, and he severely criticized Treitschke, to whose passionate one-sidedness he attributed that incapacity of judgment which marked his generation. At the same time, he was unique among the professors of his time in the courage and violence which marked his own political activity. In fact, it might be said of him what he said of the framers of the "Communist Manifesto": "In theory, if not in practice, they always refrained from moralizing. It never entered their minds (at least, so they claim) to lament the evil and infamy of the world. Yet, in reality, they were extremely passionate men who did not follow this rule at all." [4]

His style is also a study in contrasts. In the midst of magnificent pages of a nervous, dry prose, occasionally flashing with poetic insights and sarcastic thrusts at dilletantes and the literati, one is forced to wade through heavy disquisitions composed of seemingly interminable and contorted phrases.

Withal, there is a certain vigorous unity underlying the man's whole development. A first unifying strain may be perceived in the pain with which he felt and faced the antinomies of his time. He was truly a champion fighting in a world which was crumbling around him and within him. To those who might ask what his scholarly activity meant to him, he responded: "I want to see how long I can hold out." His mother was a descendant of an ancient Huguenot family and had educated him in that undogmatic faith which, in the epoch of historical criticism, had managed to keep alive something of the older Protestant spiritualism. When he attained manhood, he confessed to admiring in the church only a great historical institution. Nonetheless, he recognized that the patrimony of Christian values which he found in his mother and in himself could not and would not be shaken. He felt, as few men have, the magnificence and responsibility of political activity, but he knew that the "genius or daemon of politics lived in an inner tension, which at any moment might explode into an irreconcilable conflict with the God of love, even with the Christian God as expressed by the church." [5] And, not without a certain emotion, he cites Machiavelli's praise of the Florentines who, during the War of the Interdict, had esteemed the greatness of their native city higher than the salvation of their souls.

He criticized his father and the national-liberals for haggling over questions of principle and ignoring social questions—the only ones really worthy of consideration, in his eyes.[6] In scathing tones he denounced the pressures brought to bear by the authorities during the worker agitations, and he defended the workers' leagues as the "only real centers of idealism in the whole Social Democratic Party." But he identified socialism with bureaucratization, opposed any "dilettantish" plan for socialization, pointed out the dangers of state intervention, and, during World War I, supported state controls only as a temporary measure, necessary for the stabilization of the currency.

From the time of his doctoral dissertation—a study of the medieval trading companies—he was prone to attribute decisive importance for the history of Europe to the rationalistic liberation of business from domination by the nobility by the transition from a domestic to a business economy. Later he interpreted capitalism as one aspect of the rationalism of this civilization and diverted himself by tracing the development of the rational structure of Western music.[7] Yet it distressed him to have to watch the progressive rationalisation of life, and he frequently recalled the example of ancient Egypt which had purchased its perfect organization at the cost of its vital powers and had sterilized its existence. The current process of rationalisation seemed to him even more sinister, since it was more systematic and more mechanical.

In his studies, however, he followed an ideal which was strictly rationalistic. His investigations in the history of law were an outright repudiation of the romanticism of the older Historical School. It was his aim to comprehend the rational character of law, that is, its correlation to the exigencies of production and trade. In his essay on Roscher,[8] he rejected the mystical hypostatization of the national mind (*Volksseele*) conceived as the creation of God, and the organicist concept of the nation as expounded by Adam Müller, so that his sociology—the study of the rational relations between individuals—might free German political thought from all vestiges of Romanticism. He regarded all forms of intuitionism in science and political economy with contempt: "Let him who wants intuition go to the cinema," he is known to have exclaimed on one occasion. To those historians who exalted the creative personality and the "inner sanctum of free will" he argued that this was a most unusual "dignity" to ascribe to human activity, since it seemed to consist in its being neither intelligible nor explicable. His sarcasm was directed against any "romantic of the pen," and yet he himself transcended historical materialism precisely in his discovery that in any given economic activity there are to be found irrational motives which are often decisive. And in the end a fundamental aspect of his thought was contained in the recognition that it was irrational forces, great utopias and emotions which dominated men and moved history.

All of these disparate antinomies may be linked to a central problem in Weber's spiritual makeup, one which betrays not only the immediate and dolorous character of Weber but also of the Germany in which he lived. All of his activities centered around the nature of Bismarck's succession, that is, around the life-possibilities of the Bismarckian empire as a modern state. Weber himself could never forgive Bismarck for having refused to allow the formation around him of a group of political talents capable of assuming the burden of his legacy. In the glare of military pageantry, amid the thunder of the speeches of the "brilliant" William II, Weber refused to be blinded to the actual facts of Germany's political condition. Today there exists an extensive literature which analyzes the errors of William's foreign policy, but during the years 1906-1908, the most clamorous years of Wilhelmine *Weltpolitik*, few if any realized that a group of dilettantes and bureaucrats were only playing at power politics and were leading Germany into diplomatic encirclement and military disaster. Weber realized it and the impending tragedy forced him to take as his special theme the analysis of power techniques, of politics as a vocation. Above all, his sociology is a theory of the politician class, the absence of which in Germany appeared to him to be the gravest menace of all to the future of his fatherland.

*   *   *

Upon the occasion of his " promotion " to the doctorate Max Weber received a kind of consecration at the hands of his teacher Theodore Mommsen. That famous old scholar did not consider it beneath his dignity to cross swords with the younger man in an examination of his thesis. He immediately broke the tension, however, by declaring that often the younger generation had ideas which the older generation could not always immediately accept. And he concluded by stating: " But on the day when it is necessary for me to part this life, to no one more willingly than to Max Weber will I say, ' My son, here is my lance, now grown too heavy for my arm.' " [9]

Max Weber carried that weapon, first as historian, then as sociologist and politician. The work of the Roman historians Niebuhr and Mommsen was distinguished from that of other nineteenth-century German scholars by their interest in social history. Their histories of Rome are accounts of a peasant people which had conquered the world only to be robbed of its military vigor by a corrupt aristocracy. And by recalling the fate of the Gracchan mobs, they had formulated an indirect indictment of the landed aristocracy of their own time and country, the Prussian *Junker*. And for both Niebuhr and Mommsen the indictment was made on political rather than on moral grounds.

Niebuhr had sought to demonstrate the strict relation between the form and distribution of landed property and the
organization of the foot soldiery, the core of Roman military
power. The moral sense which led him to lament the disappearance of the ancient civic *virtù* was a purely political one, not
unlike that which had motivated Machiavelli and Möser earlier.
Mommsen, on the other hand, had sought to justify the Cae-
sarian monarchy by demonstrating the necessity of withdrawing
the direction of the state from an aristocracy which, because of
its class egoism, had become decadent and unfit to rule.

To the ideal of the free agrarian communities eulogized by
Möser, Stein and Niebuhr, the *Junker* had opposed that of the
Christian-Germanic, that is, the feudal, state. This form of
political romanticism had its greatest strength in the court party
(*Kamarilla*), not only because Frederick William IV was devoted
to it, but because it had produced " the last and greatest of the
Junkers," the one who had succeeded in founding the empire.
From one point of view, the landed gentry had demonstrated
their existence as a political class, the only one Germany had
ever known, by producing Germany's greatest political genius,
Otto von Bismarck.

Weber had grown to manhood in an age in which the figure
of Bismarck had already been consigned to the pages of history.
Reforms undertaken during the period of the restoration, which
had impoverished the peasant, had now developed into a chronic
agrarian crisis in eastern Germany. The economic decline of the
landed proprietors (*Landwirte*) had shaken the entire state
structure. Max Weber, who as Mommsen's student had begun
his scholarly career as a Roman historian, was obliged to close
the cycle of his development by abandoning his Roman studies
and devoting himself to the Prussian agrarian question, bringing
it under scrutiny from the point of view of pure power politics.

In a certain sense, Weber's *Agricultural History of Rome* [10]
was to have constituted a completion of Mommsen's work, which

Weber criticized for its failure to take sufficiently into account the economic elements of Roman history. Instead of centering his attention upon epigraphical materials, as Mommsen had done, Weber gave special attention to the methods of land survey and measurement which he reconstructed from close analysis of the works of Roman writers. From the different methods of land surveying and the different systems of property designation, he deduced the original coexistence of different types of property ownership. His main argument is that the Roman concept of private property was the artificial product of the political interests of a middle class, landed peasantry, which in the *ager privatus*, the legal and economic emancipation of landed property, had discovered the instrument for its own social and political emancipation from the rule of the patrician class. All of the great transformations which took place in the time of the republic and the empire are seen by Weber to have been linked to this fundamental change in the substructure of Roman society.

What interested him most was the formation of the great landed estates based upon slave labour. Here he deviated from the path laid out by Mommsen insofar as he attributed the birth of the *latifundia*, the destroyers of the free peasantry, not so much to the greed of the patrician class as to intrinsic economic necessity, brought on by the extension of Mediterranean culture into the interior. His historical materialism had freed him from any tendency to moralize. Thus he could account for the transition from a slave economy to serfdom—a deep and thoroughgoing restoration, bought all too dearly by the fall of the proprietors into what was often a state of permanent barbarity—as a technical necessity, brought about by the exhaustion of the slave market.[11]

The Roman social crisis, as Weber related it to the technico-economic aspects of the agrarian question, had the effect of revealing the political consequences of the German agrarian question to be even graver than Mommsen and Niebuhr had conceived them. The *Junker*, shaken by the competition of a world market, demanded from the state an increase on import duties, subsidies and emigration restrictions. The peasants, having been reduced to the status of migrant workers, preferred to emigrate. Their place was taken by Polish seasonal workers who were recruited by the landowners and deported to Poland every year after the harvest had been gathered. In 1890 the Society for Social Studies (*Verein für Sozialpolitik*) entrusted to Weber the investigation of the condition of the agrarian worker in eastern Germany. And the young historian of law was transformed overnight into an economist and sociologist.

*   *   *

In the report which resulted from these investigations, Weber did not repeat the incriminations against the aristocracy and its privileges. He did not invoke any idea of social justice. Nor did he blame the landowners for the fact that in Posen and Schlesien the rural proletariat was reduced to living on a diet of potatoes. On the contrary, he recognized the services rendered to the state by the *Junker* class in both the military and administrative branches of the government. But he pointed out that they were no longer an aristocracy. In the past, he argued, they had been qualified to wield power because they had constituted "an economically satiated group." But in the last half-century, forced to maintain themselves against a rising middle class, their political rival, they had been constrained to invest capital in the intensive cultivation of a small part of their property and to convert the remainder into pasturage. As a result, they had been transformed into a class of landed capitalist entrepreneurs. The decline of the landowner was the result of a general process of decline of products which no amount of protection could buoy up. But above all Weber felt compelled to point out that the importation of Polish workers by the landowners stood in direct conflict with the policy of Germanization advocated by the Pangermanists in the Polish districts of Prussia. The great area which hailed itself as the custodian of the most sacred national traditions stood revealed as a result of Weber's statistics and conclusions as the systematic detroyer of Germanism itself. As in ancient Rome, the agrarian enterprises of a capitalist system had, by reducing the peasant class, opened the doors to invasion.[12]

Weber recommended that the state abandon the landed proprietors to their fate and hermetically seal the frontiers against the Poles. However, since he feared that the destruction of the landed estates might create a proletariat of small holders, incapable of sustaining themselves alone, he proposed that the state intervene, purchase the lands, form domains and allot them to tenants who would be sustained by loans: a plan not at all unacceptable from a purely economic point of view. But Weber differed from the pure economists in his tendency to place the criterion of political interest above that of increased productivity. In other words, he preferred a pure German population in eastern Germany to an increased grain productivity, if the choice between the two had to be made.[13]

The agrarian research served as a point of departure for three different developments in Weber's thought. First of all, the direct contact with social reality made him cognizant of the limitations of a "purely economic interpretation" of history and led him to give his attention to an examination of the ethical evaluation of labour in social questions. The old patriarchal regime in eastern Germany was doomed also because the peasant now preferred a money wage, which would free him from his traditional subjection, to the more secure and beneficial system of shares and payment in kind: "As in the Middle Ages the money tribute was a sign of personal freedom to the peasant, so now was the money wage for the worker." The reason for the emigration of the agrarian worker was not so much the economic situation *per se* as the new structure of an agrarian society to which he did not know how to adapt himself. Thus envisaged, the class struggle took on a spiritual connotation before the realization of which Weber had difficulty concealing his surprise and even his embarrassment: "In the dark, semi-conscious yearning for foreign lands lay concealed an element of primitive idealism. The man who does not know how to interpret that feeling is insensitive to the fascination of freedom. In fact, seldom does that spirit touch us as we work in the quiet and isolation of our studies." This discovery of the psychological element in the economic struggle was the incentive to his famous investigation of the Calvinistic origins of modern capitalism.

However, for the time being the agrarian research offered a solid base from which to launch himself into a discussion of the social, political and economic issues of the time. He had been associated from time to time with the Society for Social Studies, founded by the Socialists of the Chair, had participated in the Evangelical-socialist Congress (*Evangelisch-sozialer Kongress*) and had even become connected with Friedrich Naumann, the promoter of a type of social Christianity. It was Weber's aim to take the vague and unrealistic dreams of these professors and theologians who sought to solve social problems by combining science and the Gospel and endow them with a realistic character. He thought he could do this by removing the questions with which they were dealing from an ethical plane onto a plane of power politics. Just as he had once excluded the economic principle of greater production from his discussion of the eastern German problem, he would now exclude all eudaemonistic ideals from his discussion of social problems. As he put it: "We do not engage in social politics in order to create a world of happy men. . . . We wish to transform, insofar as it is in our power, the external conditions of life, not to make men content, but to salvage out from under the burden of the inevitable struggle for existence whatever in them is worthwhile, that is, those spiritual and physical qualities which should be conserved for the national good." [14] Thus he entered into the polemic concerning the Bourse, affirming that the inconveniences caused by market speculation had to be counted among the costs of the struggle for economic supremacy in the world market. [15]

Finally, the agrarian research had the value of placing the political problem posed by Bismarck's succession and the *Junker* in a new light. He argued that it was dangerous and in the long run irreconcilable with the general interests of the nation to allow a class on the verge of economic ruin to control the reigns of political power. But then the question is raised: Which group should wield that power? The bourgeoisie, as a result of its non-political past, seemed unprepared. Its moment had already passed. And in the proletariat and its leaders Weber could not discern that " spark of the Catilinarian will to action." They lacked those grand conceptions of power which the class called to leadership must possess. Therefore, the prime problem for Weber was the formation of a politician class. Since his youth he had dreamed of a political party which could operate on a plane removed from all class and group interests. Now he sought a sociological solution to Germany's political problem in a class of professional politicians. And he turned his attention to parliamentarianism.

This son of a liberal deputy did not invoke the creation of a parliamentary state in the name of the older ethical or natural law ideals. If he demanded the concession of universal suffrage in Prussia, he did not do so because he adhered to any notion of natural equality. On the contrary, an egalitarian electoral law seemed necessary to him as the only bond which could effectively link the citizen to the state and serve as the expression of political unity in the nation precisely because there were basic natural, social and economic inequalities.[16]

He had no objections on principle to the personal rule of William II, but he felt that he could objectively show that, given the structure of the modern state, a monarch who was not a genius could only be a dilettante. He pointed out to the Germany of Bethmann-Hollweg that the bureaucracy, however efficient, competent and devoted it might be, was precisely in that degree that much less adapted to the realization of purely *political* goals. Indeed the German bureaucracy was the best in the world, but precisely for this reason it was unfit to govern, for, as Weber argued, the bureaucratic official must be concerned with impartial administration due to the very nature of his office and thus he will be unable to do what the politician must always and necessarily do, that is, *fight*.

Bismarck had received his political education in the Frankfort Diet. The new center for the training of modern Germany's leaders would have to be in a parliament.[17] But the schooling of the young political warriors would not take place in the halls of parliament proper. It would take place in the modest rooms of the commissions. There in the exercise of practical affairs and in the direct contact between man and man the future leaders would be fashioned. But it was necessary that they be guaranteed some actual control of the public administration so that their parliamentary experience would not be reduced to mere negative criticism and sterile oratory; the natural sphere of their careers, power, should not be closed to them. Germany, Weber argued, now had merely a pseudo-constitutional organization in which power, the aim of every true politician, was reserved for the bureaucracy. The result was that it was burdened with all the shortcomings of parliamentarianism and received none of the advantages.

In the discussion of this problem, Weber's originality consisted in his having turned against the monarchy of William II, not the traditional attacks on principle, but those themes of which the monarchy had made itself proponent and custodian: the interest and power of the state and the vigour and authority of political leadership. For him states were merely technical, mechanical entities.

One of Weber's critics has pointed out that the undisputed bureaucratic authority to which he attributed Germany's misfortunes was an outgrowth of the Lutheran ethic of obsequiousness to authority and the idea of loyalty to the demands of office.[18] It is a fatuous observation, because the discovery of those consequences of the Lutheran ethic was due precisely to the investigations conducted by Weber in common with his colleague and friend Troeltsch. It was unnecessary for Weber to take such considerations into account for the simple reason that the Lutheran ethic had in no way impeded the rise of the political class of the *Junker* nor the political accomplishments of Bismarck. Rather, one could argue that Weber's real error lay in his insistence upon the purely technical aspects (*tecnicismo*) of political power. Other intellectuals of that period, such as Troeltsch and Meinecke, who pointed out the urgent need for democratic reforms, avoided any appeal to natural law ideologies, but they sought to revive the Kantian tradition of the autonomy of the will and responsible liberty, the ideas of the "reform epoch," of Stein, Gneisenau and Boyen. Weber desired to avoid all contamination of politics by ethics so as to reduce the problem to solely a consideration of power techniques. In this mechanism the parliament had its place. He assigned to the parliament the control of the administration, but this control was only the opportunity offered to the future leaders to obtain practical experience in the exercise of political power. But could parliament live and function if its sole justification was that of serving as a seminary for professional politicians? And how would parliament fare once the desired political class had been formed outside and within it or once the party leader (*condottiere*) had made his appearance?

Actually, Weber did not believe in the possibility of forming a truly effective parliamentary machinery. In fact, no declared enemy of parliamentarianism ever submitted that institution to such a merciless analysis. For him true parliamentarianism was possible only in an age of local notable and aristocratic parties and was, thus envisaged, an idyll of the past. Only France and the other Latin countries appeared to be still in that arrested stage of development, while England, the parliamentary country *par excellence*, had gone beyond it long ago.[19]

In the Germany of the Weimar Republic, Weber's problem was translated into the general problem of the nature of authority in mass political regimes, of governmental unity and discipline in a total national democracy with universal suffrage. Here the rule of the notables and parliaments yields to organized parties in which power is vested in the machine politician. The question of the formation of a political class is thus seen as a question of the birth of the leader or *Führer*, who possesses the charismatic personality of the party leader, that is, the power of winning the faith of the masses over and beyond the parliament and of disposing his general staff of loyal followers (*Gefolgschaft*).

Such a plebiscitary dictatorship, Weber argued, had been realized in the countries of classical liberalism, in England and the United States. In the latter since 1824, the time of Andrew Jackson's election, in which the spoils system, the distribution of federal offices to partisans of the victor, had been openly applied, political parties had been reduced to the status of organizations of professional politicians—the ill-famed bosses—organized for the conquest of the office of President. And the President, independent of congressional control, could appoint his own ministers and officials. In England the rule of the notables had come to an end, according to Weber, already by 1866, when, upon the occasion of the democratic reform of the electoral laws, Joseph Chamberlain introduced the caucus, the gigantic electoral apparatus headed by a central office and staffed by salaried employees. Without meaning to sound paradoxical, Weber found in Gladstone's great demagoguery the final success of this Caesaro-plebiscitarian system which had reduced the members of the English parliament to a " well-disciplined voting troop," ready to return to the hall when summoned by the " whip " and vote as ordered by the leader.

Thus, almost three-quarters of a century later, Mommsen's Caesarism reappeared in his student, but it was a Caesarism totally different from that of Napoleon III. Rather it was an anglicized, constitutional brand of Caesarism which presupposed, if anything, a long parliamentary tradition in order to function in the best interests of the nation as a whole. But this tradition, in its turn, presupposed a definite ethico-religious tradition, one capable of conserving for the institution, now transcended in a practical sense, that theoretical and conventional vitality which was indispensable to it if it were to realize its modest functions. But to seek to introduce into a country which lacked such traditions an institution that had no direct relationship to the times was more than a sociological paradox; it was an historical error.

Weber took part directly in German politics only upon one occasion. It was he who was instrumental in having special prerogatives granted to the president of the Reich in the Weimar constitution. This was no small matter when one considers the use to which those extra-parliamentary powers were put by Hindenburg. But he did not live to see how the new Germany would finally resolve its problems. Physically as well as spiritually he remained a man of the Wilhelmine epoch. In 1919 he resolved to remain forever aloof from politics. In June 1920 he died.

He died in peace. In November 1918 he confessed: "I suffer much less today than I suffered in all the twenty-five years in which I had to witness the hysterical vanity of a monarch destroy everything sacred and dear to me. What was once due to human stupidity has now been resolved into fate, and with fate everything is justified." Even though he had been sympathetic to the institution of monarchy, he had implored William II to abdicate and depart with honor. The possibility that with the abdication more advantageous peace terms might be obtained was for him a matter of secondary importance and little consequence. What was important was that the dynasty remain, even if under the form of a regency, because he had little faith in the democratic experiments which were sure to follow. He felt that the new order, the product of the disaffected elements of the nation, had little chance of really taking root. He had little if any faith in the future of social democracy, which lacked all "power instincts." He foresaw "a polar night of icy darkness and hardness," no matter which party triumphed ultimately, "because, where there is nothing, not only the Kaiser but also the proletarian has lost his rights." At the same time he could affirm: "Never before have I felt so strongly the good fortune which has allowed me to be born a German as in these gloomy days of our humiliation." The state had been led to disaster by the political ineptitude of the monarch, but for four long years the nation had given proof of its inherent strength. One must wait another frightful ten years: "And then history, which has given to us and only to us a second springtime, will give us a third. Of that I have no doubt."

*   *   *

As we have seen, the underlying unity of Weber's intellectual development was his preoccupation with the principles of power and the idea of national struggle. As the heir of Niebuhr and Mommsen he had applied these ideas to the agrarian problem and to social questions in general. To a question about the aim of these studies, he responded: "Vulgar opinion has it that political science is capable of supplying formulae for the happiness of the world, for the amelioration of the general well being. But the dark seriousness of the population problem already prohibits us from embracing such a eudaemonistic attitude, from aspiring to a genuine peace and happiness in the bosom of the future, and from believing that the earthly life of man can ever be anything more than a struggle for existence." Political science was incapable of deriving its ideals from the materials and methods with which it had to work. The belief in economic ideals was an optical illusion, because it presupposed an inter-mixture of eudaemonistic and ethical criteria. Thus envisaged, the power interests of the nation were the ultimate and decisive interests and the ones in whose service the political scientist laboured. The science of economics was nothing but the science of politics, a branch of politics, not of a ruling class, but of the lasting interests of the nation as a whole. Even the question of the extent to which the state might interfere in the economic sphere was determined by the power interests of the national state.

He applied the same criterion to the evaluation of the worth of the dominant class in the nation. Its only justification was its ability to carry the power instinct. Its maturation consisted in its ability to place the power instinct of the nation above every other consideration. Thus, the true social problem for him was that of the political disposition of the dominant or ascending class. The force of the political instinct of the *Junker* had been "one of the most important capital assets that could have been employed in the service of the power interests of the state." The unification of Germany had been a youthful accomplishment, completed by the nation later, which, considering its price, would have been better left undone since it served merely as a conclusion and not as a point of departure for a world political policy in the interests of Germany as a whole. Nor was he sparing in his criticism of Bismarck, whom he berated for having encouraged France in its policy of expansion in Africa, in the vain hope of making it forget its lost provinces in Europe, and for having thereby given such a weak impulse to German colonial policy as to make every subsequent attempt at expansion appear as an unjust menace to preconstituted interests.[20] He denied to William II anything even approximating a genuine policy: "As long as this drill sergeant's manner of conceiving power lasts, any possibility of a genuine *Weltpolitik* is precluded." [21]

Seen in the light of the total development of German political thought, Weber's sociology represents a return to the consciousness of a dichotomy between politics and ethics in its most drastic formulation since the Hegelian development of Machiavelli's doctrines at the hands of Droysen and Treitschke: "Even the ancient Christians knew that the world was governed by daemons, and that involvement in politics meant becoming the servant of power and force and sealing a pact with diabolic

forces." [22] One might even argue that Weber was closer to the
ideas of Machiavelli than were Droysen and Treitschke, for
they still lived in the Bismarckian atmosphere, whereas Weber
laboured under the privation of a genuine political direction
of the nation. Just as in Machiavelli the humiliation of political
impotence gave impulse to the formulation of the doctrine of the
prince, so in Weber it gave birth to the idea of the leader or
Führer. Those pages in which Weber describes the organized
group of followers, necessary to the leader if he is to fight and
win, reflect the same calculating coldness which characterizes
the unbiased analysis of Machiavelli himself. How Machiavellian is his need to construct an empirical and technical science
of politics. How like Machiavelli is his accentuation of the
a-political character of Christianity.

He did not attempt to give any sort of ethical consecration
to the state, which, as a sociologist, he defined as a relation of
domination of men over men. If, he observed, there were any
social organisms in which violence was unknown as a means, the
concept of the state would crumble and in its place would arise
a condition of anarchy in the true sense of that word. The
modern state, unlike the medieval state in which the exercise
of violence was distributed between powers more or less autonomous, was for him " that human community which (successfully) claimed the monopoly of the legitimate use of physical
force within a given territory." [23]

To all attempts at compromise, that is, to all attempts to give
ethical legitimation to violence, he opposed political necessity,
against the laws of which it was senseless to rebel, at least if one
were not a saint and committed to complete rejection of the
world. Whatever the goal might be, even that of international
peace, it would always be necessary to recur to means which
endangered " the well-being of the soul."

It is understandable why, after Germany's defeat in World
War I, Weber was loathe to recognize the power struggle as
the judgment of God (for him " the God of battles always stood

on the side of the largest battalions ") and was indignant when the Allies sought to present their victory as a triumph of good over evil. Yet even earlier, in the period of German successes, he had been unwilling to approach power politics with the crude moral pathos of a Treitschke. He regarded politics as a "miserable duty" of nations fashioned by fate into power states. Accounting for it in the same way as had the Swiss Burckhardt, who had attributed a dialobic character to power, he thanked the gods that there was a Germanism which existed over beyond the power state itself, "where not only the genuine civic virtues and authentic democracy—things not truly realizable in the great power state—might thrive, but also values which were much more spiritual and eternal, values which flourish only where political power is renounced." [24] And he justified German participation in the war as a damned duty and a responsibility to history, that is, to the world of the future, which was the burden of peoples organized into power states and which could not be denied without a concomitant denial of their very reason for existence: "Future generations, and above all our descendants, would not hold the Danes, Swiss, or Norwegians responsible if the mastery of the world—and that means in the last analysis the power to determine the course of future civilization—were divided between Russian bureaucracy and the conventions of Anglo-Saxon society, with perhaps an interjection of Latin *raison*. It would hold us responsible and rightly so, for we are a power, and therefore, unlike the smaller nations, we are able to throw our weight into the balance of history." [25]

But was this exercise of power really outside the sphere of ethics if it could be presented as a "damned duty" and "a responsibility"? Similarly, did not politics fall under the terms of ethical judgment insofar as it had to "lose its soul"? At the same time that he proclaimed the necessity and autonomy of politics, Weber characterized it as "diabolic," that is, formulated a condemnation of it. It is here that we begin to catch a glimpse of the inner flaw in the champion of world power politics.

Here Weber reveals the fundamental religious dualism which lurked in the depths of his spirit, although he was far removed from all the conscious religious convictions of the days of his youth. He professed to accept this world, but he continued to regard it with the eye of the Christian as the realm of sin, violence and war. He regarded it, one might even say, with the eye of a Tolstoi or a Dostoyevsky. Like all of the Germans of his time he had contemplated the discourse of the Grand Inquisitor [in *The Brothers Karamazov*]. Slavic Christianity, precisely because it was oriental, seemed to him to most clearly approximate the faith revealed in the Gospels. It seemed to him to be an other-worldly faith, antithetical to all of the earthly norms of culture, power, dignity, honor and greatness of the creature, teaching a mystical communion with the Eternal for which this political, social, ethical, and scientific world had little meaning.[26] It was therefore patent that he had to consider as absurd the search made by his friend Troeltsch for a Christian social ethic. Between the world and the absolute Christian ethic of evangelical poverty and non-resistance to evil, there could be no compromise. Thus envisaged, any attempt to apply it to social reconstruction (*rivendicazione*), politics, or revolution was either vain or openly hypocritical. There was no escape from the dilemma: either one had to follow the Gospel completely, like St. Francis and the dying Tolstoi, or accept the world with all its limitations: " Any man who collects one miserable penny and thereby derives a profit from toil and commitment to the merciless economic struggle which, in the bourgeois terminology, is deemed peaceful civic activity and in which hundreds of millions of men are used up and wasted, is bound to the laws of this world which, among other things, imply the possibility and inevitability of the struggle for power." [27]

He professed to accept the world, but in reality he did not accept it at all, for it is certainly not to accept it to say that it is governed by daemons. Weber lived in a spiritual climate which was totally alien to the Hegelian acceptance of the world as an acceptance of history, which realizes that suffering, violence and war, the spirits of the earth, are elements indispensable to life, and which justifies those elements in the life-vision, that is, the good, which grows out of and triumphs over pain and death.

Unlike Troeltsch and Meinecke, he was not burdened by the hope of a compromise: between ethics and politics there was an impassible abyss. Moreover, with a sort of sadism, he pushed the two realms to the outermost limits of the antithetical relationship. He therefore excluded not only any informal compromise between the two realms but also all mediation between them. For Weber we are creatures of two worlds which are in perpetual conflict.

There was in Weber, as there was in Burckhardt, a naïve distinction between politics and ethics which became converted into a radical opposition. The famous denunciation of the diabolical character of power is, in reality, not the recognition of the autonomy of politics over against ethics, but its identification with ethical non-value, negation, evil. And since politics is a living and powerful reality, he deduced the affirmation of the wickedness and invincibility of it. Once this radical evil of the world and politics had been ascertained by Weber, he did not attempt to escape, as Burckhardt had done, into a realm of artistic contemplation. Rather, he went below the realm of the " absolute ethic," the unrealizable norm of the Gospel, in order to seek an " ethic of responsibility," a worldly ethic which was bound, because it was worldly, to the use of " ethically dangerous " means.

But to what is one responsible in this ethic of responsibility? In place of Providence and its decrees Weber posits fate and history as the forces to which we are responsible. But such empty terms could not supply the needed criteria. Something more precise was needed, and Weber found it in the old Lutheran concept of " calling " (Beruf), understood as divinely appointed vocation. Here sociology, as a science of class and class relations, is transformed into a schema of ethical norms, a modern form of the medieval ordering of estates willed by God. Thus, the professional politician, inserted into the social order as an indispensable element endowed with his peculiar *ethos*, the power instinct, found its justification. Similarly, science was also considered a calling or vocation.[28] According to the canons of this sociological ethic, Weber could see men only as men formed by their calling *(Berufsmenschen)*, who exercised their professions with competence, or as dilettantes, who, from his point of view, were outcastes. So strong was this rule for Weber as to induce him to decline when he was offered a candidacy for the *Reichstag* and when his friends had already seen in him the next national leader in place of any kind of professional politician.

It was an absurd solution. To make of politics an art, profession or technique peculiar to a special class meant to shirk one's miserable duty. Weber was anything but an aesthete or a pure scientist. He could withdraw from active politics, but he could not extinguish his anxiety as a man and as a citizen.

* * *

Divided between two laws, one of which was absolute but unrealizable, Weber ended by falling into a sort of relativism. Even here is reflected that inability to accept the world which in history orders and justifies the battle of ideas. For him immanence had to appear a chaos of irreconcilable opinions. While he did not deny his faith, he lost the apodictic certainty of a Treitschke, and recognized that he was only dealing with a faith. Beside it and against it he recognized the existence of other faiths, other values, among which it was necessary to choose if one wished to live. But he also realized that the choice had to be made irrationally, without the benefit of any rational criterion of selection. Dilthey had pointed out the modern " anarchy of values." Weber accepted it: " Anyone who lives in the world cannot avoid experiencing within him a struggle between the plurality of values, each one of which appears binding when taken by itself. It is necessary to choose which of these gods one wishes to serve, but regardless of the choice, he will always find himself in conflict with one of the other gods of the world." [29] He himself professed to be a polytheist: "As the Greeks sacrificed first to Aphrodite and then to Apollo and each of them to the gods of their own city, so that attitude, stripped of its mystical garb but intimately true, persists today. And over the gods and their battles rules destiny, not science." [30] As in Kierkegaard and the "crisis theologians," faith, for Weber, had become a commitment. And Weber agreed with Nietzsche insofar as his pseudo-acceptance of the world resolved itself into a condemnation of the Socratic claim to be able to teach men how they should live their lives.

Nevertheless, it was precisely to science that Weber turned for a solution to his problems.

*   *   *

Max Weber is the German thinker who insisted with greatest energy upon the distinction between being and obligation (*essere* and *dover essere*), between science and value judgment. For him the distinction did not arise out of an intellectual need for clarity but from practical necessity. A realistic political policy, free of all ethical, religious and natural law contaminations, demanded a rigid separation of the various "planes" of the spiritual life. However, when he came to realize that even his realism was based upon a value and that this value was bound to a subjective view of the world, then the distinction became a dyke against the irrational, a means whereby science might be removed to a point beyond the conflict of *Weltanschauungen*. In a Germany divided by party biases, questions of principle, radicalisms and fanaticisms, Weber's sociology sought to establish some solid ground for rational discussion and pave the way to some common agreement.

The hope of the positivists, that science might be able to bring order and happiness to men and serve as a substitute for their former faiths by founding new norms, he regarded as a futile dream. The " crisis of science " was underway. In order to save it, it had to be liberated from the burden of such a task. As far as Weber was concerned the possibility of constructing ideals which were scientifically justifiable did not exist: " The reason why I turn on every occasion with extreme bitterness and a certain pedantry against the contaminations of being and duty is not because I undervalue questions of duty, but precisely the contrary, because I do not believe that questions of universal importance—in a certain sense, those capable of moving the human heart—can be dealt with like questions of economics or become the object of special disciplines like political economy." [31] He regarded jurists who introduced questions of moral duty into their discipline as " the most God abandoned of men." And he derided the historian L. M. Hartmann, who claimed to have deduced ethical imperatives from his theory of social evolution, just as he criticized the chemist Ostwald for attempting to transfer the naturalistic concept of energy into the fields of ethics and politics.[32]

But the distinction did not lead Weber to a re-examination of his own system of the planes of the spiritual life. Instead, he returned once more to the so-called " philosophy of values." In his essays on the methodology of economic science he explicitly recurs to the doctrines of Windelband and Rickert, but even earlier his fundamental ideas were based upon the dualism of reality and value which was basic to that school.

This dualism did not correspond exactly to the distinction between theory and practice but rather to that of existential judgment and value judgment. Value, however much it may be a living and active force, is not being, the unique possible object of knowledge. Hence, a value judgment ceases to be a judgment and is reduced to the status of an objective attitude, to an extrinsic act of sympathy and antipathy, which determines the importance of the objective being. The realm of ethical, aesthetic, religious and emotional values is the sphere of ideals and norms with which the subject confronts reality. Since all judgment is excluded from science, it is reduced to knowledge of factual data and empirical laws. Within this domain, then, one must distinguish between the "sciences of the spirit" or of culture and the natural sciences: the first is concerned with the individuality of facts and the latter with their arrangement under various uniform laws.[33]

As was noted above, the dualism of science and value judgment allowed Weber to defend the objectivity of investigation by removing it from the realm of the irrational into that occupied solely by factual data. To exclude value judgments meant to remove political and scientific discussion from the influence of suggestion and fanaticism: a duty of both the citizen and the scientist. Once one had freed himself from the delusion that science could point the way to true being, true nature, the true God, or true happiness, the real task of the scientist would stand revealed as that of furnishing information and methods of thought, of clarifying and aiding in the rationalization of activity, and of pointing out the consequences of given actions.[34]

The limits were narrow, for precisely that inviolable realm of values was the realm of life itself from which sprang not only human actions but the very soul of science. In fact, Weber grants to our value judgments the choice of the important. Without a specific point of view empirical reality would remain undifferentiated and amorphous; no problem or interest would arise. But here we are dealing, according to Weber, with a simple, initial impulse (which gives direction to our thought), after which all should proceed objectively.

But what was the aim and purpose of a science thus conceived? Weber held that it could be useful insofar as it touched upon the realm of duty. First of all, like logic, it could dialectically dissect a value judgment in order to expose its ultimate axioms and possibly demonstrate what other hidden and contradictory value judgments might be contained within it. But above all, science would be able to indicate to whoever wished to act according to any given value judgment what means he had at his disposal and what desirable, yet unavoidable, secondary results would be brought about by the employment of those means.[35] In sum, science was a technique for the analysis of means and costs, by which the possibilities, limitations and consequences of a given action might be calculated. Its rationale was that of practical calculation, that is, economic calculation.

Weber gives an example of this procedure in his critique of socialism.[36] First of all, he sought to isolate the kernel of the "Communist Manifesto," the value judgment, that is, the hope for the elimination of exploitation of man by man. This value judgment he did not discuss. Rather, he began with that part of the doctrine which purported to see the decline of the bourgeoisie as a result of the progressive proletarianization of the masses, the numerical diminution of the capitalist class, and economic crises. Here it was a simple matter for him to demonstrate that such predictions were erroneous, that is, that the means were inadequate for the realization of the envisaged end. And what were the costs of socialism, the secondary consequences? Socialization would lead to bureaucratization, that is, rule by a class of functionaries. This meant rule by that class which tended by its very nature to separate itself from the proletarian worker. The result would be a dictatorship, not of the proletariat but of the functionary, and it would be all the more oppressive since a fusion of political bureaucracy and economic bureaucracy would remove any possibility of reciprocal control.

As for Socialists of the Chair who sought a better form of social justice through state control which shared government with business, Weber—again not bothering with a discussion of the value judgment contained in the idea of social justice—showed how such an arrangement would lead to mastery of the state by business. Under such a government, the state would be constrained to impose high prices and low wages, since it was interested alike in profits and losses. At the same time it would have to guarantee a profit to its partners. The result would be to substitute profit for justice as the criterion of production, with the added shortcoming of having the hatred of the worker now directed at the state instead of at the business interests.

*   *   *

Weber's fame rests upon his study of the relation between the Protestant ethic and modern capitalism, a thesis which has in itself produced a whole corpus of literature. He is also known as the formulator of the doctrine of the ideal type—a doctrine through which he hoped to restore the naturalistic concept of law to economic science. Furthermore, he was one of the masters of that German sociology which—it has been said—" is to be numbered among the ferments of that intellectual renaissance which reveals itself ever more clearly as an essential trait and value of contemporary German life, which in so many ways is problematical." [37] Of these more conspicuous aspects of Weber's work we have not yet spoken, it seeming more desirable to first examine the fundamental ideas which motivated him.

One might justify this procedure in yet another way. Weber has been called " the most important intellectual spirit in the Germany of the period between 1897 and 1914." [38] But what message did this master bring to his country and to his age? The answer is none, because science could not serve as a podium for the demonstration of the validity of an idea. Between empirical science, the technique of analyzing means and costs, and the arbitrary choice of a faith and a party, there was no place for thought in Weber's system. The choice itself was left to a kind of commitment, that is, to an act of will, and the victory, to dark fate.

II

Weber's essay on the Protestant ethic and the spirit of capital-ism [39] is one of the few great historical interpretations which have posed a problem where once was universal agreement or a void; in order to solve that problem, it fashioned a new method of interpretation and analysis. In its boldness and originality of conception his effort is equal to Droysen's interpretation of Hellenism, Tocqueville's interpretation of the French Revolu-tion, and Fustel de Coulanges' work on the Athenian *polis*. In Weber's study, the typical form of modern capitalism, the Anglo-Saxon variety, which up until Weber's time had seemed to be synonymous with mere greedy speculation, is presented as being united with a rigid Puritan morality. At the same time, the Puritan morality is shown to be the heir of monastic asceticism in modern, secular garb.[40] Weber's thesis has been contested, revised, and limited, but the fundamental principle has re-mained: that it is impossible to explain the development and fortunes of the economic life of peoples and civilizations by reference to economic impulses alone, that it must be correlated to the economic ethos, with the impulse to the moral evaluation of work and profit.

The particular aptitude of the believer in Calvinism for modern industrial and business activity had been observed long before Weber's time. Marx had seen Calvinism as a bourgeois religion, and many had attempted to explain the displacement of economic activity from the Mediterranean to the Atlantic seaboard by reference to religious factors. The relation between the evolution of the Christian ethic and economic activity had already been studied by Lujo Brentano, who had, however, con-sidered the religious norm with regard to its greater or lesser hostility to the business world and its progressive defeat at the hands of an advancing modern paganism.[41] But with Weber the Christian ethic in its Calvinistic form was transformed from a brake into a stimulus and an impulse. Only after the appearance of his essay were historians forced to examine the possibility of tracing economic activity back to dogmatic roots and of inserting its history into the movement of ideas and faiths.

Before we continue, it would seem desirable to clear up one misunderstanding of which many of Weber's critics have, from Brentano on, been guilty.[42] Weber's work is not concerned with the origin of capitalism. Hence, all criticism of his thesis which makes appeal to the preexistence of the phenomenon fails. He knew that enterprises conducted according to the calculation of investments and profits were old and almost universal. Capitalism, for him, meant the same thing that it did for Sombart, economic rationalization, a process which in the West, in accord with the rationalization of the science, government, law, architecture, and music of our civilization, had arrived at a stage unknown elsewhere. But for Weber the special note in Western capitalism was the organization of a formally free labor which alone allowed for exact calculation. Thus, a history of modern capitalism would have had to consist of a history of individual liberty, the various stages of which would be marked by the ancient *polis*, the Christian community, feudalism (insofar as it consisted of a free contract), the medieval corporations, and perhaps the absolute monarchy: almost the entire history of Western civilization. Therefore, it is incorrect to attribute to him a subjective or spiritualistic theory of the origins of capitalism over against an objective or technical one. It is more correct to see him as the formulator of a sociological theory of the irrational stimuli which contribute to the breakdown of traditional restraints and to the triumph of rationalism in countries which embraced the Calvinist confession.

The problem which interested Weber was peculiar to him: it was the question of the adaptability of a social type to a given economic structure. Basically, it was the problem underlying the rapid transformation of ancient, patriarchal Germany: a transformation which was not only economic but ethical and psychological as well. During his agrarian inquiries in Prussia he had realized that in the determination of the attitudes and roles of social groups there intervened psychological moments, which were often stronger than the economic moment itself, and that the struggle between the older agrarian economy and the new capitalistic one was a struggle not only of systems but of two souls, two mentalities, two different concepts of life.

Weber had already gone beyond the "antiquated" economic interpretation of history when, in the first years of the century, the Marxist theory of the superstructure forced itself on the attention of the historian and the sociologist. The scientific confutation of that theory must have developed and clarified his earlier experiences, and to this were added memories of his own family of industrialists as well as reminiscences of his Huguenot ancestors transmitted to him by his mother. [43] However, it also necessitated his including it in the theory of history and sociology which he was laboriously constructing in those years.

He considered historical materialism as a law or sociological hypothesis which had to be controlled by the sieve of experience like any other hypothesis. He refused to view it as a heuristic canon, for he did not see how a hypothesis, even if it were derived from the empirical observation of human life and verified by the facts, could ever achieve the dignity of an *a priori* canon. For him any methodological revision bespoke a scholastic confusion between the laws of nature and logical norms. In place, therefore, of a revision of historical materialism, he presented his readers with a confutation. Instead of ending his quest in a philosophy of the spirit conceived as an historical methodology, as Croce did, he ended with a sociology considered as an historical hermeneutic.[44]

The experiment which would serve to confirm his views would have to consist of an investigation of the causes of a determined historical entity strictly isolated from its context. The historical entity selected by him for study was the capitalist spirit: to demonstrate that the principal cause of this spirit was a religious dogma was to attack the enemy on his own ground and to overthrow the hypothesis with a crucial experiment.

*   *   *

That the Calvinists and members of similar sects were particularly adaptable to modern economic life because of their scrupulousness and diligence was, as noted above, an old observation and one which Weber accepted as an assumption. Furthermore, German educational statistics indicated a pronounced predilection of the members of the Reformed sects for technico-commercial studies or for realistic, over against humanistic, interests. What was the cause of this calling of theirs, of this inclination to lead their lives according to the same kind of rationalistic criteria as those demanded by modern capitalism? Weber undertook to demonstrate that their ethic, the direct expression of the dogma of predestination, far from representing an obstacle to rational economic conduct, rather resulted in an irresistible impulse to incessant labour and enrichment. Just as the monks, otherworldly ascetics, had filled their days with a rational schedule of work and prayer, so the Calvinists, ascetics of this world, had methodically organized their lives with the hope of finding therein a sign of their election. In sum, the capitalist spirit was a paradoxical joke of fate, that is, of that logic which leads to consequences unexpected by all and contrary to all intentions, which is capable of transforming an ascetic, assiduous reader of Psalms into a hard and cunning businessman. In the eighteenth century it was customary to marvel at the cunning of nature, which could transform private vices into public benefits. Goethe had, it will be remembered, placed in God's mouth the motive force for the provocation and stimulation of man. Here, in the Calvinist development, Satan took his ironical revenge.

Weber's essay was not meant to be a history of Calvinistic capitalism, however. That would have necessitated a study of the history of the great businesses of the Anglo-Saxon world. That this capitalist spirit was one of the causes of the industrial and commercial development of the Anglo-Saxon countries was self-evident in his eyes, although never demonstrated.[45]

Instead, the essay was to be considered a chapter in the history of ethics, derived not from the study of philosophical tracts but from devotional books, homilies and sermons, all of which stood in closer contact with the religious and moral life of the masses than did philosophy. Moreover, he was dealing with a special aspect of that history: that which concerned work and profit. This was a branch of ethics which had scarcely been noticed by historians of philosophy prior to that time and one which had been completely ignored by economic historians.

However, the novelty of Weber's essay did not consist in the discovery of the importance of economic ethics in the history of civilization. It lay in the new historical method there presented which had precedents only in the *Civilization of the Renaissance in Italy* (*Kultur der Renaissance*) of Burckhardt and the investigations of the religious origins of the *polis* conducted by Fustel de Coulanges.[46] In fact, once the Hegelian concept of unifying history in the unique dialectical movement of the Idea had declined, historiography had reverted to the traditional division into various areas: political history, literary history, social history, religious history, legal history, economic history, and so forth. Reciprocal influences between the various realms had been noted for some time, and in Germany a debate was underway concerning whether the political or cultural area could claim primacy. But the problem of the relationship between all the categories, that is, of the unity and continuity of the life of the spirit, really came into prominence only after the Marxists had affirmed the dependence of all other categories upon the economic. The sociological interpretation of history is based upon the transition from one category to the others.

The problem posed by Weber produced the impression of having penetrated to unknown depths, where civilizations and nations appeared called to a different destiny by their daily profession of faith. The old and almost forgotten moral theology was revealed as a keystone in the structure of civilizations, precisely because of its dual theoretical and practical nature. What appeared to be mere theological abstrusities was the result of attempts to give unity to the constituent ideals of a peculiar way of living and feeling: ideas working in social and familial relationships, in politics, in the technological and economic life, in charity, in hygiene, in sport, in love, in fashion, in the most banal conventions of society.

Along with Dilthey, who created in his immediate *Erlebnis* the common root of poetry, music and metaphysics; Troeltsch, who deduced socio-political ideologies from the dogmas of the different confessions; Sombart, who from the *forma mentis* of the Jew hoped to derive the capitalistic mentality, Weber succeeded in setting German historiography to the task of investigating the hitherto hidden reflexes, analogies, threads, and links between the various categories of the life of the spirit; his research, however, has an empirico-causal character. He not only examines the relation between the principle and the consequence, which is a logical relation; but since for him historiography is a causal science which explains the genesis of historical individualities by investigating their components, the principle becomes the cause and the consequence an effect. Thus the Marxist schema is broken, because the position of unmoved mover is taken away from the economic moment, and in its place one is presented with some sort of circular mechanism wherein what is cause becomes effect and vice versa.

However, the circle was not closed because Weber did not break through the last barrier separating the capitalist spirit from capitalism in action. The causal relation which he studied was only that which existed between the dogma of predestination and the capitalist spirit, where the mechanism exists very strongly. Furthermore, besides this dogma Weber admitted at least two causes: the socio-political ethic and humanistic rationalism. Finally, and here is the essential point, the dogma has two consequences: one logical—and that is fatalism—and one practical or psychological—the need produced in the believer for a confirmation of his election. In the clash of the two ideas it was the latter which triumphed. The capitalist spirit was the practical-psychological result of the dogma of predestination, for, Weber argues, since the Calvinist is denied the possibility of acquiring a guarantee of salvation by works, he is forced to seek in work and economic success the sign of his own *character indelebilis* as a chosen servant of God.

The criticisms of Weber's thesis most harmful to it are those which take a re-examination of Calvinist moral theology as their point of departure. Brentano had already discovered that this theology was flatly traditionalistic. In the writings of Richard Baxter, the Puritan moralist most often quoted by Weber in order to support his thesis, Brentano finds nothing which could not already have existed in the thought of the Fathers: " Paul, Clement, Basil, Jerome, Augustine, Ambrose and all the medieval doctors could not have exhorted more energetically." [47] Similarly, Robertson showed that the idea of a " calling," a vocation in which the believer is conceived to exercise his profession as a commission from God—an idea fundamental to Weber's thesis— had been adopted by sixteenth-century Protestants in order to combat the characteristic manifestations of capitalism.[48] He cites the condemnations pronounced by Huguenot synods and the Reformed churches against excessive work, which distracts from the service to God, and against the spirit of gain. Finally, he is forced to ask himself if, on the contrary, it was not the prevalence of the capitalist mentality among the middle class which forced the social ethic of Protestantism to slowly but surely take on a capitalist meaning.[49]

But even in this case the question remains as to how such a severe and rigidly observed ethic as that of the Puritan offered such slight resistance to the capitalist mentality. It has been held that capitalism found acceptance among the Protestants, not because they were Protestant but because they were bourgeois. But the problem posed by Weber still remains: why was the ascetic faith of the Calvinist embraced by a society engaged in rapid economic ascent rather than some other? [50]

In general Weber's critics have not sufficiently considered the fact that the capitalist spirit of which he spoke was not the equivalent of unbridled speculation, thirst for gain, or unhindered business activity. He explicitly distinguished the object of his study from its counterpart, the activity of the capitalist-adventurer, the speculator, the money men of the courts, the monopolists and speculators in war goods, against which the Roundheads reacted so violently. Calvin's invectives against the mammonism of Antwerp and Venice do not at all disturb Weber's fundamental thesis.

But Calvin had warned: "*Ita primum fiat ut non pernefas, et dolis ac malis artibus, vel rapacitate, cum proximorum iniuria ruamus ad captandas opes, ad honores invadendos: sed eas tantum fortunas sequamur quae ab innocentia non abducant.*" * [51] Here it is obvious that the acquisition of riches is regarded as subordinate to the moral law, but within the limits of commercial honesty it is allowed and (one might even say) recommended. Here lies the essential truth of Weber's thesis. The spirit of economic enterprise, first condemned and then tolerated in the Middle Ages, now becomes legitimized even to the most timorous conscience.

Brentano's objection, taken up by Robertson, that the idea of a calling, one's vocation as an office imposed by Providence, is already known to medieval literature is gratuitous. No doubt, recommendations to zealously fulfill one's earthly duty abound in medieval literature. [52] It is well known that the Middle Ages conceived of society as an order fashioned by God in which every form of life, every estate, every profession, had its own ethico-religious ideal to which the individual had to adapt himself if

* " First, the result will be that instead of rushing on regardless of right and wrong, by wiles and wicked arts, and with injury to our neighbours, to catch at wealth and seize upon honors, we will only follow such fortune as we may enjoy with innocence."—Trans. by L. Nixon (Grand Rapids, 1951).

he wished to be obedient to God. But it is only after Protestantism unequivocally condemned monasticism that this ideal passed
into the foreground as a norm of life subordinate to none other.
The novelty is not in the ideal, but in the place it is given in the
Protestant ethical system.

One might also point out the difference between the Lutheran
idea of calling and the Calvinist idea of vocation. Weber alluded
to the difference without really stressing its importance. The
Calvinist had to fulfill the demands of his vocation with scrupulousness and diligence, but he could change it if in so doing
he succeeded in bettering his earthly state. Thus, the medieval
idea of the order pre-established by God crumbles, as does the
conservative character of the idea as it appears in Luther, and
the idea of the moral worth of labour and honest profit remains
independent.

*   *   *

One might object to the way in which Weber attempted to
show how the terrible dogma of predestination, which Calvin,
unlike Luther, was not afraid to follow to its logical conclusion,
could be translated into a glorification of economic activity.

While he admitted, according to the tradition of Schleiermacher, the reality of the mystical experience, he granted historical importance only to the conceptual system which " confiscated " that experience and turned it in a new direction: " If
the God of the Puritans acted in history, he acted only through
those attributes which the power of thought was capable of
affording Him." [53] But in fact Weber did not consistently adhere
to this principle. The literature presented by him in support of
his thesis is not the theological writings of Calvin, but the devotional works of Bunyan and Baxter. There is no analysis of
Calvin's thought. Thus, the dogma is not examined in and of
itself at all but in the ethical mentality to whose formation it
contributed. The problem is not confronted in its true center,
in thought, but outside it, in the " psychological effects."

Protestants always regarded doubt of one's own election, from which the need of finding confirmation of salvation in one's own activity arose, as a temptation of the devil. In faith the Protestant already had the direct expression and certitude of his justification: a dogmatic principle which also provided a psychological sense of certitude. But even if one admits that the Calvinist finds in action a means of calming his anxiety, the question of how the direct activity of enrichment can be interpreted as a sign of grace still remains. In Weber's work there is no clear explanation of this subject; an explanation of it could only be drawn from an examination of the Calvinistic idea of God. But once this analysis is made Weber's subtle psychological deduction becomes superfluous, because the capitalist motif already appears in the idea of God. For a confirmation of this it is necessary only to summarize some of the ideas found scattered throughout Weber's own writings.

The Calvinist dogma of predestination concludes the process begun by the Jews of the de-magicalization [*Entzauberung*] of the world, the elimination of all ritual, operation and ceremony intended to influence the Divinity. The church no longer offers the faithful the means of salvation, and the actions of men no longer have any effect whatsoever upon the future life. This does not mean, however, that they have no value. They have an immense value: the church has the task of augmenting the glory of God, and individual actions serve the end of that glorification. In this concept of glory the capitalist idea is already present in Calvinism. It has nothing to do with martial glory, such as that won in a holy war, or with heavenly glory. God's glory consists in His will being done. But what is His will? He desires that men work, even the rich, without the riches produced being consumed in voluptuary self-indulgence or being squandered.

Here we see a transition not totally unlike that inaugurated by the Franciscans, when the world suddenly appeared in all its magnificence as a work of God, thereby initiating a spirit which ultimately flowered in the Renaissance. Here, in place of the

Cantico in praise of the Lord, is the discovery of the world as a
rational, useful creation. Precisely in the degree to which labour
ceases to be a " good " work in the Catholic sense, insofar as it
is detached from transcendental ends and is linked once more to
this earthly realm, in that degree does it attain an infinite,
intrinsic value. The idea that work represents the glory of God
means, in fact, that economic activity is consecrated and seen as
having an autonomous value.

Weber compared the Puritan obligation to work with the kind
of obligation imposed by monastic rule. But monastic rule imposes work in order to protect the monks from the excesses of
contemplation and to discourage the indolent. Here the accent
is not upon the subjective efficacy of work but upon the objective
result. Servants and administrators of the Lord, through incessant and rational labour, see that the business of the Lord
prospers, that the capital entrusted to them multiplies. But since
the glorification of God is an end in itself, the idea of the enslavement of man to production is already implied. And insofar
as this glory has a cumulative character, the concept of technico
economic advance is inherently expounded.

This idea of the relation between God and the faithful would
not have been possible if a new idea of capital had not been
tacitly set forth. Actually, the Calvinist must see himself as a
servant who has been entrusted by God with a capital which
he is obligated to increase.

Protestant asceticism could not have been translated into the
capitalist spirit if it had not removed the great ethical barrier
which separates the Middle Ages from the modern world: the
Catholic prohibition of lending on interest. Weber did not over-
look the importance of this fact, revealed by Brentano and
Sombart, but he did not seriously concern himself with it, because he did not think it apposite to his subject. Yet if one is
allowed to speak of a capitalist spirit in the history of modern
ethics, this spirit can only be identified with the modern idea of
capital. It is the idea of the means of enriching oneself which

we find expressed in dithyrambic form in Franklin's counsels, cited by Weber at the beginning of his essay as a typical manifestation of the capitalist spirit.

Although Franklin professed himself a deist and a utilitarian, Weber thought that he could attribute his basic ideas to the Calvinist spirituality of Massachusetts. But in the works of the great friend of Adam Smith there is not the least trace of the doctrine of predestination. Instead, there is the affirmation that money has a " generative and fecund " nature. From this proposition Franklin deduced a sort of categorical imperative of the skilful investment of capital. It is not only lawful, it is an outright duty to make capital multiply, while dissipation, the equivalent of a lack of profitable production, is a violation of the utilitarian ethic.

When was the discovery made that money was not sterile, as both St. Thomas and Aristotle believed? Sombart noted that in the sermons of St. Antonino the argument concerning the sterility of money was overcome. As a matter of fact, this new development was probably directly linked to the finance economy of Florence and is a Renaissance idea: to appreciate the productivity of money is to comprehend the productivity of man. However, it is a far cry from St. Antonino's tolerance to Cromwell's manifesto to the Irish in which he reminded them that it was English capital that taught them how to work. This development constitutes an important step in the history of the concept of capital. In this development Calvin also has his place.

This worldly asceticism which demanded the conscientious execution of the tasks connected with one's calling was already implied in Lutheranism and, if one wishes, even in Catholicism. The new element which upset the entire system was the principle, stated explicitly by Calvin, of the legitimacy of lending on interest. This, in turn, is based upon his distinction between productive and consumptive loans and his distinction between loan and usury.

It is true, to be sure, that Leo X had declared that loans at

2 per cent, made by the Franciscan *Monti di Pietà*, were legitimate and in accordance with the public good, but this was a
novelty, quite foreign to the general practice and allowed only
within the orbit of pious institutions. And it is likewise true
that both St. Antonino and Luther tolerated usury provided that
it was limited to a modest interest.[54] Calvin, on the other hand,
applied a distinction which was peculiarly modern, between law
and ethical norm, and ended by considering the traditional prohibition a purely legal one, that is, one which was relative to
historical conditions. Then, while examining the " papist " doctrine of the sterility of money, he discovered that only money
cached in a strong box was sterile, not that which was gainfully
employed. He therefore concluded that it was permissible to
exact interest from anyone who as a result of the loan realized
a gain or profit. However, he immediately sought to provide
limits by excluding from the rule of interest loans to the poor,
by recommending the adjustment of the rate of interest to the
nature of the employment and to the amount of profit, and by
prescribing that the rate of interest not surpass the level fixed by
the state.[55]

Weber separated the logical principles from the practical-
psychological consequences and limited the capitalistic spirit to
the latter, but in reality it was inherent in the former as well. It
would indeed be strange if there were something in the effect
which was lacking in the cause. Thus, Weber's thesis loses that
elegant, paradoxical equality in which consequences are held
to appear in opposition to the principles as unexpected and surprising results.

Some have argued against Weber, quite incorrectly, that in the
new economic mentality are to be found manifestations of the
general revolution of thought by which the individual was liberated from the bonds of the Middle Ages.[56] Calvinism is not a
pagan emancipation. Nor did it proclaim the destruction of
ethics in the face of an invincible human nature, although it did
create a new ethic in which property, enrichment, commerce,

the bank and industry all finally found a place. Only through this sanction was it able to give an indomitable energy to that economic activity which the Renaissance had regarded as an unavoidable and unfortunate reality.

The humanistic spirit of aristocratic contemplation and tranquil self-indulgence was much more the enemy of the capitalist spirit than the ethical ideals of the Middle Ages. Erasmus would have included the new spirit of voluntary servitude in his *Praise of Folly*. In fact, that spirit remained quite alien to the Arminians and in general to those circles which had taken up the humanist culture, a privilege, outside of Italy, of the courts and the nobility. Also for this reason the capitalist spirit remained scarcely sensitive to the graces of the noble arts; it remained the spirit of *parvenus*. Even today the antinomy persists in its maximum crudity.

*   *   *

The prime defect in Weber's research lies in its sociological character. He intuited the importance of Calvinistic ideas in the modern business ethic, but he limited himself to a description of a type of mentality. There is, to be sure, a kind of movement, but it is the movement of a psychological mechanism. The grand dialectic, the logical struggle, is ignored. Calvinism is seen as a moment in the history of European ethics by being isolated and studied in the moral crisis of the Calvinist who, as a victim of doubt, plunges himself into business in order to find some kind of serenity. What Hegel called " the intrusion of the divine spirit into reality and the liberation of reality into the divine spirit " [57] is thus reduced to the psychological problem of the Calvinist believer.

Weber preferred to concentrate upon the psychological consequences because only thus could he remain true to his idea of what constituted scientific analysis. For him science was a technique of analysis which, while avoiding all value judgments, showed the unforeseen consequences which the actuation of a given ideal brought about. Most important, however, was the fact that Weber took as his point of departure the sociological idea of class, in this instance a class of rising petty bourgeoisie who were hostile to the speculators and monopolists connected with the court and the Angelican church. Now, a class, a sociological type, in which ideas are important only insofar as they constitute elements of a given mentality, is susceptible only of psychological description.

Therefore, a relation between class and a specific religious ethic was assumed. It is this relation which Weber examines in his studies of the economic ethics of the world religions.

III

Weber's studies in the economic ethics of world religions (*Versuche einer vergleichenden Religionssoziologie*) [58] have a non-historical character insofar as they are an attempt to group the various religious ethics into unitary and systematic frames which admit of no development. Here in all its boldness is seen Weber's ability to deduce logical transitions, the practical and theoretical consequences through which a religious dogma is passed to a social class, from this to a legal order, to an art form, to an educational ideal, to a logical system, to a sexual ethic, to an industry, and so forth. Here cultures assume the character of isolated and almost impenetrable geometrical forms constructed with crystalline coherence and rationality according to different formulae. In fact, at one point Weber calls these studies " contributions to a sociology of rationalism."

Above all, the aim of these studies was to furnish a confirmation of the Puritan origin of the modern capitalist spirit. Here also the different religious ethics are examined in relation to the economic attitudes which they engender, so as to give better insight into that type of economic rationalism which came to prevail in the West during the sixteenth and seventeenth centuries. In sum, the studies were intended to be a series of negative experiments which would serve to establish how, given the economic, social and political conditions favorable to its development, a capitalism of the modern type could not have been realized had the Calvinist ascetic element been lacking.

Another value of these studies lies in their having revealed the economic *ethos* in all its importance. Weber derived his conclusions, not in a bookish and scholarly manner from philosophical tracts, but from all of the documents which might give insight into the moral and religious life of the poeple. Here, truly, the distance between East and West and the basic reasons for their different destinies is measured in grand perspective.

Thus, Weber describes Confucianism as more of a doctrine and a rite than a religion, one which was imposed upon China by its bureaucratic class of literati-calligraphers. It is seen to embrace a utilitarian and rationalistic ethic of conventions, self-control and rank and to be opposed to any form of mystic contemplation and orgiastic ecstasy as an irrational disorder or vulgar barbarity. Here thought remains bound to practical problems and bureaucratic interests. One abandons all attempts to communicate with the masses and dedicates himself to the mastery of a difficult calligraphy. Hence, there is no development of the art of definition or reasoning. War is disparaged as mere brigandage; the world is seen as the best possible—provided that its eternal order is not disturbed; all men are held to be naturally equal and capable of perfection; the only possible redemption is held to be that which liberates one from barbarity and ignorance; the only sins are those committed against the authority of parents, ancestors, one's hierarchical superiors, the ceremonial, and the traditional customs; the only prize of virtue is a long life, health, wealth, and (after death) a good name. With this mandarin ethic, tenaciously bound to tradition and hostile to any reform, China remained further from the capitalist spirit than classical antiquity itself. Weber was thus able to establish the fact that in precisely the country of parsimony and spirit of gain, in spite of its glorification and utilization of wealth as a means of moral perfection, in spite of the peace, tolerance, freedom of business and commerce, freedom of choice of profession and methods of production found there, China developed no rationally organized business activity, monetary system or commerce.

India seemed to offer all the conditions favorable to the development of a rational business activity. In India commerce and usury flourished; the profit instinct was never wanting; war, politics and finance were rational; public debts, tax assessment, supply and monopolies were similar to those of the West. There the rational number system was invented, rational sciences such as grammar and mathematics were cultivated, tolerance was almost an absolute and the professions were specialized. The merchant class was as autonomous as in the medieval West, and cities were developed. Nevertheless, modern capitalism did not arise in India, and when it was imported, it found no indigenous points of contact. According to Weber, this was because of the magico-ritualistic division of the populace into castes. A ritual which regarded any change in profession or even in techniques as embodying a danger of pollution and degradation was bound to frustrate any technico-economic transformation. In fact, it was the outcastes and the pariahs, not the members of the older artisan castes, who manned the modern industry of India.

A different situation obtained in Japan, where the population had received its *ethos*, not from a class of literati, such as the mandarin and the Brahmin, but from the warlike and chivalric samurai. Thus, even if it were unable to develop a rational economy by itself, Japan could easily adapt itself to modern capitalism because of the spirit of individualism which informed the feudal contract there.[59]

For Weber, however, the study of the ascetic or redemptive religions of India constituted an essential test for his thesis. Buddhism, the most radical of these religions, freed man from the " wheel," from the eternal cycle of death and rebirth, through pure contemplation and the destruction of the individual will. Consequently, it represented a type of asceticism diametrically opposed to that of the Calvinist. One Indian religion which did have a positive effect upon economic activity was that of the Jains, a monastic sect devoted to trade and labouring under a severe *ascesis* of controlled, methodical conduct, non-enjoyment of wealth, business honesty, and a strong group solidarity. But Weber does not explain why this sect of "Indian Puritans" did not create its own capitalist spirit similar to that found in the West.

One might argue that it is precisely through this examination of the Orient that the specific thesis of Weber concerning the origin of the capitalist spirit in the psychological need of the Calvinist for some sort of confirmation is shown to be invalid. The whole of Western cultural development, as opposed to the traditionalistic Orient, is shown by these studies to have been moving towards the realization of a rational economic progress from the beginning. Precisely through a comparison with the Asiatic world is modern capitalism revealed to be anything but a paradoxical, unforeseen occurrence. The Orient, with its idea of a sacred and eternal order of things, lacked the idea of the duality of ethics and politics which is presupposed in the dialectic of the condemnation of the world and its ethical reconsecration. To see this development as a kind of psychological deviation is to reduce this grandiose phenomenon to rather shabby proportions.

Even Judaism lacked these presuppositions. Against the celebrated thesis of Sombart, Weber himself denied a capitalistic spirit to the Jews. Their contribution to the development of the West rests, according to him, only in their character as a guest people who follow the petty bourgeois ethic of the prophets and psalmists towards the members of their own sect, an ethic which reflects the ancient rule of good neighborliness and solidarity, while practicing usury and speculation in their relations with the stranger. This form of capitalism is viewed as in itself reprehensible and is only conceded as a practice to be used upon strangers. Such an idea could never give birth to a professional and commercial ethic such as that which came out of Calvinism.

*　　*　　*

The real problem of these studies is not the way in which the economic ethic determines a given socio-economic order but the way in which the socio-economic order determines the ethic. Here Weber's attention is directed, not to the relation between dogma and economic activity, but to the opposite side of the cycle, to the relations between social conditions and dogma. He reascends, as it were, to the stratum which gives to the ethic its characteristic traits. That class which in his essay was only adumbrated here becomes the protagonist. Thus envisaged, Confucianism is the ethic of a class of bureaucratic literati which lives off prebends and perquisites; Hinduism is the religion of a hereditary caste of ritualist-literati who are the custodians of the sacred doctrine informing the caste hierarchy; Buddhism is the product of a patrician class and is a religion of mendicant monks completely detached from the world; Judaism was originally the religion of a confederation of semi-nomadic tribes, then of free peasants and shepherds, and finally of a petty bourgeois pariah people led by a class of intellectual ritualists; Christianity was the doctrine of a displaced artisan craftsman class and remained a bourgeois religion with its centers in the cities—political organisms peculiar to the West; Islam is the religion of a knightly order of warrior-conquerors, and its heresy, Sufism, was the religion of a petty bourgeois confraternity directed by plebian practitioners of an orgiastic mysticism.

Thus, even the most profound difference between East and West is, below all the differences of faith, primarily a question of classes.

In fact, Weber makes the fortunes of Christianity—from the first isolated communities to the medieval mendicant orders to the modern sects of Methodists and Quakers—dependent upon the city, the center of the middle class, having its own freedom and politico-military power, a political organism unknown to China. For Weber, China is essentially an agrarian culture, ultimately dependent upon a vast network of canals and dams for the control of the rivers and therefore dependent upon a patrimonial and bureaucratic monarchy. Hinduism, for Weber, is linked to a monarchical political system and it is in the service of this system that the Brahmins legitimize social rank by the ritualistic division of society into castes, thereby impeding the fraternization of the corporation and the solidarity of the bourgeoisie with the magical concept of impure contact.

However, Weber hastens to protest that he does not intend at all to consider religiosity as an ideology or a mere reflection of the material and ideal interests of a class. However deep these influences may be, he declares, the religious ethic proceeds from religious sources, and even if it adapts itself to the needs of the community, those needs are above all religious in nature. Actually, in these studies the religious life assumes concrete historical individuality only insofar as it is determined by the economico-political exigencies of a class. Its autonomy is postulated as that of an irrational and incommunicable mystical experience which acquires a physiognomy in the degree to which it is confiscated by ideas. What are the origins of these ideas? In Weber's exposition they would seem to emanate for the most part from class interest.

Except for that prejudice this sociology of religion would be differentiated from materialism only by its substitution of the concept of social class for that of economic class. Class is defined by Weber as a human group not always organized but always in some way associated through its mode of life, conventional ideas of honor, and legally monopolized economic " chances " or opportunities. It is a concept which he worked out during the agrarian inquest when he was confronted with the crisis of the Prussian peasant and the *Junker* aristocracy. And just as the German political problem seemed to him to be a problem of the ruling

class, so in the field of religion and ethical history he is concerned
with the problem of the " carrying " class.

However, the character of this sociology remains analogous to
that of materialist historiography. The spiritual life is explained
in terms of its causes, that is, is considered objectively, as a nature
deprived of any intrinsic truth. Having denied to himself any
value judgment, Weber could not construct any sort of hierarchy
and was therefore unable to perceive any sort of development.
Typical in this respect is his concept of the history of Jewish
religion, which in its various phases appears to be determined
solely by external political contingencies. In spite of Weber's
protestations, the various ethical systems here appear only as
projections of class interest—they are indelibly stamped with
designations such as " bureaucratic," " warlike," " bourgeois,"
and " petty bourgeois."

Nietzsche had juxtaposed a master morality to a slave morality.
Weber lists more moralities, as many in fact as there are social
types, and since he seeks to be objective he shows no preference
for any particular one. But since under the terms of such a view
even our moral life appears relative to the class to which we
belong or to the classes which have formed and led it (in
Judaism and Christianity the carrying class is the petty bourgeoisie) , to liberate it from such class bonds would be to push it
into a void. And one would be left with that sense of drift which
Weber himself reflects in calling himself a polytheist—at least if
one does not try to find a norm, as he himself did, in the technique of one's own profession, in responsibility to the vocation
assigned by fate.

Weber's sociology is the most coherent expression of the historiography of an epoch which has ceased to believe in history
and has banished ideas of development, unfolding and progress
to a place among the myths of optimism. In fact, Weber con-
signs any " meanings " found in history to the non-scientific
realm of value judgment. Thus envisaged, historiography has to

confine itself to the construction of a gallery containing portraits of types of civilizations.

But such a sociological view of history also raises certain problems. The first concerns the use of its instruments of analysis, those collective concepts which ordinary historiography employs but which only now stand in need of rigorous definition. The concept of class (*Stand*) belongs to the medieval world and can be applied only with difficulty, for example, to contemporary society, where the unique surviving class (according to Weber himself) is that of the cultured intellectual. Concepts such as city, patriarchal monarchy, feudalism and bureaucracy partake of the same relativity. Within the orbit of religion the concepts of church, sect, order, and the figures of the priest, prophet, monk, and master have meaning and color only within their own historical environment.

Weber realized that it was difficult to convey the fluidity and change of the historical world given the rigidity of the terms of orientation and comparison, and he sought to transcend this problem with his logic of the ideal type.

IV

Upon succeeding Knies in the chair of political economy at Freiburg, Weber found himself obliged to take a position in the dispute between Schmoller and Menger, between the young Historical School of economics, which wished to reduce economics to a science of historical facts, and the heirs of the Classical School, who sought in it a science of natural laws.

Weber realized that the economists were disputing a question of the logic of the sciences with inadequate logical tools, and he hoped to introduce into the dispute the new concepts of the historical and natural sciences which the philosophers of his time, Dilthey, Windelband, and especially Rickert, were developing.[60] Over against the positivistic desire to impose the methods of the natural sciences upon historiography, this new school had affirmed the peculiarity and autonomy of the human sciences and had consequently justified the existence of two different scientific methods or logics: that of the historical disciplines which grasped reality in its concrete individuality and that of the natural sciences which ascertained abstract uniformities and constructed both classes and general laws.

To Weber it seemed obvious that since economics was concerned with human behaviour, it belonged to the realm of the human sciences. But that did not mean that the Historical School had won. On the contrary, precisely through an investigation of historiographical method did Weber intend to restore dignity to the laws of the Classical School.

It is Weber's merit to have realized that the hope of Dilthey and his followers to free the historical sciences from the naturalistic domain was based upon an error. Despite the prohibition of the imposition of the concept of natural law, those sciences remained the ascertainment and description of empirical facts. Having assumed an historical reality made up of discrete, empirical facts, Dilthey had sought in vain to raise himself above raw experience and found a system of historiographical categories. Windelband and Rickert, founders of the so-called "philosophy of value," had excluded all value judgments from science and were therefore trapped on a road without exits. In sum, this methodology, which was professedly Neo-Kantian, contained a strong positivistic residue, which corresponded to the tendencies and practices of the age. Weber realized that along this path there could be little differentiation between the natural sciences and the historical sciences. He felt that if one did not wish to make an appeal to values—and indeed he felt that only in such a way could the objectivity and utility of science be saved—one had to consider historiography as an empirico-causal science. Therefore, both groups of sciences worked with the principle of causality as a fundamental category; both explained.

One difference however remained: besides merely explaining, historical science led to understanding, that is, it passed from the external relation to the inner meaning.

Although he had remained poised between Bacon and Vico, Dilthey had nonetheless observed that in historical knowledge there was to be found something more than what was contained in naturalistic knowledge. This was what he called " understanding through reliving " (*nacherlebendes Verstehen*). Thus was born that problem of understanding and of a new hermeneutic which so fruitlessly occupied German thought at the beginning of the twentieth century. Actually, understanding was not conceived as a judgment but as a psychological rapport (*rapporto*) between subject and object, an unhealthy dualistic relation in spite of all attempts at unification. Its unhealthiness was revealed in the fact that the esteemed new hermeneutic, the doctrine of understanding, never progressed beyond the stage of psychological description or outright prescription.

Weber pointed out that it was not enough to merely relive in order to understand. Nor was immediate and inarticulate intuition enough. History was a science and therefore had to use conceptual tools, and never could a conceptual knowledge, not even of one's own *Erlebnis*, be reduced to mere reliving, because it implied perspectives and references which are unknown in the *Erlebnis*. It was possible to understand the meaning of another person's actions intuitively, but for an historical science this was not enough. Consequently, auxiliary heuristic tools were necessary for understanding in those areas in which intuition is insufficient.

The resolute conceptualization of historiography as an empirico-causal science entailed two difficulties. The most important one was the historical problem: confronted with an infinity of indifferent, atomistic facts, lacking all value, how could science select a fact, isolate it, and adjudge it worthy of being studied in its causal origins? Weber saw that it was necessary to make a concession to values in this initial phase, that is, he saw himself forced to concede a role to the ethical, aesthetic and religious norms with which one takes his position before reality. He recognized that the scientist made his choice on the basis of his subjective interests, selected and isolated an historical individuality, a fact, and assigned an importance to it. After this, however, all should proceed objectively, without further appeal to extra-scientific principles.

The other difficulty was that posed by freedom of the will, which seemed to stand in direct opposition to the possibility of a causal historical science. Weber thought he could resolve this difficulty by identifying freedom of the will with rationality: not with Kantian rationality, which is morality, but with practical rationality as presented by the strict correlation of means to ends. The dignity of human activity as opposed to mere natural occurrence seemed to him to reside in this intrinsic rationality and intelligibility. As an impulse to action, the end was also for Weber the cause and thus the whole of human activity could be framed within the concept of causality. For him, therefore, the historical importance of a given personage is nothing but the result of his actions as a causal moment in a chain of events. This did not mean that he thus excluded qualitative novelty from history, because even the qualities of a chemical combination, for example, water, presented some novelties when compared to the qualities of the component elements.

However, a difficulty was contained in the fact that human activity was not always free and rational, but often was influenced by irrational motives, passions, affections, emotions and conventions. So it was necessary for him to divide the investigation into two parts: on the one side stands the construction of an ideal and rational activity and on the other, the description of the real, concrete activity which, in comparison with the pure schema, will reveal the irrational deviations and the intervening causes which determine them. Consequently, he held hypotheses to be heuristically useful in the degree to which they allowed one to conceive how an action would have gone had it developed rationally: the direction of a battle, for example, or the execution of a political plan. But it was not enough for him that the historian make the comparison case by case. He wished to furnish historical investigation with a series of abstract, rational operations, means of orientation, and archetypes which—with a term borrowed from Jellinek's doctrine of the state—he called " ideal types." [61]

First of all, the so-called " laws " of political economy were ideal types, not natural laws, as the Classical School held, but models which could be used for distinguishing between rational and irrational economic actions and which could thus facilitate the interpretation of human actions. As differentiated from natural laws, they did not lose their heuristic value if they were not verified in a concrete case. Indeed, they were never fully verified, because reality never fully conformed to the ideal, was never so pure or rational.

*   *   *

As can be immediately seen, this theory constitutes an abandonment of the modern concept of natural law and a return to the Classical ideal of the archetype, model or idea. Like the Platonic ideas, these ideal types also reside in a heaven of pure rationality, beyond an inchoate matter which offers the possibility of knowledge only in the measure in which it participates in that rationality. One could find an analogy between this method and that of contemporary physics, which seeks to reconcile law and the individual case with the concept of statistical probability. In fact, in Weber's theory the ideal type may be likened, not to the concept of necessary occurrence, but to " chance," the greater or lesser possibility.

However that may be, the doctrine of the ideal type, even if it is not rationalistic—insofar as it does not pretend at all that the world is rational—is a rehabilitation and defense of economic calculation. Even if men are the victims of suggestion in their practical activity, action calculated according to the strict correlation of means to ends is that and nothing else. A theorem does not lose its value if the one who applies it is confused and errs.

Weber also eliminated the antithesis of law and free will by holding that the laws of political economy presupposed that freedom of will which is the energy of character or capacity to act with fidelity to prefixed ends on the basis of an exact calculation of means. Like Kant in the sphere of the categorical imperative, Weber in this sphere of the hypothetical imperative held that decision to be freer which is less mitigated by emotions and constraints, in the degree to which it adhered to the specifically rational relation.

This relation, endowed with a special prominence, was the conformity of means to ends—what we would call the "coherence" of an action.

Since there was no guarantee that it was followed in practice, the ideal type was not to be considered an historical force. The confusion of economic laws for historical forces was the error for which Weber criticized Marx. The *homo œconomicus* was an ideal type, a heuristic construction, but nothing at all could demonstrate that men really acted according to the laws formulated by the economists. Even less could the ideal type constitute an end in itself, a practical ideal. In general, Weber felt that science had no ideals to offer, least of all economic science, which was and could only be the science of correlating means to ends. At the most it could calculate in advance the costs of any given undertaking.

Weber's economic science bears a certain similarity to contemporary physics in its relativity. Actually, Weber wished for the ideal type to correspond as closely as possible to concrete historical reality. For example, more than the act of exchange as such, he was interested in the act of exchange in the artisan or capitalist economy, because the merchant in the artisan economy had means at his disposal which were different from those available to the merchant in the capitalist economy. Thus, although the two acts of exchange were both rational, they were different.

Nor is it possible to object that the act of exchange remains the same even if legally it assumes a different form, because law, considered from the economic standpoint, was the complex of "chances" which the merchant had to have for the protection of his business and was therefore an indispensable part of the system of means which had to be included in the economic calculation.

Ideal types differ from the common concepts of empirical class, according to Weber, insofar as they are not schemata by which reality is regrouped but concepts of limits to which reality must be adjusted.

One proof that the ideal type does not correspond to the class of the natural scientist was pointed out by Weber in the possibility of formulating it on the basis of a single historical instance. For example, Christianity could be comprehended in an essence of Christianity which, as an historical illustration of the real, could have at best a problematical value, but which as an ideal type could have high heuristic value for making internal comparisons of the various Christian sects and external comparisons between Christianity and the other religions.

However, it was obvious that what Weber called "ideal types" are in this case constituted by a system of propositions of faith and ethical norms which are not a type at all but a concrete moment in the history of ideas. A type of Christian could be designated psychologically, but then one would be dealing with types like those of natural history.

Thus, Weber did not clearly perceive that the difference between the empirical class and the ideal type resided in the deductive character of the latter. Insofar as rationally deduced action, after the posing of means and ends, does not represent concrete actions, it is not an action arbitrarily chosen to represent other actions, but an unreal action, rationally constructed and not arbitrarily designated, similar to geometrical constructions. We are all familiar, in fact, with the analogy to be found in Platonic thought between the geometric figure and the idea.

Weber's doctrine could be considered as the substitution in economic science of the concept of the geometric figure for that of law. One might also add that just as contemporary physics employs different geometries, all equally true according to the gravitational field, so Weber's economic science modifies its own laws according to the socio-economic regime in which they operate.[62]

*   *   *

In the biography written by his wife, Weber's transition from political economy to sociology is not very clearly delineated.[63] So, too, in his thought, the dividing line is not marked with great precision. Moreover, the division of the realm of the sciences into individual disciplines which order the factual data was considered by Weber to be an " accidental division." His break with the Classical School, in virtue of which he went over to ideal types historically relative to sociological regimes in preference to abstract theorems, already marked a passage to considerations of a more thoroughly sociological nature. Rather than a distinction, one might more correctly speak of an absorption of economic science by the broader " science of relations." Economic activity *per se* was not yet a social activity, for Weber. Being directed to the satisfaction of the desire for things useful, economic activity was social only when it was oriented according to the predictable behaviour of others. Thus, money was a means of exchange accepted by the seller because he was oriented according to the faith that others would have accepted it in their turn.[64]

It has been held that the so-called " German sociology " is distinguished from the older French and English sociology by a greater philosophical sophistication and psychological insight.[65] The validity of the appraisal may be questioned. It is true, to be sure, that the sociological systems of Simmel, Tönnies, and Vierkandt apply Neo-Kantian analytical and descriptive psy-

chology and the phenomenological method of investigation to the
analysis of society as form, relation, and structure, but it is also
true that this use of refined distinctions revealed the vanity of a
sociology conducted with speculative pretensions and the error
of expanding formal logical categories into laws and empirical
concepts. A theory of relations should result in a practical philosophy. But in such a case the category of sociality would appear
arbitrary, since placing oneself in relation to a man or to a
human group would not be formally different from placing oneself in relation to animals, plants and inanimate things.

Weber never succeeded in liberating himself from all of these
psychological-philosophical pretensions. His rational sociology
(*verstehende Soziologie*) aspired to the dignity of an empirical
science insofar as it sought to free itself from all *a priori* constructs and to limit itself to the understanding of historical
reality. But while history seeks to understand the meaning of a
single historical case, it constructs pure conceptual types of
action, as does economic science. Its object is no longer only
economic activity, oriented toward the means necessary to the
satisfaction of needs, but activities in general—including those
which hinder as well as those which support the realization of the
end—according to a meaning (*senso*) and with constant reference to the behaviour of others.[66]

As can be seen, Weber above all admitted (without very deep
analysis or justification) a distinction between economic activity
and practical activity in general. Moreover, he limited this
practical or "social" activity by assigning to it, as a special characteristic, constant reference to the behaviour of others, even
though he knew (as a result of his explicit objection to Stammler)
that formally such a criterion was insufficient. He limited himself, therefore, to requiring that in the realm of sociology action
have a meaning, that is, be intelligible, and for this reason he
insisted on the obscurity of the animal psyche. Physical facts
were excluded because they lacked any meaning. Thus envisaged, social actions were the relations between men insofar

as they acted in mutual understanding, according to the meanings which give rationality to their actions.

On the other hand, Weber insisted that his sociology presumed to be nothing more than a hermeneutical instrument for the examination of historical knowledge. He abstained from constructing any system, but he did submit some sociological concepts to systematic elaboration in *Economics and Society (Wirtschaft und Gesellschaft)*, in which book there is little unity or continuity. However much this lack of unity can be attributed to its posthumous publication, the fact remains that he held any attempt at a definitive system of concepts to be absurd, since reality constantly manifested itself in new forms.

In sum, he did not conceive his sociology as a science in itself, but saw it as a construction of concepts useful to the orientation of historical investigations. Even if this book has a certain systematic appearance, being divided into one part which is systematic and another more completely historical, such a division would seem to have little foundation. In fact, one might easily be led to suspect that the two parts were only different drafts, the one schematic and summary, the other abounding in historical references.

In relation to history this sociology might be viewed as a kind of terminology. It offered an unequivocal accentuation of concepts, a series of abstractions relatively empty of content but which might serve towards the end of defining concrete historical phenomena. Weber spoke openly of a casuistic sociology, of a comparative procedure, with which the historian could establish the propriety of the use of one or more terms in his interpretation. That is, it seemed to him profitable to determine with a certain rigour the degree in which a given historical phenomenon might be called " feudal," " bureaucratic," " ecclesiastical," etc.

It is impossible to understand Weber's sociology if one does not juxtapose it to the Romantic concept of the collective soul and above all to the organological doctrine which goes back to Adam Müller and which was recently taken up again by the

sociologist Othmar Spann. Weber admitted that it was possible
for scientific purposes, for example, for legal reasons, to consider
the social formations—state, commune, corporation, etc.—as single
individualities, subjects of rights and duties, but from a sociological point of view such entities had to be reduced to specific
activities of individual human beings. For his sociology there
were no collective personalities; there were only the specific
social operations of individuals. The employment of functional
concepts on the part of the organologists was an imitation of the
science of physiology, but for him the determination of the
function of a cell was not enough to constitute understanding of
its inner behaviour. And this was precisely the aim of Weber's
sociology: to understand the behavior of individuals not simply
as a function of the whole but with regard to the meaning which
they gave to their activity. On the other hand, those collective
concepts entered into sociological investigation insofar as they
were effective representations in the minds of men who organized
their activities on the basis of them. Thus, a modern state consisted, to be sure, of the cooperative action of men, but it was a
cooperative activity oriented according to the idea which that
politico-legal order had to enforce.

Weber did not fail to point out that it would be a misunderstanding to identify this individualistic method of his with some
individualistic ideal. The reduction of collective concepts to
concrete human actions was not meant to loosen or to destroy
any bonds, but to rediscover them there where they were real,
in the hearts and minds of men, and to observe their effective
historical worth in the way in which they conditioned life.
Thus, in this sense, the sociological investigation of a socialistic
regime would have to be individualistic insofar as it would be
obliged to investigate the ideal and practical motives which determined the components active in the formation and maintenance of life in a socialist community. Similarly, concerning the
concepts of nation and race, Weber set himself the task of discerning how these concepts were manifested in human activity,

and when he distinguished the church from the sect he was only seeking to distinguish the mode of behavior of the member of the church from that of one affiliated with a sect and reasons for this difference. That the sociologist might take sides during this investigation was of course rigidly prohibited.[67]

* * *

It has been stated that sociology goes back to the time of Hammurabi. In reality, it is even older, going back to the moment when language first became enriched with terms such as " city," " tribe," " family." Is it possible to assign to these terms, of which historiography makes such frequent use, a more precise meaning than that conveyed by traditional usage?

First of all, it is necessary to distinguish between concepts encountered in economic science and those of sociology. According to Weber's own declaration, economic science is the most perfect part of sociology. In it activity is rationally correlated to an envisaged end (*zweckrational*). Any intrusion of heterogeneous elements, such as ethics, politics, religions, emotions, aesthetics, is a cause of deviation and error. Instead, in social relations, insofar as they are not economic, those irrational values which in economic activity have a negative character, intervene as specific motives. Here action is rationally correlated to value (*wertrational*). It is worth noting that for Weber it becomes completed in a given way, not only because of interest, but for its own, intrinsic, absolute value. Here Weber can construct some schematically deduced types of action, not according to the simple and unequivocal economic principle, but according to the values by which individuals orient their actions. But it is clear that the heuristic utility of such types will be much less than that of the economic types. Nonetheless, it is undeniable that Weber obtained some original insights into the realm of the political by this method. Those chapters in *Economics and Society* which concern sovereignty can be considered an essay in a new political science which, in place of the traditional Aristotelian classification of political forms, provides a classification of pure types of sovereignty deduced from the principles upon which sovereignty is founded. The superiority of such classifications is due to the superiority of deduction over external, qualitative description.

Sovereignty is defined by Weber as the "chance" of finding obedience among a human group, a "chance" which can be based upon the possession of definite economic goods but which in general is based upon authority. Every sovereignty seeks to legitimize itself, to give justification to its own exercise of power. This is the premise of Weber's deduction: according to the type of claim of legitimacy, there will be a different exercise of power, a different structure of the executive machine, a different form of obedience on the part of the people. There are three principles of legitimation: *rationalistic,* which recognizes the validity of ordinances and statutory rules; *traditionalistic,* which invokes the sacred authority of the past; and *charismatic,* that is, faith in the exceptional gift (*charisma*) of the prophet, the leader or hero. From these three principles are deduced the three pure types of sovereignty, the combinations, mixtures, and transformations of which then result in the historically real forms. In the first type, the ruler and the ruled obey an impersonal system of regulations, the executive is a bureaucracy which functions according to jurisdictions and written orders, and the ruled are in principle equal to the rulers. In the second, sovereignty assumes the form of a patriarchal monarchy in which the sovereign is seen as the lord, surrounded by his bodyguard and mercenary troops, governing by means of a general staff of servants, clients, freemen and *ministeriales,* who are bound to his person, and the ruled are subjects. In the third, the exceptional quality of the leader consists in his being presented as the servant of God who demands unconditional obedience, and the exercise of sovereignty is specifically revolutionary in character insofar as it ignores precedents and creates new laws, while the general staff is composed of the leader's disciples, the faithful, the men who trust him implicitly. On the basis of this schema,

Weber then proceeds to an analysis of the transition from one type to another.

As is obvious, this political science is very far from the construction of a genuine economic science. Here there is no calculation, but deduction of practical-psychological consequences from principles. Nor is there lacking any margin of free will in the choice of the criteria of discrimination. Instead of the principles of legitimacy, one could assume as a premise of deduction some other trait or moment deliberately isolated and accentuated. Such an artifice, essential to all sociological constructions, would in no way detract from its heuristic utility, according to Weber. On the contrary, they are capable of serving as terms of orientation in historical interpretation precisely in the degree in which they are unreal abstractions.

*   *   *

Is it possible to construct, besides the ideal types of economic science and those of political science, also some new types which are specifically sociological? A long chapter in *Economics and Society* dedicated to the concept of the city would seem to suggest such a possibility. The city is a central theme in Weber's thought. In his studies on the economic ethic of religions he saw in the city the primary origins of the uniqueness, not only in the realm of politics and economics but also in those of religion and intellectual endeavour, of our culture as compared with that of the Orient.

Here, however, the ideal type is identified with a specific historical phenomenon: with the medieval city of transalpine Europe. Such a type is differentiated from the ancient city and the Oriental city by a legal usurpation, that is, by the freedom which every new inhabitant of it acquires there as a result of his escape from his feudal lord and through a revolutionary act, the oath (*coniuratio*), by which the commune is formed. Moreover, compared with the ancient classical city and those of medieval Italy, where the city is born as a seat of the nobility, in northern Europe the feudal nobility is excluded, and only later is a city patriciate formed, bourgeois both in origin and character.

The sociology of the city is thus reduced to the sociology of a determined, specifically urban class, endowed with privileges and politically organized: the bourgeoisie. The reason why Weber finds in the northern European medieval city the ideal type is because of the exclusive and typical presence of the bourgeoisie from the beginning. In the Orient the artisan and merchant corporations never arrive at the politico-legal organization of the commune. The classical *polis* is born as a result of the transition from monarchical authority to that of the nobility. In medieval Italy the *coniuratio* was the work of the noble families who, even after the victory of the *popolo*, continued to live in the city and enjoy prestige there. Only in the north was the bourgeoisie separated from the feudal nobility from the very beginning. This difference was maintained even in the later phases: the *demos* which won power in the *polis* was a class of peasant proprietors which had organized itself into an army of hoplites and broken the power of the aristocracy by the use of a new military technique. Sparta was a typical example of a city in which the aristocracy ceased to exist and which was turned into a military camp. In Italy, where already Rome was distinguished from the *polis* by the existence of its economic class of knights, the commune, especially with the victory of the great guilds (*arti maggiori*), represented an intermediary type, neither properly classical nor wholly bourgeois. Only in the cities of France, the Low Countries, England and Germany was the urban class oriented in an economic rather than a politico-military sense. It did not achieve political independence nor even aspire to it. Its artisan and mercantile autonomy was protected and favoured by kings and princes, and therefore it created, not *homo politicus*, the citizen of the classical *polis*, but *homo œconomicus*, the bourgeois.

This sociology of the city is, therefore, nothing but a comparative history of the urban class, useful for showing how political, economic, and legal peculiarities distinguish the ancient citizen from the bourgeoisie, how the *demos* and the *plebs* differ from the *popolo*, and how the ancient proletariat, the classless citizen despoiled of his property, has little in common with the medieval proletariat, a small artisan excluded from the great guilds, and nothing in common with the modern industrial worker at all.

Similarly, the sociology of religion and the sociology of law, in *Economics and Society*, are concerned with the relation between cults, rites, norms, and legal institutions, and the formation and structure of determined professional classes. Consequently, it would seem that sociology, insofar as it seeks to construct some types, which are neither strictly economic nor yet strictly political, must be considered merely a class theory, a typology constructed from the viewpoint of social position. Now this is not what Weber's sociology is. Why was it not possible for him to construct a theory of social class similar to the Marxian theory of economic class, which then could have constituted the basis of his sociology of religion, law, and so forth?

It is because the heuristic value of the ideal type is completely negative, as is seen in the sociology of the city summarized above. Here a deduction is not possible. The comparison of the classical type, the Italian type and the northern European type, demonstrates that one is dealing with different historical phenomena which have in common only the name city. The most important of the class concepts, that of the bourgeoisie, seems to be directly connected only with the development of medieval northern European states. The comparisons throw into bold relief the error of extending such terms to other urban phenomena. The ideal type of the bourgeoisie, identified with the artisan and merchant population of the medieval northern European city, is useful only for an analysis of this population in its historical individuality, and as such, it is no longer ideal but real. And then sociology is completely resolved into history.

This history is not, however, identifiable with economic history, for Weber's class is not an economic class. Weber recalled attention to the importance of class conventions, to that area of human life which is governed by what is termed (with etymological inaccuracy) " a lesser ethic," that is, etiquette: privileges and obligations, the sentiments of pride, prestige, dignity, and honor, which are sometimes anti-political (as in the case of knightly warfare), often anti-economic (as in the case of the prescription of prodigality), and even anti-ethical (as in the case in which it is joined to caste hatred). Overcoming an obsolete intellectualism which saw in all this mere empty prejudices Weber saw there some ideal forces of major importance. Consequently, one can view his sociology in the same way as Croce and Sorel viewed historical materialism: as a canon of historical interpretation which prescribes the consideration of the conventions of society for the explanation of educational ideals, literary styles, and political, military, religious and economic movements themselves.[68] Only in this limited sense, that is, only insofar as there are some relations between class sentiment and religio-ethical ideals, can the scientific value of the so-called sociology of religion be recognized for the historical investigation of such relations.

Chapter 5

JOHAN HUIZINGA

When it first appeared in 1919, Johan Huizinga's *The Waning of the Middle Ages* was hailed as a performance in the grand manner of Jacob Burckhardt.[1] It seemed to many that the Dutch historian had succeeded in doing for fifteenth-century Franco-Burgundian civilization what Burckhardt had done for the Italian Renaissance, that is, had discovered in it a new type of humanity. In the gallery of great historical portraits, the perfect knight took his place beside the medieval man and the man of the Renaissance.

And yet Huizinga's work, in order to be truly understood, must be viewed as the direct opposite of Burckhardt's history of civilization (*Kulturgeschichte*) in both aims and method. Huizinga's divergence from the Burckhardtian pattern is clearly seen in two essays appearing in *Reflections on Cultural History* (*Cultur-historische Verkenningen*): "The Renaissance and Realism" and "The Problem of the Renaissance."[2] In these two essays Burckhardt's happy formula, in which the Renaissance found a sort of unitary physiognomy in realism and individualism, is resolutely rejected. Huizinga holds that individualism was only one of the many characteristic traits of the period and that realism itself is a tendency common to every art cycle in its earliest stages. Furthermore, he notes that the realism of the earliest phases of Renaissance art was later replaced by the grand style of the High Renaissance. Taking his point of departure from the history of art and probably working under the influence of

185

Wölfflin's studies of the Renaissance and the Baroque,[3] Huizinga regards civilizations as forms, ideal types, styles of life which are raised above raw reality. For him the Renaissance is the world of the courtier (*il cortegiano*) and therefore of Raphael: the expression of an ideal harmony. It is, thus, like every civilization, the formal quest for a type and consequently the subordination of the individual to a convention and norm.

Yet even thus understood, a cultural period cannot be described by formulae. In fact, Huizinga rejects any attempt at definition. For him a definition is always the equation of an infinitely heterogeneous reality with a necessarily generical concept. His work revives on a somewhat different plane Ranke's protests against attempts to subsume historical reality under generalized concepts like "movement" and "class" or under generalized categories of the spiritual life. But Ranke still spoke rather vaguely of "tendencies" and "ideas." Huizinga flatly refuses to admit any concept, and in the end he embraces a thoroughgoing nominalism. Even the idea of the Renaissance is offensive to him: "The [term] 'Renaissance' is only a label used by historians when they bottle their wine." Any schematic division of cultural history into periods is to be rejected. The Renaissance, like the rest of the Middle Ages, like any other age, is a composite of heterogeneous elements, a totality of changes, revolutions, variations, transitions and mixtures. They can be described pluralistically, but it is impossible to collect them under any formula.

Having excluded the formula and the concept from the civilization which he describes, Huizingà really ought to exclude thought as well. While the history of ideas (*Geistesgeschichte*) from Hegel to Dilthey had sought the connecting thread of history in the religio-philosophical development, Huizinga attempted only to describe states of mind, emotional motifs, aspirations, dreams. Between the utilitarian rationality of economic man and the speculative rationality of metaphysical and religious man, he chose the irrational intermediate zone of emotion and fantasy.

Thus his history is not a history of ideas, nor even of interests, but of sentiment and feeling. He is a master at correlating episodes, phrases and documents to the end of creating an affective atmosphere in which both individuals and masses are immersed. He makes extensive use of citations, not because of any pedantic devotion to the ideal of objectivity but only because thus can he avoid the sterile formula and allow the world which he describes to present itself through the immediacy of its own modes of expression. Here we are presented with insights into the folklife and the life of the nobility. Into his work is incorporated a masterful knowledge of legal acts and the diaries and letters of the time, yet he is not merely a social historian. In fact, for him there is no dividing line between the private and public life in any given civilization.

I should think that there is only a coincidental similarity between Huizinga's approach and that of the sociologist Max Weber. Yet in his way Huizinga reacted to the economic interpretation of history by seeking to demonstrate how man is often governed by ideal impulses and movements of a purely conventional nature, concepts of rank and honor, and ethical precepts. And he often spoke of his research as sociological investigation.

The subject of which Huizinga writes would seem to place him in the tradition of de la Curne Sainte Palaye and Barante. In reality his work is an ironic commentary on that of de la Curne, the eighteenth-century eulogist of the ancient chivalric *virtù*, and on Barante, the romantic, fallacious and naïve historian of the feats of the Dukes of Burgundy. Nonetheless it is true that in Huizinga there is something of the same spirit as that which moved Barante to attempt the re-evocation of the Burgundian local color. But in place of the eighteenth-century naïveté which permeated de la Curne's work and the romantic ingenuousness of Barante, with Huizinga we are in the presence of one who is not only extremely subtle in his perceptions but is also a master at the investigation of the sources of modern economic history. He saw the fifteenth century as an age of harsh extremes, rich in violent contrasts and ugly in its brute reality, and he felt that over the whole landscape the rapid vicissitudes of fortune and constant warfare cast a mood of general disquietude. But what he describes in his history is fundamentally an illusion. Among the contemporary sources of the period under investigation he turned to the most naïve and unreliable: to Chastellain, Oliver de la Marche, and Molinet.

The result of his work is, however, more than a picture; it takes on the character of a great stained glass panorama in which are associated kings, saints and bishops, princes and knights, ladies and concubines, burghers and peasants. Huizinga had a strong sense of his rights as an artist. That unitary picture which he denies to the concept is here admitted in the harmony of composition: to those who objected to his having omitted any mention of Joan of Arc in his *The Waning of the Middle Ages*, Huizinga responded that he had specifically excluded her from his narrative because the presence of a heroine would have destroyed the proportions of his work.

Thus envisaged, Huizinga's work raises a question: Could the creator and narrator of such picaresque scenes really come to grips with the problem posed by the transition from medieval to Renaissance civilization? Actually he does have a thesis: that of the continuity between the Franco-Burgundian twilight of the Middle Ages and the Renaissance. But his idea of transition refers not so much to ideas as to forms. According to him, cultural history (*Kulturgeschichte*), for all its links with other branches of history, must pursue its own proper goal. Its aim is not to reconstruct the whole of the history of art, philosophy, science, religion and technology, but to grasp the " forms of life, creativity and thought." Thus the description of social convention is deepened so as to reveal the general tone, the common form, which is revealed in all the products of an age, in its art, its literature, its philosophy and its religion.

*   *   *

The extent to which form can be detached from reality is seen precisely in the epoch studied by Huizinga, in the period which extends from the middle of the fourteenth to the middle of the fifteenth century. This was an age full of contradictions (as is any age of transition) —an age in which the substance of life had already become modern while the forms, still medieval, had been raised to the level of sublime, albeit empty, ideals. The unique aspect of the late Middle Ages—the Middle Ages of the tournaments, of the splendid cavalcades, of the grandiose undertakings—if it were not a historical reality, was at least the form in which society desired to see itself. And it is precisely this great goodheartedness of the knights, this dream of a beautiful life, all chivalry and honor, which Huizinga took as his special field of interest.

He did not criticize those historians who refused to take the chivalry of the age seriously or who saw behind the ostentatious scenery the hard reality of the economic and political struggle. He knew very well that the men of that age already presented the characteristic features of the cold politician and the cunning merchant, just as he knew that in this age of incipient capitalism, national monarchies and agrarian revolts great social forces were on the move. But he was not interested in these forces. Above this real and vulgar level unfolds the grand chivalric game, the expression of the ideal form of life—not merely a fashion. He found that the rules of the game were observed not only by the knights but in a certain measure by the entire populace. And he felt that it was the task of cultural history to investigate it, not because the utopian dream constitutes a socio-political force, but because the style of life sets the tone of the age, suggests the norms of art and thought, of private and public life, informs the communal ethic, and influences religion itself. Thus envisaged, civilization is all convention and play, an exquisite and fragile product of society, the Ariel who ignores Caliban. A society must be in some way idealistic in order to take its fictions seriously, but this idealism must be abstract, doted upon, and blind, without any tendency to movement as a result of its tenuous character. One dotes upon the ideal in all its vagueness and is satisfied with it thus. Instead of any effective movement towards a new ideal in society, there is only the progressive dessication of convention, the rarification of the dream, the autumn. It is boredom which kills the play, a sense of vacuity and uselessness which destroys the game. If the uselessness or emptiness of the game is grasped only for an instant, there is a breakthrough of the crude reality of life, bringing in its train the feeling of bitterness, disillusionment, and despair. This disillusionment will lead to the construction of new games, new dreams: the Middle Ages exhausts its reserves of ideality and the noble game of the Renaissance begins. The new game is also a straining toward an ideal, but according to new rules and through the utilization of other themes. After it will follow the game of the Baroque, the Enlightenment, the Romantic period, and so forth. Thus, of the seventeenth century Huizinga writes: "There is no other century in which the ideal has weighed so heavily upon the real, in which life cast such an image of earthly perfection upon the mirror of the spirit. In the recitation and performance of a role, who can compare with Louis XIV?"

The noble game always has its fixed rules. The Duchy of Burgundy, within the temporal and spatial limits of which Huizinga studied the dissolution of the Middle Ages, seemed created expressly to represent a culture in the extreme stage of the abstraction and rigidity of such rules. Born of the absurd gesture of a French king who wished to reward his valiant younger son with an almost independent state, Burgundy became the land of the Golden Fleece and of a courtly etiquette which was later called Austrian and Spanish and fashioned the ideal of the perfect knight from which, according to Huizinga, descended the *cortegiano*, the *gentilhomme*, and the gentleman. Its entire history is an epic of gallantry, pride and folly. Its destruction, upon the death of Charles the Bold, defeated by the intrigues of the bourgeois King Louis XI and the force of the plebeian Swiss infantry, signalled the end of an epoch.

The criticism made by some, that Huizinga limited himself to the study of the nobility and ignored the middle class, which was just as rich and active at that time, is gratuitous, because the chivalric ideal was not the exclusive property of a single class. If etiquette as such reached its apogée at the court, the sense of form, the sentiments of honor and fidelity which were demanded by the code of chivalry were common to all the people. One might even go so far as to assert that the Burgundian courtly life which appealed to the eye, the imagination and the heart, was so constructed as to be understood and loved by the people and that it had a genuinely popular character. The house of Burgundy incarnated the ideal of royalty which the masses had always envisaged. There was little difference in spirit between the soul inspired by the complicated court ceremonial, those sublime and absurd vows of the knightly orders, the rule of conduct for the tournaments, and feudal warfare with its characteristic embellishments, and the popular spirit which demanded the solemn processions, ornate funerals, and capital executions which assumed the character of fairs. It is the world which, if I am not mistaken, has been immortalized on the playing card.

It might be noted that in order to account for the abstract rigidity of these forms, Huizinga was forced to recur to their social and economic content. He realized that gold was still the instrument of power, even in the world of noble knights, and that everyone was subject to its malignant charm. Life itself was precarious, a prolonged sequence of struggles, risks and hardships. At another time in history such a harsh state of affairs might have resulted in an ascetic flight from the world and its renunciation. But in the lusty society of fifteenth-century Burgundy and gay Flanders there existed a robust will to life, a will revealed in the horror manifested of death itself, as shown in the dance of death motifs invented there. This deep seated affirmation of life and urge to gratification rendered necessary, accord-

ing to Huizinga, some kind of brake, an "etiquette which en-
compassed every event in life with fixed forms and rules which
had been elevated to the dignity of ritual."

Such an explanation is too simple. The urge for gratification
is a fundamental fact of life and common to all ages. Its
emergence to life in the land of Cluny was more than likely a
result of the slackening of older restraints which had once
obtained there. The evil of that world was the result of the
liberation and development of economic interests, new ideas, and
unbiased and individualistic interests. In the literature of the
time Huizinga detected a certain scepticism and noted how the
weight of such a fatuous and artificial social life was already
being felt. But what was this reality which threatened to break
through the world of convention? Huizinga does not say. Yet
this too may be considered a way of seeing, a spiritual and moral
climate. In history there are no transitions from spirit to reality;
there are only transitions from spirit to spirit.

So intent was he upon describing the elegant comedy of the
knights, Huizinga paid little attention to the political, philosophic and religious currents of the time. Of religious movements themselves Huizinga devoted time only to the *Devotio
Moderna*. Thus, he could not become aware of the deepest
reasons for the sadness of the "autumn," an age of schisms and
councils, an age in which the financial interests of the national
churches strained against the old unity of the West and in which
Europe ceased to consider itself a Christian community. William
of Ockham had long since struck at the roots of a faith in the
rationality of the world. Men felt themselves to be abandoned
and isolated. Already that ethics of desperation was growing
which, one day, would be codified by Machiavelli. The melancholy colors of the "autumn of the Middle Ages" should have
been applied to the breakdown of institutions and ideas rather
than to the fine rules of the chivalric code. The drama of
chivalry is merely one aspect of a drama of infinitely wider scope,
a drama which Huizinga knew intimately, but which he believed

to be able to exclude from cultural history as he understood it. At the end of his work, in an analysis of the thought of Diony-sius the Carthusian and other mystics, he pointed out with extra-ordinary finesse the similarity between medieval metaphysical realism and the symbolism of medieval art. In the realm of logic he could have revealed the internal crisis of the Middle Ages, the disintegration of the entire edifice of an ordered system. Instead, he limited himself to a more static description of a primitive mentality by observing it more with the eye of an ethnologist than that of an historian. Here is manifested an influence of the sociological method of a Levy-Bruhl.

By adopting the term " autumn "—or more exactly " autumnal hour " (Herbstij) —Huizinga hoped to avoid using the dangerous concept of decadence. In the preface he was careful to point out that the title is to be regarded figuratively. The period that he describes is truly one of tension and uneasiness, but the problem of whether or not this represents a decline à la Gibbon is not even skirted. However, the image of the autumnal hour brings to mind a feeling of a movement which, although enjoying its last flowering, is nonetheless coming to an end. Having begun with a study of the art of the Van Eyck brothers and their rela-tions to the life of the time, he was aware that this period in France and the Low Countries lent itself to the construction of some concept of the end of the Middle Ages. The state organiza-tion of the Dukes of Burgundy was a typical representation of this end. None of the traits of Burgundian society is unique to it, so one cannot really hold that Huizinga discovered a Burgundian culture (civiltà) which was only dimly perceived up to his own time. The courtly life, the communal burgesses, the chivalric ideals, and the popular superstitions were all common to the Europe of that time, even if in Burgundy they appeared in bold relief. Thus, Huizinga has reversed the usual procedure: instead of following the development of the movement from its origins, he preferred to observe the final stages, because according to his view the salient features of it were more visible at that time. In

reality, in his picture that which is usually considered characteristic of the medieval world—the predilection for the symbol, the
cult of relics, belief in daemons and witchcraft, the ideas of sin
and death, and the sentiments of loyalty and honor—is carried to
a stage of extreme exaggeration and overripeness.

Here the nominalism of Huizinga meets it most difficult test.
After an ennervating tightening, the dissolution should occur
precipitately. The realization of the difference from the modern
world, the disenchantment, the awakening from the dream,
should be sudden. The distinctions between the two periods,
medieval and Renaissance, have been exaggerated, he argues, for
the most part because of the influence of Burckhardt. Huizinga
himself finds humanists in the Franco-Burgundian courtly society,
who enact, like the knights, a mannered comedy. Indeed, Huizinga does perceive the advent of a new spirit at the end. But
the transition is slight and gradual. Even that thirst for glory
which Burckhardt considered characteristic of the man of the
Renaissance is, from Huizinga's position, considered to be only
the chivalric ambition of an earlier age and as Franco-Burgundian
in origin.

The thesis has a certain paradoxical ring about it. Huizinga
was able to formulate it only because he had made the Burgundian court the center of medieval development, just as he had
evidently considered the courts of Urbino, Ferrara, Mantua and
Milan the center of the Renaissance. Undoubtedly, the Franco-
Burgundian courtly life exerted a strong influence on the Italian
court of the Renaissance. One could also admit that after Huizinga's book it is possible to understand more clearly the sources
of *Orlando Furioso* and how the atmosphere in which Ariosto
lived, at least as an artist, was something besides the product of
his imagination. But here one is dealing with the Renaissance
of Ariosto, or better of Castiglione, not that of Machiavelli. It
is precisely here that the limitations of historiography as sociology are manifested: useful for an elucidation of the importance
of social conventions, it is prone to exaggeration when it brings

under investigation the fundamental principles of civilization. Burckhardt had studied the individualism of the Renaissance and seen in it a new note, a new force of the epoch. But he had not followed it through to the recognition of the more profoundly secular character of the Renaissance which was radically opposed to the medieval transcendental ideal.[4] The institution of chivalry was strictly bound to this transcendental ideal. Huizinga remained under the influence of Burckhardt's interpretation insofar as he did not perceive the difference between the new desire for earthly glory and the older, chivalric ambition. It is impossible to understand the Renaissance desire for glory if one fails to grasp its relation to the pagan concept of the value of this world; this is the novelty of the Renaissance. Furthermore, it is difficult to imagine it without that classical culture which was not available to the knight: if among the knightly models, among the so-called "new heroes," are to be found the names of Caesar and Alexander, these names, as Gundolf points out, were merely symbols of abstract chivalric virtues, impersonal types, whereas the man of the Renaissance took as his models concrete figures and historical personalities.[5] And if one wishes to remain solely within the orbit of courtly society, in the world of Castiglione, it would not be difficult to discover in that desire for worldly perfection, musical harmony and grace a reflection of humanistic Neo-Platonism.

Huizinga went even further: he asserted that the spirit of the Renaissance, its aspiration to beauty, had its roots in the chivalric ideal. But the Renaissance, for all of its obeisance before the world of art, guarded itself well against the transformation of life into a series of *beaux gestes*. And here a crucial difference emerges: Huizinga demonstrated how politics and war, carried on in Franco-Burgundian civilization under the aegis of the chivalric ideal, led to tragic errors. But such magnificent follies were inconceivable in the Renaissance, which, if anything, erred in the opposite direction by glorifying cold diplomacy, a tendency which could only be regarded as a decline from the

chivalric point of view and a triumph of bad taste. The sense
of art has very little to do with the sense of etiquette: the whole
of Burgundian society, plumed and resplendent, provides scarce
examples of good taste, beginning with Huizinga's hero, Charles
the Bold, who on solemn occasions sported a vest quilted with
flowers.

*   *   *

Also, in his life of Erasmus, which appeared in 1924, the dualistic motif of the separation of reality and the world of the
spirit returns.[6] After having expressed his admiration for the
limitless curiosity of Erasmus and his experience in the world,
Huizinga then asked himself what consistency this realism might
have had: " Were not Erasmus and his circle on the wrong path?
Were they searching for genuine reality? Was not their superb
Latinity in itself a fatal error? " Erasmus and his followers had
created a spiritual world completely alien to their own time,
because the stormy history of the sixteenth century " was not
played out with classical phrases and noble gestures." Moreover,
Erasmus was able to write only in Latin: " the vulgar tongue
would have rendered everything too immediate, too personal,
too real for this delicate soul. He needed that light veil of the
far distant and indefinite which Latin extends over all."

The world of chivalric conventions, ornate ceremonial, and
splendid tautness is here replaced by the bookish world of those
handsome volumes issuing from the presses of Aldus and Fro-
benius, the world of subtle and learned disputation, of philological collation, and of epistles elevated to the status of
literature, wrapping themselves in elegance and lingering over
the vicissitudes of life and the most discrete movements of the
heart. All of this is play which is all the finer the more it attains
to the character of abstract convention and rises above the crude
reality of the age. Naturally, in his *Erasmus* Huizinga did not
repeat himself and present us with a kind of " Autumn of Hu-

manism." But the analogies, perhaps involuntary, are obvious: here elegance, propriety, clarity and fidelity to authentic rendering of texts correspond to the chivalric virtues encountered in *The Waning of the Middle Ages*. And when Huizinga describes Erasmus' fervor for the critical revision of the Vulgate, which was to have represented the great reform awaited for centuries, it is impossible not to think of the naïve social ideals of the knights.

Huizinga admired in Erasmus the "man of the half tones," of the *nuance*, of the word never fully spoken, "who dreamed of a life of harmony, decorum, and courtesy and who held in horror anything violent or extravagant"; who detested pathos and partisanship; the perfect example of the *fin de siècle* man, because such are distinguished by their disinterested sapience, tolerance and human indulgence. The author of the *Antibarbari* (*Book Against the Barbarians*) well knew that passion was a youthful folly, and thus Erasmus could never bring himself to participate in the Reformation nor experience the passions of love, political partisanship, and religion. Erasmus was too sophisticated to allow the murky subjects to arise, too much the finished litterateur to concede them any right of expression. It is reticence and reserve which predominated in his code of behavior.

Such a man could never bring himself to participate in the Reformation. Huizinga had no need to reexamine the accusations of the reformers in order to defend him. Erasmus could not assume the role of hero precisely because the essential characteristics of the hero, violent intransigence and divine tactlessness, were completely alien to his spirit. His educative, moral, and political ideals were perfectly expressed in the *bonae litterae*, which symbolized honest clarity and propriety of language, and above all, a healthy knowledge of life and human nature. He never justified his convictions by the construction of a specific metaphysical base. They assumed the optimistic view that once the follies of passion and barbarism in general were eliminated, the dignity of human life could be realized. Hence, Erasmus' view had to be presented as constituting an absolute antithesis of the Lutheran conviction of the enslavement of the will and the infirmity of human nature.

Also, this aristocratic ideal was projected, as that of the knights had been formerly, into an idyllic myth common to the Renaissance: this was the ideal of the colloquy, that is, the light and yet serious conversation among congenial and learned friends in the cool shade of the summer house. As Dante had described it in the noble castle of great minds, he had denied any real joy to it. And, in fact, real joy, overflowing passion, was foreign to these dialogues and symposia, to this *otium cum dignitate*, which was born for the first time in Elysium and was reborn in the villa at Tusculum and in that of the Careggi.

In Praise of Folly is adjudged by Huizinga to be " a masterpiece of humor and sapient irony." According to him, Erasmus saw that the world was the scene of universal folly: this was a view already expressed in *The Ship of Fools* and was certainly not original. But Huizinga pointed out that the novelty of the book lay in its exaltation of folly as an element indispensable to life and society. However, for him, this discovery pointed up the necessity of social conventions: here " folly becomes wisdom, resignation, and clemency of judgment." It is the basis of that fiction necessary to communal existence. Erasmus himself wrote: " He who wrenches the mask from others in the game of life will be ostracized. What is this mortal life if not a kind of comedy in which each person plays out his role with one mask after another until he is asked to retire? He acts badly who does not play the game or asks that the play be abandoned."

Actually, the elaboration of the idea of folly found in *In Praise of Folly* is much more interesting than the traditional motif of the eternal human comedy, for here folly is regarded as everything constituting the impulse or will to life. This fact did not escape Huizinga's view, but he did not stress it because it ran counter to his interpretation. Indeed, we are here in the presence of such a strange innovation that the utmost caution is to be prescribed in its evaluation. The sister of folly, argues Erasmus, is Philantia, the self-love which is the spice of life and without which nothing is produced, nothing at least of that aspect of life which is universally considered noble and grand. The man who follows the injunctions of pure reason, who is devoid of passions, is like a stone image, obtuse and devoid of human feeling, a spectre and a monster, oblivious of the movements of the heart.

At first glance, there would seem to be an open contradiction between this completely modern feeling (we were about to say romantic) for the irrational and Erasmus' general philosophical position, that is, his total condemnation of barbarous passions and all aspiration to higher wisdom. The humanistic worldly experience, sharpened by satire, is not limited to the admission with a kind of indulgent resignation of the irresistibility of foolish passion. Instead, it arrives immediately at the positive celebration of its fecundity and of self-love. The instincts and impulses of youth are already exalted as ferments and stimuli of action and art. For Erasmus sin is the source of civilization and history, just as it later became for the libertines, Möser and Goethe. In a fable cited by Huizinga, Erasmus dares link the Christian myth of the Fall with the classical myth of Prometheus. In this tale he places in the mouth of Cain, along with words of scorn for the Paradise lost, words of defiance and at the same time hope of a better future, a future conquered by men through their labour and ingenuity.

In his inquiry into the profundity of the Erasmian experience of the world, Huizinga did not really perceive the significance of Erasmus' secular humanism. Erasmus was anything but on the wrong road: if one desired to draw up here what Lord Acton called a pedigree of ideas, it would be possible to draw a direct line from the Erasmian *Praise* to the psychological research of Montaigne, thence to the moralistic observations of Addison, and ultimately to the discovery of fantasy and politics.

*   *   *

Huizinga attempted to defend his methodological criteria in some essays collected in *Reflections on Cultural History*.[7] As noted above, he belonged to that current of German historical thought which insisted on the subjectivity and freedom of historical interpretation by identifying artistic subjectivity with historical subjectivity, which is both subjective and objective. But while there are many historians who followed this path into the idea of history as myth and legend, for example, the so-called school of Stefan George, Huizinga clung to the feeling of the scientific dignity of the discipline, fled from aesthetic dilettantism, and strove for objectivity. In his writings there is a healthy common sense attitude which allowed him to maintain with amiable serenity a position which is theoretically untenable. Citing Dutch historiography as a typical expression of the mentality of his country, he wrote: "If a German historian examines Dutch historical studies, he will often have the feeling that Dutch science does not really examine the problem thoroughly. Above all, he will deplore the absence of a tight and theoretically formulable argumentation. . . . The Dutch spirit is and remains quietly contemplative more than philosophical. Its need of strict definition is minimal."

This absence of rigour is evident in his definition of historiography, which is based upon an idealistic premise. Historiography, he argues, is never the exact reproduction of a given past, for the past is never given; it is only " an attempt at a certain representation, the image of a determined piece of the past." If one objects to the phrase " piece of the past," there is still the idea that history is always concerned with a particular problem. Vaguely it is also assumed that one is not dealing with a simple representation or with an image but with an act of thought: " To know the history of a period does not mean to possess it, but to be capable of entertaining new representations of it, of criticizing them and assimilating them." However, since the problem is indispensable to the inauguration of work, any distinction between the preparatory critical analysis of sources and the later synthesis falls: " Already in the course of scholarly research, the interpretation is forming, while the document, in itself mute and amorphous, furnishes answers only when questioned."

From this subjectivism to relativism is a short and simple step, but Huizinga does not seem particularly bothered by that. For him, historiography is " rendering account of the past," and since one may render account according to categories as various as those of "virtue and vice, wisdom and folly, friend and foe, force and law, order and freedom, interest and idea, will and determinism, personality and mass," a different image will result from every new investigation. Everyone renders " account " according to his conception of the world.

Once this relation between historiography and philosophy has been posited, one would expect an examination of the antitheses or categories by which accounts are rendered. But Huizinga considers his historiography a " cultural phenomenon " and therefore bound to the form of the civilization to which it belongs. Every civilization creates its own form of historiography and defines the questions that it wishes its historiography to deal with. The historian must be aware of this legitimate multiplicity of forms and must recognize the relative value of his own work. This is also a result of the object of consideration, of that past which is in itself a chaos and which is limited every time by the subject which seeks to understand it: every civilization has its own peculiar past, that is, that which is intelligible to it.

How then can Huizinga salvage the scientific dignity of historiography? As a social product, like fashion or etiquette, it cannot pretend to a validity which transcends the moment. But he purports to find one method of salvation precisely in the link which he holds to exist between historiography and history, in his concept of historiography as a cultural phenomenon which seems to justify relativism. Our civilization, he argues, has a scientific character. Therefore, the type of historiography adapted to it can be nothing but a critically scientific historiography. But it can be legitimately asked if every historian from Herodotus on has not also aspired to such a historiography. The success of mythical and romantic historiography he regards as a retrogression of the historical consciousness and as a grave symptom of a decline in seriousness and sincerity. But if these interpretations are popular today, are they not thereby justified —especially since every historiography is justified as a function of its own culture?

Historiography, Huizinga insists, has to satisfy the demands which give birth to it, the demand for understanding. But what will be his answer to the defenders of mythical and aesthetic historiography when they affirm that their method is best for understanding the past? Huizinga is a relativist who, reacting to the threat against the discipline which is dear to him, himself rebels against relativism.

His relativism is a direct result of a rebellion against positivism. Against Bernheim he denies that one can apply to history methods borrowed from the natural sciences. And likewise he excludes any form of determinism, any kind of causal explanation: for him to understand does not mean to be able to give the why of an event. In the end, he even excludes the idea of development, an idea which he imagines to be derived from the natural sciences: "To the degree that history is spiritual, that much more does it rebel against any concept of development." "Development" is a concept borrowed from biology and bound to a biological concept of organisms: it can be employed by the naturalist, since he conceives of organisms as individuals endowed with intrinsic traits which the environment cannot change, while historical phenomena cannot be isolated, for historical organisms do not exist.

Evidently, Huizinga does not even suppose that next to and in opposition to the crude concept of organic, biological development, there could be a spiritual development, an unfolding of ethical and philosophical ideas. Ignoring any kind of continuity, he is reduced to accepting the " Cleopatra's nose " theory of historical change. External factors intervene, he argues, to render impossible any kind of organic development. Unforeseen accidents, like the arrival of Cortez and Pizzarro in Mexico, bring about essential, terminal catastrophes. When he turned to the political history of the Low Countries, he remained faithful to the idea of caprice and destiny: " It was mere circumstance (and basically what else does history know?) which caused the line of separation to follow linguistic borders. Destiny wished that the free Low Countries should develop without Flanders and Brabant." For him, the Low Countries constituted a potentially great national state which was stillborn. It could have been a state made of the fusion of German and French elements, but it failed because of a series of fortuitous catastrophes. The Burgundian kingdom of which Charles the Bold dreamed could have become a reality: " Only completely unforeseen vicissitudes, like the death of the princes, their capacities and their passions, and a thousand other circumstances determined in the particulars the growth process of the Low Countries."

Thus, in reality, the vicissitudes of the Burgundian state appear bound to the career of a dynasty, because he deals precisely only with the ambition of a dynasty. The chivalric, fantastic and passionate character of the Duke himself is a sign of the lack of a solid base. If one considers the fate of that border territory not in itself but in relation to the process of development of the French monarchy and the decline of the Empire, and in general to the history of western Europe, fate appears to be less capricious. At the beginning of the modern age, a state like Burgundy, lacking geographic and economic unity, without a national consciousness, sustained only by old feudal sentiments of loyalty and honor, sooner or later had to fall through the same kind of dynastic machinations as those which had brought it to life in the first place.

The idea of a capricious destiny as an explanatory principle is a denial of historical interpretation. Seen as a sum of atomistic accidents, no historical process is intelligible. It is understandable why Huizinga, who sees in political history only the rule of chance, preferred cultural history, the history of cultural forms. Here he could imagine that he was not furnishing the why's but only describing the how's of historical occurence. But is description merely reproduction, re-evocation, depicting? Huizinga, like Dilthey before him, warns that one cannot stop at mere reliving: intuitive contact with the past is only the primary phase of historical understanding. More important is the second phase: the interpretation of the forms in which the past is presented to our spirit. Historiography is this morphology.

But what are these forms behind which thought grasps the chaotic material of the past? Here one is not dealing with categories true and proper, such as Dilthey, a Kantian, claimed to have found, but with schematic attitudes of a common mentality which the historian finds already made and finished in the ordinary life about him. Sometimes, Huizinga admits, the historian is forced to produce them. But by what criterion can the historian evaluate new forms offered by the common needs and shape new ones? Huizinga limits himself to a recommendation of prudence: precisely because the historian is aware of his autonomy in this selection, he must guard himself against phantoms and idols. He avoids attempting to embrace whole epochs and civilizations with a single concept and contents himself with determining the aspects, motifs, themes, ideals, styles, and symbols of an age.

It is evident that Huizinga does not resolve the difficulty with this clever pluralism, because even in the description of the aspects of a period, a unitary concept of that period (even if unadmitted) presides over this description. And besides, does not the same question arise for the partial forms as that which he hoped to avoid by the suppression of the general forms?

In his nominalism, Huizinga has to deny any validity to the division of history into periods. Such division, he recognizes, is inevitable, but since one is dealing with pure names, it only remains to use them moderately. Indeed, in order to avoid mis-understandings and to be perfectly clear that one is using simple expedients, it would be preferable to employ the progressive numeration of the centuries and the names of dynasties.

How was it possible for him to write *The Waning of the Middle Ages*, given the canons of such a view? It is true, avers Huizinga, that they are names and expedients up to a certain point: what unites them and renders homogeneous the aspects of a given epoch is something which always stands before us and is never totally grasped, so that it is permissible for us to assign it a name in order to indicate it, without any pretense of having defined it.

This explains the panoramic character of his reconstruction of a state of mind or a series of states of mind which stamps his work as historian. Concerning his *Waning of the Middle Ages*, the comparison to a great stained glass window or a painting springs immediately to mind. Perhaps it would be more exact to use the simile of a symphony, so much the more so since he himself adopted a musical terminology. History, as he imagines it, is a series of great polyphonic concerts, each of which is ruled by a dominant theme accompanied by other minor motifs which appear as successions of infinite variations, unexpected turns, and developments. The historian, like the musicologist, must know how to distinguish and follow the thread of the plot, while at the same time he gathers together and savours the inexpressible effect of the whole.

*   *   *

Huizinga's last work, up to the present writing, consisted of a diagnosis of our time and was a protest against the irrational forces which threatened our civilization.[8] The aggravation of the European situation presented new problems to the gentle historian of the chivalric dream, to the scholar of the Van Eycks' art. It made him more conscious of the European role of his homeland, of its role as mediator.[9] Here he sees it as the land of tolerance, of Erasmus and Grotius and the Arminians, which raises its voice against violence, fanaticism and irrationalism: " Today we are witnessing with our own eyes how almost everything which once appeared to be solid and sacred has become tenuous and unstable: truth, humanity, reason, law." However, his historiography was itself a symptom of the evil which he deplored. He sharpened the dualism between civilization and nature, and then argued that civilization was mere form, stylized convention, play, comedy. And history was nothing but a succession of these brilliant ceremonies. Should one be surprised if, from time to time, raw reality intruded, disrupted the play, and put the comedians to flight? What sort of spirit can be demanded of the participant in a play called upon to defend that which he knows to be nothing but a fatuous game? And how is it possible to lament the fact that all things " which once stood firm and sacred " have now been shaken? Especially if one has asserted the relativity of all cultural phenomena and the legitimate plurality of all forms?

Chapter 6

HEINRICH WÖLFFLIN

One of Goethe's observations in his *Italian Journey* (*Italianische Reise*) might well serve as the motto for the work of Heinrich Wölfflin. Goethe wrote: "It is evident that the eye forms itself by the objects which from youth on it is accustomed to look upon; and so the Venetian artist must see all things in a clearer and brighter light than other men. We, whose eye when out of doors falls on a dingy soil, which, when not muddy, is dusty, and which, always colorless, gives a sombre hue to the reflected rays, or who at home spend our lives in a close, narrow room, can never attain to such a cheerful view of nature." Wölfflin's theoretical problem, the problem of the eye of the artist, is a product of the Italian *Erlebnis* which every German from Goethe on brought back with him when he returned from the land of clear and perfect forms into a "formless Germany." It was this Italian experience which gave the German nation its greatest nineteenth century artists, Feuerbach, Böcklin, Marées, Hildebrand, and its two greatest dilettantes, Goethe and Burckhardt. Here, in fact, the German could enjoy beauty as pure and immediate visual stimulation, and by forgetting his inner problems in a sort of vacation of the soul, he could delight in the spectacle of life in its simplicity and its variety. Not having realized the extent to which the literary and artistic tradition forced him to apprehend men and things in an idyllic light,[1] the German artist attributed the power of rendering the soul

207

clear, serene, measured, and classic to the nature of the country itself, to its lines and light. Only here, he believed, was it possible to learn the discipline of pure form: Goethe himself later wrote, " My greatest joy is the fact that my eye was educated through contact with stable forms and was easily habituated to forms and their relations."

Thus, as early as Goethe, the Italian experience was seen as a problem of form. But precisely because the form to which the German eye had to be educated was Italian, it came to be regarded as something purely external, something merely visual, and above all, as something completely alien to the Nordic nature (natura). Confronted with the Italian triumph of forms, the German came to regard himself as "living" art in some internal sense. Soon this notion was translated into the idea that the German had sacrificed the desire to perfect the external covering of the art object to a desire to express its inner emotional and ethical quality. Thus, a dichotomy was posited in which, throughout the nineteenth century, the problem of art was confused with nationalistic passions. From this confusion descended a long series of problems which were theoretically ill formulated and only partially resolved. If, for example, German art seemed to be rich in content yet weak in formal values, what criterion of judgment could be used for the evaluation of German figurative art? Goethe had denied to the German painter a pure delight in seeing. A century later, Henry Thode had flatly denied to the German people a vocation in the figurative arts and had banished their talents in emotional expression and fantasy to the realm of music. Could one conclude, therefore, that German painting had been merely one grand error, a deviation of the national genius into forms of expression congenitally denied it? Even worse: if the German artists of the Renaissance, men like Dürer and Holbein, had acquired a taste for the line of the Italian school, was one to consider their art a break in the national tradition, a betrayal of the German nature? And if so, what constituted this nature?

In his own way, Wölfflin answered all of these questions by beginning again at their origins, that is, with the Goethean concept of the eye which is educated through the contemplation of a figure or landscape. He accepted the fundamental assumption of the complete difference between the two natural environments, but he did not conclude therefrom that the sense of form was a prerogative of Italy. There had to be a type of education of the eye, a visual experience, which corresponded to the German physical environment. That excessive realism which Thode had considered an unhealthy deficiency in German art in Wölfflin achieves its justification as a peculiarly German sense of form. He held that the German artists of the Renaissance had indeed fallen into temptation, but they had been able to resist it and had remained faithful to the Nordic nature. And it was Wölfflin who finally succeeded in defining this famous nature or essence. In a sense, the problem of form was for the German a problem of his very humanity and destiny. Confronted with his *alter ego*, the Italian form, the German is forced to define his own national individuality: " The more often one goes to Italy and the more intimately one comes to know it, the more alien it appears. However, it is possible that these experiences make the traveler more clearly and intimately aware of the special worth of the things of his own country." [2]

It was on this encounter of the two forms that Wölfflin loved to linger. Notwithstanding the fact that he gave the Germans a key to the understanding of their art—and perhaps even a way of exalting it above Italian art—he himself made little use of that key. Of his master Burckhardt, he observed how the only Nordic artist with whom he had been concerned was Rubens, "who, more than any other, was nourished on Latin culture without sacrificing himself." [3] Of Wölfflin it could be said analogously that the motive force in his development was Dürer.

Since the age of Romanticism no formula had had such a fortunate career as his. It was not only applied by art historians, among whom it became a dogma or a commonplace, but also by literary historians,[4] students of pre-history and even by political publicists.

Some hailed him as "the first great and authentic art historian." In reality, in those works which had the greatest circulation, he examined only the premises which would serve for the interpretation of painting, sculpture, and architecture. He himself speaks of "auxiliary constructions" which in no way seek to usurp the role of art history in its traditional sense. His famous demand for "a history of art without names," which caused such a scandal, did not mean that he conceived of a history of art which could ignore personalities, but only that in order to understand a work of art, it was necessary to take into account that unity of atmosphere and style which it has in common with other works of its time and society. Thus, his investigation does not really move into the sphere of art history *per se*, but penetrates below that sphere into the zone of the distinctive character of civilizations, nations and races. He makes no value judgments, not because he considers them unscientific, but because they have no place in the investigation of a collective psychology, even if conducted on the ground of art.[5]

From the time when Dilthey had attempted a compromise between his spiritualism and his positivism in a theory of the types of world views and, after him, Max Weber and Troeltsch had introduced the concept of type into the historiography of religion and economics, the idea of the type became the nodal point around which everything revolved that was active or at least exciting in German historico-philosophical activity: the "life forms" of Spranger, the "soul types" of Jaspers, the "tribal types" [*Stammentypen*] of Nadler, the "types of mysticism" of Otto, the "types of humanity" of Worringer, the "cultural types" of Spengler, the "character types" of Klages, and the "racial types" of the anthropologists.[6] In this intellectual atmosphere were Wölfflin's forms of vision born and nurtured.

*   *   *

Burckhardt had answered those who criticized him for having avoided any reference to the history of culture in his *The Art of the Renaissance in Italy (Kunst der Renaissance)* : " The great spiritual facts belong to the history of the artists, not to the systematic investigation which seeks to describe the impulses and conditions governing the whole." [7] Here was an outright rejection of the romantic conception of art as a translation of life or as a historical document. The new historiography which organized its data into events and their types was obliged to see in the history of art the solution of merely formal problems, anchored in life to be sure, but capable of being broken down into two parallel lines: one, the narrative history, that is, the biographies of the artists, and the other, the anonymous systematic history.

What constituted the anchorage or what sort of relationship existed between the two parallels Burckhardt did not ask; indeed, he prohibited himself from asking. Yet at the beginning of his systematic description of Renaissance architecture he had inserted a brief note on the monumental sense of the Italians of that epoch, and he had attributed the existence of this sense to their modern individualism and ambition. But there was little organic connection between this chapter and the rest of his work. His formal analysis went its own way, oblivious to any historical consideration.

Wölfflin, Burckhardt's disciple and successor in his chair at Basle, remained faithful to this dualistic view. In 1888, while still quite young, Wölfflin asked with a suppressed smile: " What sort of relation could there be between the Gothic style, feudalism and scholasticism? What sort of bridge could link together the Baroque and Jesuitism?" [8] Later, after he had become interested in the question of the origins of the Baroque, he observed that it was born of an epoch which enjoyed the sensation of discovering new vistas, was possessed of an eye which was well disposed toward whatever was detached from the classic rule, and which used the terms "new," "capricious," "extravagant," and "bizarre" honorifically. But this *ante literam* futurism of the late Renaissance was not for him the main reason for the emergence of the new style. It seemed to him to be a necessary transformation, not a development brought about by the creative free will and experimentation of individuals, but by a process which was, so to speak, spontaneous, in which the forms changed almost by themselves under the hands of the artists.[9] Finally, in his book on Dürer,[10] although he did make mention of Dürer the man and his relation to the violent passions of the Reformation, he ignored any relations which might have existed between this and his work as an artist. At the very most the religious crisis is reflected in Dürer's selection of themes.

Yet Wölfflin is distinguished from the positivistic art historians of the late nineteenth century who, in opposition to the Hegelians and Romantics of the earlier part of the century, devoted themselves solely to the problem of formal analysis. Wölfflin is distinguished from them by a trait which is also found in Dilthey. In his dissertation, "Prolegomena to a Psychology of Architecture" (*Prolegomena zu einer Psychologie der Architektur*), Wölfflin reminds one of Dilthey in his lamentation over the fact that the human sciences—and among them art history— still lacked the solid foundations which only psychology could provide. The type of psychology which he had in mind was the theory of empathy (*Einfühlung*) as it had been developed by Thomas Lipps, Volkelt, and Robert Vischer.[11] Here he asks how architectonic forms can be considered expressions of states of mind. Bodily forms send back to us only what we put into them. In the case of stone we can put into it only those feelings which come to us through the body, that is, the feeling of heaviness, balance, and so forth. Therefore, the laws of architecture would have to be based upon our own bodily experience. The architectonic effect, thus envisaged, will be nothing but the feeling of an achieved balance, the feeling of the victory of our inner *vis plastica* over inert matter, the realization of our organic well-being.

This was a psychological justification of Burckhardt's classicism. In reality, Wölfflin deplored the fact that in his time movement and excitement were preferred to simplicity, balance and serenity: all this appeared to him as a deficiency similar to that of Dürer's "Melancholy I" where he found "the unrequited frustration which comes of the failure to achieve form." [12]

The classic sense of form was for the Wölfflin of that time an absolute: the uniformity of our bodily structure guaranteed its uniformity. There still remained, however, the fact of change in styles. In order to surmount this difficulty, he recurred to the variation of the ideal of beauty, that is, the variation of the ideal of the body, its attitudes and movements. For him architectural style could be correlated to the mode of dressing peculiar to any given epoch insofar as dress indicated how men desired to hold and carry themselves. And he concluded with some remarks about the relation between medieval pointed shoes and Gothic spires.

This criterion was easily applied by Wölfflin to the history of art in general. Having forgotten his aim of describing how style was transformed by itself according to those inner laws of form which his master Burckhardt had wished to reduce to the "clearest possible formulae," [13] he asked himself, in the essay on the origin and essence of the Baroque, what determined transformations of style. The explanation of the positivists, who found the cause of stylistic changes in the external limitations of the materials and practical aims, seemed to him too materialistic. Here also it would be necessary to discover the effect of the new corporeal sense. What, in fact, was the corporeal ideal of the Baroque? In place of the slim and austere figure of the Renaissance, we are now met with the massive Herculean body, swollen with muscles, in both painting and sculpture. Art meekly obeys and offers a swollen heaviness in place of an ethereal lightness.

For a moment it seemed as if Wölfflin had succeeded in finally erecting a bridge between art and the general spiritual disposition of life. The corporeal ideal of the Baroque seemed to him to correspond to the mood of an epoch which was no longer happy but had become serious: "In all spheres the element of seriousness is the supreme value: in religious thought, where the world turns and confronts the sacred and ecclesiastical, there is a cessation of cynical, sensual gratification; Tasso chooses a hero who is tired of life as the central character of his Christian poem; in society and in all forms of communal experience, a heavier and more reserved tone is evident; one no longer finds the light and careless grace of the Renaissance—only seriousness and dignity; instead of a ludic lightness, one finds an ostentatious and deadening pomposity; everywhere the grandiose and the important is sought." [14] Perhaps it was this passage which inspired Huizinga to formulate his theory of the ideal forms of life which stamp every aspect of the culture of an age. When Wölfflin comes to the point of affirming that the nucleus of the Baroque spirit is its craving for the sublime, its tendency to break through to the infinite, one has a presentment of the motif so dear to Dvořák, who saw spiritual crisis as the impetus to revolution in style. However, when Wölfflin concludes that it is not by chance that Palestrina was contemporary with the Baroque, that is, that architectonic forms have been absorbed by music— a more adequate mode of expression for vague and formless states of mind—one is led to suspect that Wölfflin has succumbed to the seductions of the romantic Nietzsche.

But the heresy—if it existed—was short lived, for in *Classic Art* (*Die klassische Kunst*) ,[15] when confronted with the problem of the transition from the fifteenth to the sixteenth century, he turns to a concept of style as a projection of a definite corporeal sense. Here he can point to the code which informs the new corporeal ideal: the *Cortegiano* of Castiglione, the collection of rules in use at the court of Urbino, the recognized school of the new gentility. The scornful grace of carriage, the modesty and pomp (*grandezza*) of the sedate walk, the air of self possession and the flaccid delicacy of gesture are translated into the art of the sixteenth-century in which sky and earth, madonnas, saints, angels and *putti*, are all characterized by a sense of distinction and refinement, like the new dominant class, the aristocracy of the courts. Wölfflin argues that it is this new manner of feeling and observing the body which brings to the new style its famous classic serenity. And yet the essay on Dürer presents the encounter between German art and Italian art, between the influences of Schongauer and Mantegna, as a conflict between two different senses of corporeality: between the delicate and graceful gesture, the elegant, dance-like walk, and the leanness of the late Gothic body and the monumental solidity of Renaissance bodies.

Thus Wölfflin has maintained that bifurcation of form and spiritual content by which Burckhardt hoped to save the autonomy of beauty and thus remove himself from the demands of documentary art history. However, Wölfflin felt it necessary to attribute to form a psychological and a sociological origin. Between the psychological factor, the feeling or ideal of the body, and style he placed a mediating factor, one less compromising than that of causality, that is, the concept of determination. Form is historically determined and is thus a document—if not of the spirit of an age, at least of the rules of etiquette and fashion. It is etiquette and fashion which the artist serves, as much as does the tailor. One can easily understand, therefore, how Wölfflin could regard as " a refreshing shower upon a dry earth " and at the same time as " a little crown of thorns " an improvised affirmation of the freedom of art, the producer of forms, the theory of pure visibility.

* * *

The theory of pure visibility is distinguished from the aesthetics of its own time by its origins, born as it was of the researches of a painter, Hans von Marées, a sculptor, Adolf von Hildebrand, and a patron of the arts, Conrad Fiedler. Having met in Rome around 1870, these three friends breathed the air which Goethe had breathed and, like Goethe, they found themselves confronted with the problem of the classic line. Motivated by

the ideal of form for form's sake and immune to any naturalistic, sentimental, literary or social contamination, they reverted
to a transcendental aesthetics and perhaps even more to Kantian
ethics: the power (virtù) of the artist seemed to them to be the
power of man himself, the force of character which, as plastic
force (Gestaltungskraft), dominates a formless and elusive matter
presented by sensations, by producing "truly determined, tan-
gible, and sensibly demonstrable forms." [16]
     What they wanted, however, was an a priori aesthetics of the
figurative arts. For them the aesthetic synthesis was something
different from, but analogous to, scientific knowledge, and since
this was presented as a concentration of sense data in the abstract
concept, the artistic act was conceived by them as a process of
abstraction which began with individual representations and
ended in pure visibility. And just as science obeyed logical
laws, so every art had to have its coherence, imposed by the
a priori conditions of sensibility. In the case of the figurative
arts, coherence had to result from the a priori structure of the
eye. Fiedler concentrated upon the investigation of the " way
in which the eye progressed, singling out, isolating, combining,
ordering, and creating its autonomous, rich, infinite real-ideal
world." [17] Hildebrand, using the stereoscope as an archetype,
sought to separate tactile from visual elements by opposing ordinary close range vision to long distance, two dimensional vision
in which the artist was pure " seeing " (vedere) .[18]
     It was this theory of art (Kunsttheorie) which awakened
Wölfflin from his dogmatic slumbers. While all around him
positivistic historiography continued to chart the derivations and
transformations of styles, he now perceived in form the free
activity of the artist and began to consider the eye as an image-
producing organ which continually educated and perfected itself.
Now the historical consideration only seemed to lead up to a
certain point; in fact, one might even say that the historical
consideration led up to the point where art itself began.[19]
     Standing on the shoulders of Fiedler and Hildebrand, he now

determined what values this formative activity brought into existence: the simplicity and clarity of figures, the richness of intuitions, the unity of the manifold and the necessity of relations. However, Wölfflin departed from those who had inspired him at the point where they began to search for an "a priori structure" of the eye. For him the formal values were not the representations of a universal and eternal beauty, but the characteristics of the art of the sixteenth century as compared with that of the fifteenth. He admitted that they were not exclusive to the Italian sixteenth century, and he discerned their presence, for example, in Ruysdael, but he sought to avoid identifying them with art per se. Instead, he reduced them to the status of "characteristic moments" of a definite type of art; that is, he saw them as characteristics of classic art. At the base of this type, he argued, there was a definite eye-structure, a particular mode of seeing, which does not exhaust all of the possibilities of art itself.

Having been raised in a Kantian atmosphere, Wölfflin immediately fell into the concept of type. He seems to have understood Kant in a psychological sense, if not in a physiological one. Psychology lent itself to classificatory methods of analysis. In this case, it served to render account of that purely formal evolution, independent of any spiritual disposition of artists, which Burckhardt had held to be the true object of art history. In fact, clarity, richness and organic quality of expression became the "inexpressible moments" of a given art style, standing beside the older "expressible moments" which were envisaged as a product of the particular corporeal sense. As Croce remarked, it was a strange sort of dualism [20] and one which was not destined to endure: little by little the expressive moments disappeared before those which were conceived as purely optical. In place of the anonymous corporeal sense there now appeared the "feeling for visual forms"—also anonymous. What Wölfflin undertook to describe was the conditionedness (conditionatezza) of the artist, his belonging to a type of seeing, to a pattern. Instead of a history of art, he developed a psychology of the "forms of vision" in which abstract entities instead of men became the object of study. The subject matter of this discipline was not the creative artist but line, contour, figure, drapery, the boundaries between light and shadow, that is, the particulars of the spatial configurations.

Wölfflin already possessed one type: classic art. It remained to define the other, non-classic type—a type just as truly artistic as the former even though it was a response to another manner of seeing things. Thus, instead of an antithesis of beautiful and ugly as categories of art, one is presented with a bifurcation of the concept of the beautiful. Whatever appeared to be ugly and defective from one of the categories became beautiful and complete from the other. Strictly speaking, the distinction between beauty and ugliness really no longer had any reason for being, for the rehabilitation of the so-called decadent ages, promoted by Burckhardt and completed by the "Viennese school," had placed all art styles on the same qualitative plane. Now, if the classic land was Italy, if in Italy, in the south, an unrivalled form of classic art had flourished, where was one to look for the other type if not at the opposite geographical pole, in the north?

*   *   *

In 1905 Wölfflin published his book on Dürer. His thesis is that Dürer was not the most German of all German artists, but that he, more than any other German artist, had looked with longing beyond the frontiers of his homeland to that great foreign beauty which was responsible for the "great insecurity" of German art. Thus envisaged, the problem is not merely that of the encounter and resolution within the spirit of a genius of the influences of Schongauer and Mantegna, a clash between late Gothic and Renaissance: it is the story of a dramatic concourse of two totally different natures, the Nordic and the Southern, the Germanic and the Latin. Thus, although Wölfflin had opposed himself to the Romantics, he developed the discussion in their terms, that is, in terms of the national genius (*Volksgeist*). He might have asked himself if the difference were due to a fundamentally different spiritual disposition. But that would have led him back to the biography of the man, not into the history of the artist. It is true that Wölfflin admitted a difference in corporeal sense, but the real, the essential, difference was for him in the seeing (*vedere*).

In the young Dürer he discerned one who already possessed an unusual sensitivity for plastic form, for visual values. Later, Italy had taught the artist to see in terms of greater forms, to mold the figure with a sense of visual clarity, and to enrich his innate plastic sensitivity. But alas, the Nordic had to pay the price of his infidelity: his art became formalistic and lacking in color and immediacy. He was unexpectedly rescued by a trip to Holland: the painter returned to reestablish a living contact with nature, to regard every living thing, every head and every individual, with an attentive and loving eye, almost as if he had awakened to the world for the first time. The terrible spell of Italy was broken: the man of the north had rediscovered his own true nature.

To render this moving tale, Wölfflin employed two pairs of distinct and, in a certain sense, opposed concepts: plastic-painterly and Latin-Nordic. He then proclaimed the essential correspondence of the two concepts. All of this was, of course, an assumption, a postulate, but Wölfflin spent the rest of his life in the elaboration of the distinctions.

That stylistic movements might vacillate between two opposite poles was an old idea.[21] Burckhardt had defined Renaissance architecture as "painterly," that is, as one which worked with forms and geometrical relations of a purely optical value, whereas the Gothic church and the Greek temple were organic, structural and functional expressions. Alois Riegel had organized his history of style around the fundamental antithesis of optical and tactile, assigning to tactile values a chronological precedence over optical ones. Riegel's student, Jantzen, had even attempted to demonstrate that the Flemish were predisposed toward tactile perceptions while the Dutch were oriented optically.[22]

And while on the subject, it might be recalled that polarities are by no means an oddity in recent German art historiography: plastic-painterly (Schmarsow), being and becoming (Frankl), fullness-form (Panofsky), cubist-organic (Coellens), technical-contratechnical (Scheltma), naturalistic-anti-naturalistic (Dvořák), and, if one wished, it would be a simple matter to extend the list almost indefinitely.[23]

In his *Renaissance and Baroque* (*Renaissance und Barock*), Wölfflin himself juxtaposed painterly to linear-plastic-architectonic, and he pointed out the predominance of the painterly in the Baroque. But he would not identify painterly with Baroque because he believed that Baroque corresponded to a general orientation of the sense of form and was not a prevalence of one form or art over others. He had surmounted the difficulties of the problem by 1912, in which year he submitted a communication to the Academy of Sciences in Berlin which later became his *Principles of Art History* (*Kunstgeschichtliche Grundbegriffe*).[24] Here he argued that painterly and linear have no particular links with a determined art style but are two optical types, two different orientations of the sense of form.

However, since there are two poles, the history of style must necessarily oscillate rhythmically from one to the other extreme. Like certain positivistic historians who were his contemporaries, for example, Breysig and Lamprecht, Wölfflin succumbed to the idea of the cycle, the Vichian motif of recurrence. The transition from one pole to another he sees as a law of periodic evolution of the optical pattern which is necessary, natural, inevitable. He examines a typical case of this evolution in the transition from the Renaissance to the Baroque, but he holds that the transitional pattern has already been verified in the movement which led from Romanesque to Gothic style and could be verified in every individual artist, every idea and every emotion coming under examination. However, Wölfflin did not maintain his thesis with any sort of rigorous orthodoxy. With his usual eclecticism triumphing, he admitted that the ideal of beauty might exert some influence upon the visual disposition, and in the transition from Renaissance to Baroque he also hoped to find a transformation of the practical ideal (*Lebensideal*), a concept which was never clearly defined by him but which is probably a residue of his older corporeal sense. Thus, the criticism of the theory of visual forms put forth by Dehio is not wholly justified: Dehio had objected to Wölfflin's asking how men *had* to see, instead of why do men see thus.[25] It would have been much more apposite to observe that Wölfflin had neglected to examine the relations between the visual forms and the practical ideal—a much more acute problem since in his terms it is unclear how far the ideal can influence the evolution of style, which is supposedly at the same time self-actuating by virtue of an inner, objective necessity.

The processes (or the aspects of the process) which lead from Renaissance to Baroque are five: from linear to painterly, from superficial plane vision to recessional vision, from a closed form to an open and less rigidly limited one, from a multiplicity of the parts to their fusion into a unity, and from clarity of composition to relative clarity. This process is supposed to have reached its apex in the sixteenth century, the acme of linearity, to have descended towards the painterly, and then to have veered upwards once more at the end of the eighteenth century, when the line once more predominates.

There are some who have objected that these categories are not *a priori* deductions, some who have found them too subjective and too complex, and others who have denied the existence of any real polarity between linear and painterly. Actually, they are abstract schemata empirically arrived at through generalization, vague and indefinite by the admission of their formulator.[26] Their deduction or justification in any formal sense was never attempted by Wölfflin. Behind them there is only the negation of the thesis of the limitation of nature and the consequent assertion of the eye's productivity. But why this productivity is conditioned by determined optical possibilities and is not free is never stated. Wölfflin had the good taste not to follow the path set by Hildebrand's research on the physiology of the eye.

On the other hand, L. Venturi, while recognizing the provisional character of such classificatory schemata, confessed that after having become acquainted with Wölfflin's work one had a much clearer understanding of many art works of the sixteenth and seventeenth centuries.[27] These abstract schemata have therefore, some use. According to Venturi, they are only intellectual cues, the theories of the artists, which the historian rediscovers. They are useful for determining the viewpoint of the artist, for understanding how he thought and conceived his own work. Wölfflin's mistake was in having given a rigidity to schemata which did not tally perfectly with the thought of the artists of which he spoke.

In reality, underlying all of Wölfflin's work there is a fundamental error—one which is common to a large part of modern art historiography. This error lies in his considering art merely as stylistic phenomenon, that is, as some objective reality. When Wölfflin declares that he hopes to offer us a natural history, he has quite correctly stated his aim. His procedure is that of the natural scientist insofar as he seeks to subsume art objects under general, abstract concepts. Art history, thus conceived, can never produce anything but abstract patterns, just as biology and mineralogy can never produce anything but abstract patterns. It is obvious that such schematizations can never be a priori, absolute, or universal, even though they may be useful in bringing some order out of chaos—at least when one is confronted, not by the work or art itself, but by the artistic production of an epoch, nation or the human race as a whole. And, in fact, this is Wölfflin's concern: he is not interested in the individual work of art, but in style, that is, in the common mean, the mediocre uniformity and generality of an epoch. Thus envisaged, the real nature of the so-called polarity becomes patent. That art admits of no descriptive adjectives is self-evident. Adjectives such as " linear " and " painterly " point to limitations and defects in the work of art. The two poles are, in reality, slopes which rise to the peak which is art. If they were genuine poles, then extreme linearity and extreme painterliness would have to be considered the purest and highest forms of art: instead, the two extremes are nothing but geometricity and confusion.

Since any *limitatio est negatio* the adjectives can only be conceived as indications of incompleteness and defectiveness. When the historiography of art has recourse to naturalistic schemata, it blinds itself to beauty and perceives defects without realizing that they are such. That art which springs from the originality and creative genius of the artist defies classification, and all that remains is the uniform, the common, the mediocre, the art which is bound to the taste, fashion and prejudice of an age.

Venturi observed that such schemata were cues to the theoretical or intellectual orientation of the artist. But if such intellectual, that is to say, non-artistic, elements are discernible in a work of art, they constitute defects, bonds from which the artist has failed to free himself.

However, besides the doctrines and canons which make up the aesthetic precepts of an age and which more or less weigh upon the work of the artist, there is in Wölfflin's concept of the artist's eye yet another element. The artist strives for a definite ideal of beauty through suggestion as he moves from image to image. According to Wölfflin, only a dilettante would believe that an artist could work without presuppositions. In fact, a master teaches his pupils to see in a certain way and imposes upon them his own manner of observation and entertainment of objects. Thus envisaged, every epoch must be considered a school. There is an evolution of taste, that is, of the capacity to enjoy beauty, and the educators, the creators, are the great masters. Wölfflin was working out of the realization that the taste of an epoch presented a unified whole: " The columns and arches of the High Renaissance speak as intelligibly of the spirit of the time as the figures of Raphael." Only in this sense can one speak of an optical schema and the style of an age. But the true artist, the creator who is not a disciple but a teacher, is his own master and breaks through the pattern to open the way to a new concept of the beautiful.

*   *   *

Having determined the two forms of vision, the linear and the painterly, Wölfflin could finally define the Italian and the German sense of form.[28] Here the two schemata are transformed into or are identified with two distinct, permanent and essential ethnic types: " Italy revealed its national genius in the Renaissance, Germany in the Baroque."

However, in order to raise what had formerly been variable stylistic forms to the dignity of permanent racial structures, it was first necessary to link them with something solid. At this point Wölfflin utilizes an idea which he had hitherto ignored, that is, the concept of the *milieu*, the geographic environment.[29] He had already found in the Italian landscape that exactitude (*determinatezza*) and measure which are characteristic of Italian art. Here things were offered in stable proportion, in defined figures, whereas the German came from a world of the " linked, dependent, intricate, where everything was a part of a whole." [30]

For the five conceptual dualities noted above, Wölfflin substitutes two opposed senses of form. The conceptual dualities are maintained but are extended in number. Moreover, the new dualities acquire the greatest importance. Above all stands the duality of " techtonic-vegetal ": " There is a beauty of the column and a beauty of the plant; the Italian sees the column in the plant and the German the plant in the column." Then, the duality of " proportion-function ": Italian art strives for the

effect of proportion and conceives the human body as a problem
of measurement ("measurement is primary not secondary"),
while the German "rebels against the use of the compass" and
strives to attain the ultimate in functionalism. Third, the duality
of "ideal-real": Italian art seeks the typical and believes in
eternal models of the beautiful, whereas the German grasps life
in its particularity and is much more penetrating in portraiture:
"It is as though metaphysical reality consists for the Italian in
the universal and for the German in the individual." Fourth,
the duality of "static-dynamic": in the German picture there
is a movement which is lacking in the Italian. Fifth, the duality
of "regularity-variation" (arbitrarietá): in Italy rules are followed with decision and coherence; in German art there is a
capricious looseness, because the German has a sense of the
spontaneity and irrationality of nature. Finally, there is the
duality of "limited-unlimited": in German art the outline is
vague and fluctuating, for the German sees the isolation of the
figure in Italian painting as a limitation, and he always seeks to
plunge once more into his own proper element, that is, into
the unlimited, the indefinite, the complicated.[31] There is no
need to examine here the extent to which these categories correspond with those mentioned earlier and with themselves:
Wölfflin considered them to be variations of a unique antithesis.

At the base of the sense of form Wölfflin ended by admitting—
possibly under Dilthey's influence—a particular life mood (Le-
bensstimmung), a definite life and world view. There could be
little objection to such a conclusion. Undoubtedly the nation,
the product of, and a factor in, history, imparts its own peculiar
accent or gives an affective coloration to life. Also the nation
may hypostatize certain traditional virtues from which (it may
be believed) its greatest powers flow. But that does not mean
that the national genius or spirit can be turned into a static
schema. The national spiritual physiognomy which is a function
of a peculiar destiny and which grows out of the diversity of
political, economic and religious experiences becomes, thus

envisaged, a limitation on the growth of the nation itself. To rigidly schematize that physiognomy would be to turn it into a burden which the nation has to carry with it throughout the course of its existence and which would have limited its activity from the time of its origin. The nation, thus conceived, would have no power over its own will; in fact, the history of the nation would be determined by it. The writing of history, true and proper, would have to be preceded by a study of national psychology in order to establish valid interpretative criteria.

In fact, Wölfflin did assert that it was absolutely necessary to establish the ethnic sense of form prior to undertaking historical investigations. It is a singular notion, for it is difficult to imagine anyone seriously holding that before one can undertake a religious or political history of a people, it is necessary first to define their political or religious sense. If anything, such formulae would be the result of a history already narrated, standing as a sort of conclusion. Instead, Wölfflin chose the period 1490-1530, the period from Leonardo to Titian and from Dürer to Holbein, and assigned to it the function of a "specimen" in which was reflected the whole of the art history of the two nations.

The result is that he assumes as a typical characteristic of Italy that Platonic canon of divine proportion which historically was formed during the Renaissance. Italian idealism is the result of a whole complex of spiritual elements which indeed has accompanied the development of the Italian intellectual world. But it remains nonetheless merely a moment of the total history of Italy. Nothing at all justifies identifying it with any morphological characteristics such as those which, according to Linnaeus, characterize the animal and plant kingdoms.

On the other hand, it is obvious that the new dualities, like the old ones, indicate a weakness and a one-sidedness in the two national cultural traditions. It is probably in this, their negative character, that they have their value: it is true that the Platonic ideal weighed heavily upon Renaissance art, just as German art has traditionally tended to realistic particularism and has, thereby, lost a sense of order and unity.

Yet even if we admit that the two senses of form represent two opposed unilateral entities, it is difficult to see what value the recognition of their existence might have. The older distinction between classic and romantic at least was justified by a distinction between feeling and form as two different moments. In place of that distinction Wölfflin posits a distinction within form itself. He no longer deals with the prevalence of one or the other of the two moments, but of two different types of classicity. Do they correspond to the two senses of form described by Wölfflin? Are they two moments of form itself?

Wölfflin's criterion of discrimination is furnished by the concept of line and thus by the antithesis of definite and indefinite (or linear-painterly). Now, it may be argued that art is the experience of the world in its totality, the totality being enclosed in an image. The artist finds himself confronted with the infinite world, but he does not remain in a state of aesthetic contemplation. What to the Romantics seemed to be an infinite approximation of the inexpressible infinite, infinite nostalgia, and presentiment is a single moment of creation. The artist can linger and indulge himself in an uncertain, magical atmosphere in which everything is attenuated and confused or in which all, even the insignificant, takes on a strange importance. But in a second moment, the world will assume outlines, will become a plastic image, definite and clear. Not that one perceives an isolated part of it: the artist always grasps the whole universe which is then broken down and consolidated into a concrete image. This process of determination turns upon a center: the world is concentrated and organized in an individuality. This individuality can remain faded and evanescent. Instead of having a nucleus, it can be dispersed into many creations and directions, especially if the artist is not afraid of imposing limits upon his experience. When reality is presented with such distinctness, the spectacle is transfigured into a starburst of ideality, while remaining at the same time truthful and real. The cosmic experience continues to flutter around the image, to circulate in it and to nurture it. The finite is not the negation of the infinite, because if that were so, the finite would be dead and abstract; it is always the infinite itself which the artist perceives and offers to us. But if the original experience is defective and the plastic intervention too violent, the finite will seem to be detached from the whole and thus geometrically defined and limited.

Now, since the destinies of nations are diverse, one might even admit that northern and southern vacillate between the two moments, one moving out of the cosmic moment of infinity, the other being based upon the victorious affirmation of the limited. It will not surprise us that the land of humanism seems inclined to favour the figure and that the land of mysticism and the Reformation remains fascinated with the diffuse and unlimited, with the mysterious in nature. Only in such a sense and within such limits could the atavistic optical schemata of Wölfflin be justified as a description of the dialectic of the creative act.

Notes

INTRODUCTION

[1] Ernst Cassirer, *The Myth of the State* (New Haven, 1946), p. 254.

[2] *Ibid.*, p. 225.

[3] The best discussion of historicism as a concept peculiar to German thought may be found in Walter Hofer, *Geschichtschreibung und Weltanschauung: Betrachtungen zum Werk Friedrich Meineckes* (München, 1950), pp. 326-411. The best discussion of historicism in the general frame of European thought is Carlo Antoni, *Lo storicismo* (Roma, 1957) and his *La lotta contra la ragione* (Firenze, 1942). See also the exhaustive compendium of Pietro Rossi, *Lo storicismo tedesco contemporaneo* (Firenze, 1956) and Manlio Ciardo, *Le quattro epoche dello storicismo* (Bari, 1947). It is unfortunate that Karl Popper chose the term "historicism" to denote an intellectual frame which is only a species of the genus. He regards historicism as any form of monism, failing to recognize that historicism may take many forms. See his perceptive study of this one aspect of historicism in *The Poverty of Historicism* (London and Boston, 1957).

[4] See R. G. Collingwood, *The Idea of History* (New York, 1956), pp. 88-93.

[5] Benedetto Croce, *History as the Story of Liberty*, English translation by Sylvia Sprigge of *La storia come pensiero e come azione* (New York, 1955), pp. 132-38.

[6] See the excellent analysis of Burckhardt's thought in *ibid.*, pp. 93-103.

[7] Collingwood, *op. cit.*, pp. 165-170.

[8] *Ibid.*, pp. 190-94, for a discussion of Croce's essay. See the *Estetica come scienza dell'espressione e linguistica generale* (9th ed., Bari, 1950), pp. 28-36.

[9] Collingwood, *op. cit.*, p. 194.

[10] *Ibid.*

[11] *Ibid.* See Croce, *Logica come scienza del concetto puro* (3rd ed., Bari, 1917), pp. 91-120, 189-222.

[12] *Ibid.*, pp. 210-21.

[13] *Ibid.*, pp. 223-43.

[14] Carlo Antoni, "Benedetto Croce. In Memoriam: Three Years after his Death, November 20th, 1953," *Scienza Nuova*, nos. 3-4 (1956-57), p. 102. See also Antoni, *Commento a Croce* (Venezia, 1955), p. 66 ff.

[15] Croce, *History as the Story of Liberty*, p. 35 ff.

[16] *Ibid.*, pp. 312-17.

230   FROM HISTORY TO SOCIOLOGY

CHAPTER I

[1] Preface to *Der junge Dilthey. Ein Lebensbild in Briefen und Tage-bücher, 1852-70* (Leipzig and Berlin, 1933).

[2] G. Misch, " Vorbericht " to Vol. V of *Gesammelte Schriften* (Leipzig and Berlin, 1924), p. xxxi.

[3] G. Masur, " Wilhelm Dilthey und die europäische Geistesgeschichte," *Deutsche Vierteljahresschrift f. Literaturwissenschaft u. Geistesgeschichte,* IV (1934), 502.

[4] " Das achtzehnte Jahrhundert und die geschichtliche Welt," *Deutsche Rundschau* (May, 1911); reprinted in *Ges. Schrift.* (Leipzig and Berlin, 1927), III, 224.

[5] G. Masur, *op. cit.,* p. 483.

[6] *Briefwechsel zwischen W. Dilthey und dem Grafen P. York v. Wartenburg* (Halle, 1923), p. vi.

[7] *Das Leben Schleiermachers,* Vol. I (1867 and 1870; 2nd ed., 1922).

[8] G. De Ruggiero, " Note sulla piu recente filosofia europea. IX. G. Dilthey," *La Critica,* XXVIII, No. 6 (1930), 433.

[9] Rigutini-Bulle translates *Erlebnis* as " life experience." In reality the word belongs to that group of expressions so peculiarly German that it is untranslatable.

[10] See E. Rothacker, *Einleitung in die Geisteswissenschaften* (2nd ed., Tübingen, 1930).

[11] " Einleitung in die Geisteswissenschaften," in *Ges. Schrift.* (Leipzig and Berlin, 1922), I.

[12] " Die Einbildungskraft des Dichters " (1887), in *Ges. ,Schrift.* (Leipzig and Berlin, 1924), VI.

[13] " Die drei Epochen der modernen Aesthetik und ihrer heutige Aufgabe " (1892), in *Ges. Schrift.,* VI.

[14] " Beitrage zur Lösung der Frage vom Ursprung unseres Glaubens an die Realität der Aussenwelt und seinem Recht " (1890), in *Ges. Schrift.,* V.

[15] " Erfahren und Denken " (1892), in *Ges. Schrift.,* V.

[16] " Das geschichtliche Bewusstsein und die Weltanschauungen," in *Ges. Schrift.,* III.

[17] *Ideen über eine beschreibende und zergliedernde Psychologie* (1894).

[18] There have been many recent attempts to interpret Dilthey's thought in an extensive sense and to turn it into metaphysics. See G. Misch, *Lebensphilosophie und Phänomenologie* (2nd ed., Leipzig and Berlin, 1931); O. F. Bollnow, " Die Lehre von den Typen d. Weltanschauung," *Neue Jahrbücher,* 4 (1934); J. Stenzel, " Dilthey und die deutsche Philosophie der Gegenwart," *Philos. Vorträge d. Kant-Gesellschaft* (Berlin, 1934), p. 33; D.

Bischoff, *Wilhelm Diltheys geschichtliche Lebensphilosophie* (Leipzig and Berlin, 1935). It has been argued that the ego and the world are, according to Dilthey, conjoined in the indissoluble unity of life, because he used the terms *Weltanschauung* and *Lebensanschauung* indiscriminately. But he did this much too infrequently to justify the belief that to him they were identical. On the contrary, the two terms were not at all synonymous for him: he used the first term to indicate the presence of the cognitive moment; with the second he stressed the emotive moment. Since the whole never lacks either of the two moments, Dilthey could use the terms indifferently, recurring from time to time to the term *Welt-und Lebensansicht* for purposes of exactitude.

When Dilthey affirms that the inner life and the pure external world are never given but are always presented in a vital relation, he only means to put forth the obvious principle that there is no subject without an object and vice versa. But he gives a psychophysical meaning to the principle. That is, he never denied the psychophysics of Fechner, which he cultivated in his youth: the external stimuli act on consciousness, which, in its turn, reacts with sentiments and acts of will. Therefore, there is, for Dilthey, an incessant relation of action-reaction between the ego and the environment in a physio-psychological sense. From time to time he evinces a hope that the multiplicity and variety of our spiritual life can offer us some indications of the nature of objective reality, but beyond this he is unwilling to go. However, the two terms " ego " and " world," even if life is a fecund exchange between them, remain, for him, two entities: objective reality is derived from our direct consciousness, and life does not embrace and comprehend it. To claim that for Dilthey life and the world are the same thing is to attribute to a few individual sentences (existing for the most part in manuscript notes) an importance which is justified neither by their context nor even less by the general attitude informing Dilthey's thought.

[19] " Beitrage zum Studium der Individualität (1896) , in *Ges. Schrift.* V.

[20] " Die Entstehung der Hermeneutik " (1900) , in *Ges. Schrift.,* V.

[21] " Zur seelischen Struktur " (1905) , in *Ges. Schrift.,* V.

[22] " Die Abgrenzung der Geisteswissenschaften," in *Ges. Schrift.,* V.

[23] " Der Aufbau der Geisteswissenschaften," in *Ges. Schrift.,* V.

[24] " Entwürfe zur Kritik der historischen Vernunft," fragments published in *Ges. Schrift.* (Leipzig and Berlin, 1927) , VII.

[25] In the discourse delivered on his seventieth birthday, Dilthey stated that he regarded as his greatest claim to fame his discovery of real time. The analogous discovery of Bergson comes immediately to mind. However, no matter what similarities may be found between *Erlebnis* and *durée*, the anti-intellectual character of Bergson, who tends to deprive *durée* of any

conceptual element, is completely opposed to Dilthey's concept insofar as the latter is intent upon discovering the seeds of the "construction" in the *Erlebnis*.

[26] G. Misch, "Vorwort" to Vol. II of *Ges. Schrift.* (Leipzig and Berlin, 1921), p. vi.

[27] Collected under the title "Weltanschauung u. Analyse d. Menschen seit Renaissance und Reformation," in *Ges Schrift.*, II.

[28] "Zur Würdigung der Reformation," in *Ges Schrift.*, II.

[29] "Das natürliche System der Geisteswissenschaften im 17. Jahrhundert," in *Ges. Schrift.*, II.

[30] "Die Autonomie des Denkens, der konstruktive Rationalismus u. der pantheistische Monismus nach ihrem Zusammenhang im 17. Jahrh.," in *Ges. Schrift.*, II.

[31] *Die drei Grundformen der Systeme in der ersten Hälfte des neunzehnten Jahrhunderts.*

[32] *Das Wesen der Philosophie* (1907).

[33] "Die Typen der Weltanschauungen u. ihre Ausbildung in den metaphysischen Systemen" (1911), in *Ges. Schrift.* (Leipzig and Berlin, 1931), VIII.

[34] In 1905 Dilthey considered writing a biography of Hegel, but he stopped while still working on the first chapter. The impulse behind the composition of this "Youth of Hegel" was provided by the abundant papers available in the Berlin State Archives. He wished to repeat the sort of work he had done on Schleiermacher, reconstructing the formative process from the sources. As early as 1888, in a review of an edition of Hegel's letters, he had written: "The time of battle is over; the time for an historical appraisal of Hegel has come. Historical investigation will reveal what is living and what is dead in his thought." However, Hegel always remained for Dilthey a dark zone in the history of the German spirit. As a specialist in metaphysics he limited himself to a study of the Hegel "case."

To Hegelian studies he brought a contribution not unlike that which he had made to the understanding of Schleiermacher: also, in the life of Hegel he discovered a hitherto ignored youthful phase, a period of mystical pantheism.

The polemical strain of the biography is curious. Dilthey proposed to confute the creator of the dialectical method not *ex ore suo* but *e vita sua.* Thus, he demonstrates the absence of a linear development from Fichte, stressing instead a plurality of formative factors: first among all is that pantheism borrowed from Shaftesbury and Hemsterhuys, which had operated also in Schleiermacher. In Hegel, such pantheism had a more decisively mystical character, so as to allow his immersion in the Johannine Gospel (from which the concept of the "Spirit"), Eckhart and Tauler, and the construction of a system akin to that of Plotinus.

J. Stenzel, in a study of the relation between Hegel and Dilthey, " Ueber Diltheys Verhältnis zu Hegel," in *Die Idee* (Haarlem, 1934), insists upon a generic affinity which, in our view, is to be found in every major thinker of the nineteenth century.

[35] P. Ritter, " Vorwort " to " Studien zu Geschichte d. deutschen Geistes," in *Ges. Schrift.*, III.

[36] " Die germanische Welt," in *Von deutscher Dichtung u. Musik* (Leipzig and Berlin, 1933).

[37] " Die grosse deutsche Musik des 18. Jahrhunderts," in *Von deutscher Dichtung u. Musik.*

[38] " Friedrich der Grosse u. die deutsche Aufklärung," in *Ges. Schrift.*, III.

[39] " Leibnitz u. sein Zeitalter," in *Ges. Schrift.*, III.

[40] " Pädagogik, Geschichte und Grundlinien des Systems," in *Ges. Schrift.*, IX.

[41] *Briefwechsel zwischen W. Dilthey u. dem Grafen P. York v. Wartenburg*, p. 125.

[42] *Ibid.*, p. 139.

[43] *Ibid.*, p. 146.

CHAPTER II

[1] " Meine Bücher," in *Die deutsche Philosophie der Gegenwart in Selbstdarstellungen* (Leipzig, 1922), II, reprinted in *Gesammelte Schriften* (Tübingen, 1925), IV.

[2] See " Protestantisches Christentum und Kirche in der Neuzeit," in *Die Kultur der Gegenwart* (2nd ed., Leipzig and Berlin, 1922).

[3] See *Der Historismus und seine Probleme* (Tübingen, 1922), p. ix.

[4] *Vernunft und Offenbarung bei Johann Gerhard und Melancthon* (Göttingen, 1891).

[5] Only one of them is contained in Vol. II of *Ges. Schrift.*: *Zur religiösen Lage, Religionsphilosophie und Ethik* (Tübingen, 1913).

[6] " Religion und Kirche," *Preuss. Jahrbücher* (1895), reprinted in *Ges. Schrift.*, II.

[7] For Troeltsch, Nietzsche was, like Spinoza, the *philosophus atheissimus*, who would appear one day as a religious spirit athirst more than any other for the divine. See " Aus des religiösen Bewegung der Gegenwart " (1910), in *Ges. Schrift.*, II.

[8] See Troeltsch, " Rückblick auf ein halbes Jahrhundert der theologischen Wissenschaft," *Zeitsch. f. wiss. Theologie* (1908); reprinted in *Ges. Schrift.*, II.

[9] See L. Salvatorelli, " Da Locke a Reitzenstein," *Rivista Storica Italiana*, XLVI, 1-2 (1928-29).

[10] " Prot. Christentum u. Kirche in d. Neuzeit," in *Die Kultur der Gegenwart*," p. 742.

[11] " Die christliche Weltanschauung und ihre Gegenströmungen," *Zeitsch. f. Theologie und Kirche* (1894) ; reprinted in *Ges. Schrift.*, II.

[12] " Meine Bücher."

[13] See A. Liebert, " E. Troeltsch, Der Historismus und seine Ueberwindung," *Kant-Studien*, XXIX, 3-4 (1924).

[14] " Die Bedeutung des Begriffs der Kontingenz," in *Encyclopedia of Religion and Ethics* (1910) ; reprinted in *Ges. Schriften*, II.

[15] " Voraussetzungslose Wissenschaft," *Die Christliche Welt* (1897) ; reprinted in *Ges. Schrift.*, II.

[16] " Aus der religösen Bewegungen der Gegenwart," *Die neue Rundschau* (1910) ; reprinted in *Ges. Schrift.*, II.

[17] " Gewissensfreiheit," *Die Christliche Welt* (1911) ; reprinted in *Ges. Schrift.*, II.

[18] " Religion und Kirche," *Preuss. Jahrbücher* (1895) ; reprinted in *Ges. Schrift.*, II.

[19] " Richard Rothe," in *Gedächtnisrede* (Tübingen, 1900).

[20] " Die Zukunftmöglichkeiten des Christentums im Verhältnis zur modernen Philosophie," *Logos* (1910) ; reprinted in *Ges. Schrift.*, II.

[21] " Religiöser Individualismus und Kirche," *Prot. Monatshefte* (1911) ; reprinted in *Ges. Schrift.*, II.

[22] *Die Kirche im Leben der Gegenwart, in Weltanschauung, Philosophie u. Religion*, ed. by Friescheisen-Kohler (Berlin, 1911) ; reprinted in *Ges. Schrift.*, II.

[23] " Die Mission in der modernen Welt," *Die Christliche Welt* (1906) ; reprinted in *Ges. Schrift.*, II.

[24] " Die Religion im deutschen Staate," *Patria* (1912) ; reprinted in *Ges. Schrift.*, II.

[25] " Der Modernismus," *Die neue Rundschau* (1909) ; reprinted in *Ges. Schrift.*, II.

[26] K. Heussi has questioned the appropriateness of the title of the German edition of the lectures destined for the English public but never given due to Troeltsch's death: " Der Historismus und seine Ueberwindung." See *Die Krisis der Historismus* (Tübingen, 1932), p. 14.

[27] " Die Zukunftsmöglichkeiten des Christentums," in *Ges. Schrift.*, II.

[28] *Die wissenschaftliche Lage und ihre Anforderungen an die Theologie* (Tübingen, 1900).

[29] See Troeltsch, " Die theologische und religiöse Lage der Gegenwart," *Deutsche Monatschrift für das gesamte Leben der Gegenwart* (1903) ; reprinted in *Ges. Schrift.*, II.

[30] *Das Historische in Kants Religionsphilosophie* (Berlin, 1904).

[31] " Wesen der Religion und der Religionswissenschaft," in *Kultur der Gegenwart* (2nd ed., 1909), I, 4.

[32] " Religionsphilosophie," in *Die Philosophie im Beginn des Zwanzigsten Jahrhunderts, Festschrift für Kuno Fischer* (Heidelberg, 1904), Vol. I.

[33] " Ueber historische und dogmatische Methode in der Theologie," *Studien des rheinischen Predigervereins* (1898) ; in *Ges. Schrift.*, II.

[34] " Die Dogmatik der ' religionsgeschichtlichen Schule,' " (1913) ; in *Ges. Schrift.*, II.

[35] "'Was heisst ' Wesen des Christentums ' ? " *Die Christliche Welt* (1903), in *Ges. Schrift.*, II.

[36] Tübingen, 1902.

[37] " Ueber historische und dogmatische Methode in der Theologie," *Studien des rheinischen Predigervereins* (1898), in *Ges. Schrift.*, II.

[38] *Die wissenschaftliche Lage und ihre Anforderung an die Theologie* (Tübingen, 1900).

[39] *Die Bedeutung des Protestantismus für die Entstehung der modernen Welt* (Munich and Berlin, 1906; 5th ed., 1928).

[40] *Kultur der Gegenwart.*

[41] " Meiner Bücher."

[42] In *Ges. Schrift.*, I (Tübingen, 1912; reprinted, 1919 and 1923).

[43] See the review of *Calvinismus und Kapitalismus* by Rachfals in *Ges. Schrift.*, IV, 783-801.

[44] " Religion, Wirtschaft und Gesellschaft " (1913) in *Ges. Schrift.*, IV.

[45] *Glaubenslehre*, a course held at Heidelberg in 1911-12, published by Martha Troeltsch (Munich and Leipzig, 1925).

[46] Collected by H. Baron in *Ges. Schrift.*, IV (Tübingen, 1925).

[47] See A. Passerin d'Entreves, " Il concetto del diritto naturale cristiano e la sua storia secondo E. Troeltsch," *Atti di R. Accademia di scienze di Torino*, LXI (1926), 644-704.

[48] However, there is lacking in the *Soziallehren* any discussion of Eastern Christianity, as there is lacking a discussion of Anglicanism and post-Tridentine Catholicism.

[49] See besides the *Soziallehren*, the essays " Epochen und Typen der Sozialphilosophie des Christentums," and " Das stoisch-christliche Naturrecht und das moderne profane Naturrecht," in *Ges. Schrift.*, IV.

[50] *Augustin, die christliche Antike und das Mittelalter* (Munich and Berlin, 1915).

[51] *Der Historismus und seine Uberwindung* (Berlin, 1924).

[52] See Heussi, *Die Krisis der Historismus.*

[53] " Der Historismus und seine Probleme," *Ges. Schrift.*, III. The works collected in this volume belong to the period 1917-21.

[54] *Die neue Rundschau*, XXXIII (1922), 573.

[55] *Der Historismus und seine Uberwindung*, p. 66.

[56] See G. Gentile, " The Transcending of Time in History," in *Philosophy and History, Essays Presented to Ernst Cassirer* (Oxford, 1936).

CHAPTER III

[1] *Leben des Generalfeldmarschalls von Boyen* (Stuttgart, 1896-99), II, 390. Earlier, Meinecke had published an investigation of an episode in Prussian history, *Stralendorffsche Gutachten und Jülicher Erbfolgestreit* (Potsdam, 1886), and a monograph on the political associations of the era of the anti-Napoleonic wars: *Die deutschen Gesellschaften und der Hoffmannsche Bund* (Stuttgart, 1891).

[2] " Boyen und Roon," *Historische Zeitschrift*, LXXVII (1896); reprinted in *Von Stein zu Bismarck* (Berlin, 1909).

[3] " Heinrich von Treitschke," *Hist. Zeitsch.*, LXXVII (1896); reprinted in *Von Stein zu Bismarck.*

[4] Meinecke denies any influence on Boyen of his master Christian J. Kraus, the apostle of Adam Smith in Germany. However, it is impossible to deny the influence of English politico-economic thought and practice on Stein.

[5] This is the theme, as is well known, of the *Römische Geschichte* of Niebuhr, the patriot and collaborator of Stein.

[6] Published in *Der Protestantismus am Ende des XIX Jahrhunderts*, ed. by C. Werkshagen (Leipzig, 1901); reprinted in *Von Stein zu Bismarck*. The title may be translated as " Patriotic and Religions Uplift in the Early 19th Century."

[7] Munich and Berlin, 1907.

[8] *Hist. Zeitsch.*, LXXXII (1898); reprinted in *Von Stein zu Bismarck.*

[9] In a popular volume, *Das Zeitalter der deutschen Erhebung* (Leipzig and Bielefeld, 1906), Meinecke renewed his criticism of the ideas informing Stein's faction which had been "more ethical than political." Stein had erred, it was argued, in extolling Germany as a powerful political community which would serve to protect the civil life from despotism and Europe from the threat of French tyranny.

[10] " Preussen und Deutschland im neunzehnten Jahrhundert," a lecture delivered at the Congress of German Historians in Stuttgart, April 19, 1906, and published in *Hist. Zeitsch.*, XCVII (1906); reprinted in *Preussen und Deutschland im neunzehnten und zwanzigsten Jahrhundert* (Munich and Berlin, 1918).

[11] *Radowitz und die deutsche Revolution* (Berlin, 1913).

[12] "Landwehr und Landsturm seit 1814"; reprinted in *Schmollers Jahrbuch*, Vol. XL, and in *Preussen und Deutschland im neunzehnten und zwanzigsten Jahrhundert*.

[13] "Am Vorabend der Revolution," *Deutsche Allgemeine Zeitung*, November 20, 1918; reprinted in *Nach der Revolution: Geschichtliche Betrachtungen über unsere Lage* (Munich and Berlin, 1919).

[14] "Der nationale Gedanke im alten und neuen Deutschland," written in December, 1918 and published in *Deutscher Wille* (February, 1919); reprinted in *Nach der Revolution*.

[15] *Ibid.*

[16] "Weltgeschichtliche Parallelen unserer Lage," in *Gerechtigkeit* (August, 1919); reprinted in *Nach der Revolution*.

[17] *Geschichte des deutsch-englischen Bündnisproblems* (Munich and Berlin, 1927); *Probleme des Weltkrieges* (Munich and Berlin, 1927). See also the collection edited by Meinecke, *Deutschland und der Weltkrieg*.

[18] Third ed. (Munich and Berlin, 1929), p. 488.

[19] *La Critica*, XXIII, 118-22, and *Storia della età barocca in Italia* (Bari, 1929), p. 95. See also F. Chabod, "Uno storico tedesco contemporaneo: Frederico Meinecke," *Nuova rivista storica*, XI (1927).

[20] Already in "Persönlichkeit und geschichtliche Welt," a lecture delivered in January, 1918 (2nd ed., Berlin, 1923), Meinecke discussed the "obscure fates and subterranean powers which invade the life of the spirit" and asserted that "freedom and necessity act not only against one another but also in one another."

[21] "Aus der Entstehungsgeschichte des deutschen Nationalstaatsgedankens," *Velhagen und Klasings Monatschrifte* (1907); reprinted in *Preussen und Deutschland im neunzehnten und zwanzigsten Jahrhundert*.

[22] "Jakob Burckhardt, die deutsche Geschichtsschreibung und der nationale Staat," *Hist. Zeitsch.*, XCVII (1906); reprinted in *Von Stein zu Bismarck*.

[23] "Herder, Goethe, Wilhelm von Humboldt and the Romantics discovered the inexpressible worth of the individual which grew originally and singularly in life and history. . . . Frederick the Great possessed a physiognomy almost totally foreign, even antipathetic, to Goethe, Schiller, Kant and Fichte . . . but he was for them a life experience. . . . He not only strengthened their national consciousness and their pride in being Germans, but— of this they had even greater need—he strengthened their opinion that it was a task and a duty to break the barriers of convention, the prejudices of the age, and to become men according to one's own law."—*Persönlichkeit und geschichtliche Welt*.

[24] K. Heussi has listed six meanings of the term in *Die Krisis des Historismus* (Tübingen, 1932).

238 FROM HISTORY TO SOCIOLOGY

²⁵ (Munich and Berlin, 1936).

²⁶ E. Seeberg, " Zur Entstehung des Historismus: Gedanken zu Friedrich Meineckes jüngstem Werk," *Hist. Zeitsch.*, CLVII (1938).

²⁷ In *Persönlichkeit und geschichtliche Welt*, he defined personality as " a world in itself which is still linked organically to the great world," spoke of the " solid barriers between internal and external which ought to be maintained without hermetically sealing the internal from the external while at the same time regulating the traffic between them," and added: " in their reciprocal action, in their affirmation of themselves the one against the other and in their indissoluble cooperation the historical life evolves."

CHAPTER IV

¹ K. Jaspers, " Max Weber, deutsche Wesen im politischen Denken," *Forschen und Philosophieren* (Oldenburg, 1932).

² Marianne Weber, *Max Weber, ein Lebensbild* (Tübingen, 1926). See also *Bedeutende Männer* (Leipzig, 1927); H. Schumacher, " Max Weber," *Deutsche biographische Jahrbuch* (Berlin and Leipzig, 1928); E. Sestan, " Max Weber," *Nuovi studi di diritto, economia, e politica*, VI-VII, nos. 3-6 (1933-34).

³ *Zur Geschichte des Handelsgesellschaft im Mittelalter* (Stuttgart, 1889); reprinted in *Gesammelte Aufsätze zur Sozial-und Wirtschaftsgeschichte* (Tübingen, 1924).

⁴ *Der Sozialismus* (Vienna, 1918); reprinted in *Gesammelte Aufsätze zur Soziologie und Sozialpolitik* (Tübingen, 1924).

⁵ *Politik als Beruf* (Munich, 1919); reprinted in *Ges. politische Schriften* (Munich, 1921); *Wissenschaft als Beruf* (Munich, 1919), reprinted in *Ges. Aufsätze zur Wissenschaftslehre* (Tübingen, 1922).

⁶ *Jugendbriefe* (Tübingen, 1937).

⁷ " Die rationalen und soziologischen Grundlagen der Musik," in *Wirtschaft und Gesellschaft* (Tübingen, 1922).

⁸ " Roscher und Knies und die logischen Probleme der historischen Nationalökonomie," *Schmollers Jahrbuch* (1903-1906); reprinted in *Ges. Aufsätze zur Wissenschaftslehre* (Tübingen, 1922).

⁹ Marianne Weber *op,. cit.*, p. 121.

¹⁰ *Die römische Agrargeschichte in ihrer Bedeutung für das Staats-und Privatrecht* (Stuttgart, 1891). Italian translation Pareto, *Biblioteca di storia economica* (Milan, 1907), II, 2.

¹¹ See *Die sozialen Gründe des Unterganges der antiken Kultur* (Stuttgart, 1896); reprinted in *Ges. Aufsätze zur Soz.-und Wirtschaftsgeschichte*.

¹² See " Die ländliche Arbeitsverfassung " (1893), and " Entwicklungsten-

denzen in der Lage der ostelbischen Landarbeiter" (1894); both reprinted in *Ges. Aufsätze zur Soz.-und Wirtschaftsgeschichte.*

[13] Weber returned to the agrarian problem in order to combat the growth of the so-called enfeoffment in trust in which he saw a capital investment for the formation of assured high incomes which, through the purchase of the best lands, would force a rise in prices and trap the peasant in the sterile zones. See his "Agrargeschichte und sozial-politische Betrachtungen zur Fideikommissfrage in Preussen" (1904), reprinted in *Ges. Aufsätze zur Soziologie und Sozialpolitik.* This institution was particularly offensive to him in that it was a means by which an enriched middle class might aspire to the brevet of nobility; this meant that thousands of hectares of the best land of Germany were sacrificed to the vanity of the new rich. During the World War, the Prussian government could think of nothing better than to undertake the revival of the enfeoffment in trust. Weber protested against the plan because it would withhold land from the peasant soldiery and redound to the benefit of profiteers, who sought to screen their motives and gains under the guise of aristocratic investment. See "Die Nobilitierung der Kriegsgewinne" (1917); reprinted in *Ges. pol. Schrift.* (Munich, 1921). The project was withdrawn.

[14] "Der Nationalstaat und die Volkswirtschaft" (1895), in *Ges. pol. Schrift.*

[15] This was the time in which the preacher Stöcker launched his attacks against financial speculation. The struggle was taken up by the *Junker,* who wished to see the time contract on wheat abolished. In a work composed for Naumann's "Worker's Library," *Die Börse* (Göttingen, 1894), Weber argued that the bourse was the typical form of modern business transaction and indispensable to large scale commerce. He examined the question of speculation from the viewpoint of the financial power of the nation, and, while demanding restrictive measures which would exclude speculators without funds, he held that the elimination of the time contract would undermine the national economic market to the advantage of foreign financiers.

[16] "Wahlrecht und Demokratie in Deutschland" (1917); reprinted in *Ges. pol. Schrift.*

[17] "Parliament und Regierung im neugeordneten Deutschland" (1917); reprinted in *Ges. pol. Schrift.* Italian translation by E. Ruta (Bari, 1919).

[18] E. Ruta, *op. cit.,* preface.

[19] *Politik als Beruf.* See O. F., "Democrazia e capitalismo nell'opera di Max Weber," *Lo Stato,* IX, nos. 7-9 (1938).

[20] "Bismarcks Aussenpolitik und die Gegenwart" (1915); reprinted in *Ges. pol. Schrift.*

[21] Letters to F. Naumann of 1906-1908; in *Ges. pol. Schrift.*

[22] *Politik als Beruf.*

[23] *Ibid.*

[24] "Deutschland unter den europäischen Weltmächten" (1916), in *Ges. pol. Schrift.*

[25] "Zwischen zwei Gesetzen" (1916), in *Ges. pol. Schrift.*

[26] "Diskussionsreden auf den Tagungen d. Vereins für Sozialpolitik" (1905); reprinted in *Ges. Aufsätze zur Soziologie und Sozialpolitik.*

[27] "Zwischen zwei Gesetzen."

[28] *Wissenschaft als Beruf.*

[29] "Zwischen zwei Gesetzen."

[30] *Politik als Beruf.*

[31] "Diskussionsreden."

[32] "Energetische Kulturtheorien" (1909); reprinted in *Ges. Aufsätze zur Wissenschaftslehre.*

[33] See G. De Ruggiero, "La filosofia dei valori in Germania," *La Critica*, IX-X (1911-12) and *La filosofia contemporanea* (Bari, 1920), I, 78-86.

[34] *Wissenschaft als Beruf.*

[35] *Ibid.*

[36] *Der Sozialismus.*

[37] E. R. Curtius, *Deutscher Geist in Gefahr* (Stuttgart, 1932), p. 83.

[38] R. Michel, *Bedeutende Männer* (Leipzig, 1927).

[39] "Die protestantische Ethik und der Geist des Kapitalismus," *Archiv für Sozialwissenschaft und Sozialpolitik*, 1904-1905; reprinted in *Ges. Aufsätze zur Religionssoziologie*, I (Tübingen, 1920, 3rd ed. 1934). See also "Die protestantische Sekten und der Geist des Kapitalismus" (1906).

[40] There is an excellent resumé of the argument and estimates of the polemic (Troeltsch, Fischer, Sée, Wünsch, Sombart) in M. M. Rossi, *L'ascesi capitalistica* (Rome, 1928). There is a bibliography in A. Fanfani, "Riforma e capitalismo moderno nella recente letteratura," *Rivista internazionale di scienze sociali* (July, 1930). See also Fanfani's *Cattolicesimo e Protestantesimo nella formazione storica del capitalismo* (Milan, 1934) and E. Sestan, "Max Weber," *Nuovi Studi di diritto economica e politica*, III, nos. 4-6 (1933-34).

[41] "Ethik und Volkswirtschaft in der Geschichte" (1901); reprinted in *Der wirtschaftliche Mensch in der Geschichte* (Leipzig, 1923).

[42] L. Brentano, "Puritanismus und Kapitalismus," in *Wirtschaftende Mensch in der Geschichte* (Leipzig, 1923).

[43] Another descendant of the bourgeois patriciate, Thomas Mann, found in the idea of the ascetico-protestant origins of the modern business man the ideas to which he gave expression in the figure of Thomas Buddenbrook. See G. v. Below, *Probleme der Wirtschaftsgeschichte* (2nd ed., Tübingen, 1926), p. 434.

[44] See the reviews by Croce and Weber of Stammler's *Wirtschaft und*

Recht nach der materialistischen Geschichtsauffassung: B. Croce, " Il libro del prof. Stammler," in *Materialismo storico ed economia marxistica* (5th ed., Bari, 1927) , pp. 115-30; Max Weber, " R. Stammlers ' Ueberwindung,' der materialistischen Geschichtsauffassung," in *Ges. Aufsätze zur Wissenschaftslehre.*

[45] " But he never succeeded in overcoming the last barrier and bringing under examination a concrete case of a thorough-going follower of these determined doctrines, one who was also notoriously an asserter of life and of capitalistic sentiments in his economic activity."—E. Sestan, *op. cit.*, p. 389.

[46] One should not forget the interest aroused among the theologians and sociologists of the Heidelberg group—then discussing Marxist theory and centered around Weber and Troeltsch—by Volpe's studies of the heretical sects of the Middle Ages.

[47] L. Brentano, *op. cit.*

[48] H. M. Robertson, *The Rise of Economic Individualism* (Cambridge, 1933) .

[49] See A. Fanfani, *Cattolicesimo e Protestantesimo,* which gives a summary of the criticisms advanced by Robertson, Tawney, Bains, etc.

[50] Fanfani's thesis is most unconvincing. Here Calvinism is presented as having furthered the triumph of the capitalistic phenomenon with its idea of predestination by making the individual feel himself authorized to act according to his own selfish interests and to ignore former fears and scruples. It is impossible to see Calvinism as a religion of license: " puritan " and " Quaker " are still synonyms for rigid morality, even for narrowmindedness and heartlessness; but it always included distinctions between licit and illicit actions.

[51] Calvin, *Institutiones*, III, 7.

[52] It may be noted, however, that it was found preeminently in the mystics of the late Middle Ages. See J. Huizinga, *Herbst des Mittelalters* (2nd ed., Munich, 1928) .

[53] " Die protestantische Ethik," p. 112.

[54] See M. M. Rossi, *op. cit.*, p. 78.

[55] In the Ordinances of 1547 it is stated that no one might lend usuriously or at a profit greater than five per cent without suffering confiscation of property or a fine set at the discretion of the authorities. See R. Freschi, *Giovanni Calvino* (Milan, 1934) , II, 682-87. At the same time, the Catholic, De Moulin, justified interest in his *Traité de l'usure et des rentes constituées,* and many therefore wish to attribute to him the honor of having surmounted the objections. However, it is well to remember that the authority of a simple publicist is one thing; that of the founder of a new church and a famous teacher is another. The coincidence does show, however, that the idea was already in the air.

[56] G. Luzzatto, *Storia economica, L'età moderna* (Padua, 1934).

[57] See B. Croce, "Calvinismo e operosità economica," *La Critica*, XXXVI, no. 5 (1938).

[58] "Die Wirtschaftsethik der Weltreligionen," *Archiv für Sozialwissenschaft und Sozialpolitik* (1915-19); reprinted in *Ges. Aufsätze zur Religionssoziologie*. The entire work is composed of one volume on the religions of China (3rd ed., Tübingen, 1934), a second on the religions of India (2nd ed., 1923), and a third, uncompleted, on Judaism (2nd ed., 1923). Ultimately the work was to have included a volume on Christianity and also one on Islam.

[59] Also Weber attributed a decisive historical importance in the development of the West to the rationalistic character of the feudal contract, seeing it as the destroyer of the irrational bonds of the *Sippe*.

[60] "Roscher und Knies und die logischen Probleme der historischen Nationalökonomie," *Schmollers Jahrbuch* (1903-1906); "Die Objektivität sozialwissenschaftlicher und sozialpolitischer Erkenntnis" and "Kritische Studien auf dem Gebiet der Kulturwissenschaftlichen Logik," both in *Archiv für Sozialwissenschaft und ,Sozialpolitik* (1904-1905) and reprinted in *Ges. Aufsätze zur Wissenschaftslehre* (Tübingen, 1922).

[61] On the history of the concept of the type, see H. Grab, *Der Begriff des Rationalen in der Soziologie Max Webers* (Karlsruhe, 1927); W. Bienfait, *Max Webers Lehre vom geschichtlichen Erkennen* (Berlin, 1930); A. von Schelting, *Max Webers Wissenschaftslehre* (Tübingen, 1934).

[62] Ultimately Weber's theory results in a conclusion not unlike that of Croce, according to which economic laws are mathematics applied to the concept of action, which submit to calculation certain determinations of actions in order to discover in them necessary configurations and consequences to the end of orienting oneself in empirical reality.

[63] Marianne Weber, *op. cit.*

[64] *Wirtschaft und Gesellschaft* (2nd ed., Tübingen, 1925), p. 11.

[65] R. Aron, *La sociologie allemande contemporaine* (Paris, 1935).

[66] "Ueber einige Kategorien der verstehende Soziologie" (1913); reprinted in *Ges. Aufsätze zur Wissenschaftslehre*.

[67] "Methodische Grundlage der Soziologie," in "*Grundriss der Sozialökonomie*," Part III of *Wirtschaft und Gesellschaft* (Tübingen, 1920); reprinted in *Ges. Aufsätze zur Wissenschaftslehre*.

[68] The canon is also the practical rule for social politics. Weber promoted some investigations in the selection and adaptation of the industrial workers, concentrating upon their provenance and life-traditions and studying the effects of industry upon their way of life. By such investigations he hoped to clarify the situation for both the worker and management and to advance suggestions for labor legislation. See "Methodologische Einleitung für die

Erhebung des Vereins für Sozialpolitik über Auslese und Anpassung der Arbeitsschaft" (1908) and "Zur Psychophysik der industriellen Arbeit" (1908-1909); both reprinted in *Ges. Aufsätze zur Sozialwissenschaft und Sozialpolitik.*

CHAPTER V

[1] *Herbstij der Middeleuwen* (Leyden, 1919, 3rd ed., 1928); German translation, *Herbst des Mittelalters*, by T. Wolff-Monckeberg (Munich, 1924, 2nd ed., 1928); French translation, *Le declin du moyen âge*, by J. Bastin (Paris, 1932); Italian translation, *Autunno del Medioevo* (Florence, 1940); English translation, *The Waning of the Middle Ages*, by F. Hopman (London, 1924, 2nd ed.. 1927, other English editions 1937, 1948, 1950). Huizinga's previous works: *Het aesthetische bastanddeel van geschiedkundige voorstellungen* (Haarlem, 1905); *Over historische levensideal* (Haarlem, 1915).

[2] *Wege der Kulturgeschichte* (Munich, 1930).

[3] *Renaissance und Barock* (Munich, 1888, 2nd ed., 1907).

[4] See B. Croce, *La storia come pensiero e come azione* (Bari, 1938), p. 98.

[5] F. Gundolf, *Caesar*, Italian translation by E. Giovannetti (Milan and Rome, 1932).

[6] (2nd ed., 1925); German translation by W. Kaegi (Munich, 1928).

[7] Also of this period are: *Tien Studien* (Haarlem, 1926); *Leven en werk van Jan Veth* (Haarlem, 1927); *Amerika levend en denkend* (Haarlem, 1927); *Mensch en menigte in Amerika* (Haarlem, 1928).

[8] *Im Schatten von Morgen*, German translation by W. Kaegi (Bern and Leipzig, 1935); Italian translation (Turin, 1937).

[9] *Holländische Kultur des siebzehnten Jahrhunderts* (Leipzig and Berlin, 1933); *Die Mittlerstellung der Niederlande zwischen West und Mitteleuropa* (Leipzig and Berlin, 1933): "La formazione del tipo culturale olandese," *Studi Germanici*, XIII (1935), pp. 22-38.

CHAPTER VI

[1] It would be interesting to study the origin of the Arcadian myth of the Roman Campagna which is the center of the landscape image of Goethe, Humboldt and countless painters. On the image of Italy as a classic land, see C. von Klemze, *The Interpretation of Italy during the Last Two Centuries* (Chicago, 1907), and W. Waetzoldt, *Das klassische Land* (Leipzig, 1927).

[2] H. Wölfflin, *Italien und das deutsche Formgefühl* (Munich, 1931), p. vi.

[3] Preface to *Erinnerungen aus Rubens*, in *Gesammtausgabe der Werke Jakob Burckhardts* (Berlin and Leipzig, 1934), XIII, 369.

[4] For its influence on the interpretation of the German literary baroque, see the article by L. Vincenti in *Studi Germanici*, I, 39, and for its influence on the interpretation of Romanticism, see F. Stritch, *Deutsche Klassik und Romantik* (Leipzig, 1922), and O. F. Walzel, *Idee und Gestalt* (Potsdam, 1925).

[5] Wölfflin defined the tasks and limits of art history in a short essay entitled *Das Erklaren von Kunstwerken* (Leipzig, 1921). He also defined the limits of his theory, which he wished to have coexist with others in a peaceful division of labor. The tasks of art history are four: 1) to teach how to see form by leading to the discovery in works of art of the unity and rhythm of color, line and design and to the correlation of the artist's standpoint to the type of his generation, his regional type, and his national genius; 2) to interpret art historically by taking into account the technical conditions of the material and the socio-economic conditions of the public (but as secondary factors) and by considering art as an expression of a life view, although not always and everywhere in the same degree; 3) to explain why a given form of art developed by rendering account of the organic process of forms, that is, the logic of artistic development; 4) to explain why a work of art is beautiful. For this fourth task Wölfflin appealed to the idea of reliving (*Erleben*), concluding with the words of Burckhardt: "If it were possible to express in words the deepest content or idea of a work of art, art itself would be superfluous, and all buildings, statues and paintings could have remained unbuilt, unfashioned and unpainted."

[6] See K. Joel, *Kant Studien*, XXXII (1927), 491.

[7] See Wölfflin's preface to Burckhardt's *Die Kunst der Renaissance in Italien*, in *Gesammtausgabe der Werke Jakob Burckhardts*, VI, xxvi.

[8] *Renaissance und Barock: Eine Untersuchung über Wesen und Entstehung des Barockstils in Italien* (Munich, 1888, 2nd ed., 1907).

[9] *Ibid.*, p. 53.

[10] *Die Kunst Albrecht Dürers* (Munich, 1905).

[11] Munich, 1886. See Croce, *L'estetica della Einfühlung e Robert Vischer* (Naples, 1934).

[12] *Prolegomena*, p. 34.

[13] W. Waetzoldt, *Deutsche Kunsthistoriker* (Leipzig, 1924), II, 189.

[14] *Renaissance und Barock*, p. 62.

[15] *Die klassische Kunst, Eine Einführung in die italienische Renaissance* (Munich, 1898, 3rd ed., Munich, 1904).

[16] See B. Croce, "La teoria dell'arte come pura visibilità," in *Nuovi saggi di estetica* (2nd ed., Bari, 1926), pp. 233-50.

[17] *A. von Hildebrands Briefwechsel mit C. Fiedler*, ed. by G. Jachmann (Dresden, 1937), p. 172.

[18] A. von Hildebrand, *Das Problem der Form in der bildenden Kunst*

(Strasburg, 1893, 4th ed., 1903), reviewed by Wölfflin upon its appearance in the *Münchener Allgemeine Zeitung*, no. 157 (1893).

[19] *Die klassische Kunst*, p. 2.

[20] " Un tentativo eclettico nella storia delle arti figurative," in *Nuovi saggi di estetica* (2nd ed., Bari, 1926), p. 253.

[21] O. Walzel has sought to demonstrate how the dualities of Wölfflin can be found in W. Schlegel's thought. Schlegel supposedly derived them from the Dutch thinker, Hemsterhuys. See *Vom Geistesleben alter und neuer Zeit* (Leipzig, 1922), p. 85.

[22] See E. Heidrich, *Beiträge zur Geschichte und Methode der Kunstgeschichte* (Basle, 1917).

[23] See W. Passarge, *Die Philosophie der Kunstgeschichte in der Gegenwart* (Berlin, 1930).

[24] Munich, 1915, 5th ed., 1921.

[25] *Geschichte der deutschen Kunst* (4th ed., Berlin and Leipzig), p. 16.

[26] Croce, *Nuovi saggi di estetica*, p. 257.

[27] " Gli schemi del Wölfflin," *L'Esame*, I, no. 1 (April, 1922).

[28] *Italien und das deutsche Formgefühl* (Munich, 1931).

[29] One of the strangest aspects of contemporary German culture is the tendency to attribute importance to the mysterious bond between the land and the soul of its inhabitants: the motif is found in Sombart's economic hisory, in Nadler's literary history, in the touristic-philosophical fantasies of Keyserling, and in the so-called " geopolitics."

[30] It is worth noting that in his *Voyage en Italie* Chateaubriand found that the Italian landscape was characterized by the absence of any precise contours: " Une teinte singulièrment harmonieuse marie la terre, le ciel et les eaux: toutes les surfaces, au moyen d'une gradation insensible de couleurs, s'unissent par leur extrémités, sans qu'on puisse déterminer le point où une nuance finit et où l'autre commence."

[31] This motif has been adopted recently by German historians of philosophy to define the tradition of German thought. See, for example, the work of E. Rothacker.

Index

247